MILITARIZATION
AND DEMILITARIZATION
IN EL SALVADOR'S TRANSITION
TO DEMOCRACY

MILITARIZATION

AND

DEMILITARIZATION

IN

EL SALVADOR'S

TRANSITION TO

DEMOCRACY

Philip J. Williams
and
Knut Walter

UNIVERSITY OF PITTSBURGH PRESS

Published by the University of Pittsburgh Press, Pittsburgh, Pa.
15261

Copyright © 1997, University of Pittsburgh Press
All rights reserved
Manufactured in the United States of America
Printed on acid-free paper

10 9 8 7 6 5 4 3 2 1

Library of Congress Cataloging-in-Publication Data
Williams, Philip J., 1959–
     Militarization and demilitarization in El Salvador's transition to
democracy / Philip J. Williams and Knut Walter.
         p.   cm. — (Pitt Latin American series)
     Includes bibliographical references (p.   ) and index.
     ISBN 0-8229-4041-8 (cloth : acid-free paper). —
ISBN 0-8229-5646-2 (pbk. : acid-free paper)
         1. Civil-military relations—El Salvador. 2. El Salvador—Armed
Forces—Political activity. 3. El Salvador—Politics and government—20th
century. I. Walter, Knut. II. Title.
III. Series.
JL1566.C58W54 1977   97-4920
322' .5'097284—dc21

A CIP catalog record for this book is available from the
British Library.

CONTENTS

ACRONYMS

ABECAFE	Asociación de Beneficiadores y Exportadoras de Café
ACM	Acción Cívica Militar
ACS	Asociación Cívica Salvadoreña
ADEFAES	Asociación de Desmovilizados de la Fuerza Armada de El Salvador
AGEUS	Asociación General de Estudiantes Universitarios Salvadoreños
AIFLD	American Institute for Free Labor Development
ANDA	Administración Nacional de Acuaductos y Agua
ANSESAL	Agencia Nacional de Seguridad Salvadoreña
ANSP	Academia Nacional de Seguridad Pública
ANTEL	Administración Nacional de Telecomunicaciones
ARENA	Alianza Republicana Nacionalista
BIRIs	Batallónes de Infantería de Reacción Inmediata
CACM	Central American Common Market
CCE	Consejo Central de Elecciones
CD	Convergencia Democrática
CEL	Comisión Ejecutiva Hidroeléctrica del Río Lempa
CEMFA	Centro de Entrenamiento de la Fuerza Armada
CENITEC	Centro de Investigaciones Tecnológicas
CEPA	Comisión Ejecutiva Portuario Autónoma
CETIPOL	National Police Technical School
CGR	Consejo de Gobierno Revolucionario
CGTS	Confederación General de Trabajadores Salvadoreños
CODEM	Comando de Doctrina y Educación Militar
CONARA	Comisión Nacional para la Restoración de Areas
COPEFA	Consejo Permanente de la Fuerza Armada
DNI	National Intelligence Directorate
EMC	Estado Mayor Conjunto
ENI	Escuela Nacional de Inteligencia
ESAF	El Salvadoran Armed Forces
ESF	Economic Support Fund
FAN	Frente Amplio Nacional
FECCAS	Federación Cristiana de Campesinos Salvadoreños
FMLN	Frente Farabundo Martí para la Liberación Nacional

FUDI	Frente Unido Democrático Independiente
INCAFE	Instituto Nacional de Café
INSAFI	Instituto Salvadoreño de Fomento Industrial
IPSFA	Instituto de Previsión Social de la Fuerza Armada
ISSS	Instituto Salvadoreño de Seguro Social
ISTA	Instituto Salvadoreño de Transformación Agraria
MAP	Military Assistance Program
MILGROUP	U.S. Military Group
MJM	Movimiento de la Juventud Militar
MNR	Movimiento Nacional Revolucionario
MU	Movimiento de Unidad
OIE	State Intelligence Organ
ONUSAL	United Nations Observer Mission in El Salvador
ORDEN	Organización Democrática Nacionalista
PAR	Partido de Acción Renovadora
PCN	Partido de Conciliación Nacional
PDC	Partido Demócrata Cristiano
PNC	National Civilian Police
PPS	Partido Popular Salvadoreño
PRAM	Partido Revolucionario Abril y Mayo
PRN	Plan for National Reconstruction
PRUD	Partido Revolucionario de Unificación Democrática
PRUDA	PRUD Auténtico
PSD	Partido Social Demócrata
PUD	Partido Unión Demócrata
SENCO	Secretariado Nacional de Comunicaciones
SIU	National Police Special Investigative Unit
SRN	Secretariat of National Reconstruction
TSE	Tribunal Supremo Electoral
UCA	Universidad Centroamericana
UCS	Unión Comunal Salvadoreña
UDN	Unión Democrática Nacionalista
UEA	Special Anti-Narcotics Unit
UNO	Unión Nacional Opositora
UPR	Unidos para Reconstruir
USAID	United States Agency for International Development
USAL	Universidad Salvadoreña
USGAO	U.S. General Accounting Office
USSOUTHCOM	U.S. Southern Command
UTC	Unión de Trabajadores del Campo

ACKNOWLEDGMENTS

A generous grant from the North-South Center at the University of Miami provided funds for the bulk of the field research and for a conference on civil-military relations in San Salvador. The Centro de Investigaciones Tecnológicas (CENITEC) cosponsored the conference in October 1993. A grant from the United States Institute of Peace made it possible for Williams to spend much of 1994 working on the manuscript. The Division of Sponsored Research and the College of Liberal Arts and Sciences at the University of Florida also provided support for a graduate research assistant during the 1993–94 academic year.

We thank Tommie Sue Montgomery, Manuel Vásquez, Amanda Wolfe, and an anonymous reviewer for their valuable comments on the manuscript. We are also grateful to the many retired and active-duty officers who shared with us their stories and insights, some of whom must remain anonymous. Throughout the course of the project, the authors benefited greatly from the insights and encouragement of fellow Salvadoranists, Tommie Sue Montgomery, Jack Spence, David Holiday, Elisabeth Wood and Bill Stanley, and our colleagues at the UCA.

Williams would like to thank Melida Porras and Miguel Arrieta for their hospitality and support during his research visits to El Salvador. Also, a special thanks to the residents of Mejicanos, whose probing questions and healthy skepticism were a constant source of inspiration throughout this endeavor. And finally, to "mi flaquita," thanks for your patience and understanding during the best of times and worst of times these last few years.

MILITARIZATION
AND DEMILITARIZATION
IN EL SALVADOR'S TRANSITION
TO DEMOCRACY

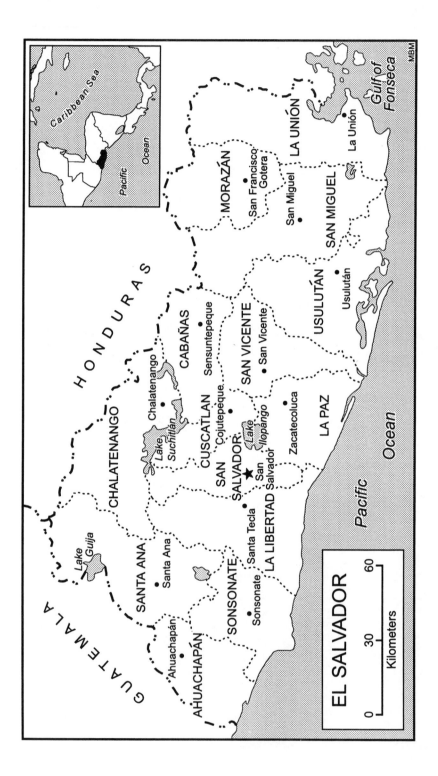

INTRODUCTION

"I DO THIS as a soldier who wants to serve his country. I do it because I have to live in El Salvador." With those words, Salvadoran defense minister, Gen. René Emilio Ponce, offered up his resignation just days before the release of the long-awaited United Nations Truth Commission report.

General Ponce's resignation in March 1993 marked the end of an era in El Salvador—an era in which the Salvadoran military dominated the political sphere with total impunity. The Truth Commission's findings unmasked for all to see the sheer brutality with which the Salvadoran armed forces conducted themselves during the twelve-year-long civil war. For a military that already had lost many of its prerogatives under the terms of the January 1992 peace accords, the report was a bitter pill to swallow.

The peace accords went a long way toward ending the military's political domination. Under the accords, the military's constitutional role no longer included public security; the security forces were dissolved and a new civilian police force created under executive control; the military-controlled intelligence agency was disbanded and a new one set up under civilian control; the military academy was now accountable to a civilian-military council; and, for the first time in history, officers had to submit to an external evaluation conducted by civilians. Nevertheless, despite the significant progress that was made in circumscribing the military's traditional political power, the road ahead is not without obstacles. As Alfred Stepan has suggested, prolonged military rule can leave important legacies that present powerful obstacles to democratic consolidation.[1] Understanding these legacies and the problems they present is essential in developing strategies aimed at transforming civil-military relations.

The onset of democratic transitions in Latin America has brought to the fore difficult questions regarding the role of the armed forces. Whereas some scholars arrive at the conclusion that the core interests of the armed forces must be preserved in order to guarantee "successful" transitions, others argue that negotiated pacts that protect the military's vital interests present serious obstacles to democratic consolidation. For example, O'Donnell and Schmitter contend that one of the lessons of recent transitions is that the Left must accept that the armed forces' "institutional existence, assets, and hierarchy cannot be eliminated or seriously threatened."[2] In exploring the role of pacts in Brazil's transition, Frances Hagopian, on the other hand, demonstrates how pacts enabled the military to solidify its predominant position within the state and to preserve its institutional autonomy vis-à-vis civilian authorities.[3] Although scholars may disagree as to the best way to guarantee the military's compliance with the democratic system, most would agree that the fundamental challenge for policy makers is to craft policies that reduce the military's political power but at the same time limit the potential for conflict.

In El Salvador, the prospects for peace and democratization are closely linked to the future of the country's armed forces. The unique legacy of some sixty years of military domination of the political sphere provides a key to understanding the possibilities for transforming civil-military relations in the wake of the January 1992 peace accords between the government of El Salvador and the FMLN (Frente Farabundo Martí para la Liberación Nacional). Yet, despite their central role in the country's political life, to date there has been no systematic study of the Salvadoran armed forces during the period of direct military rule nor during the more recent transition from authoritarianism.

As with other Central American transitions from authoritarianism, El Salvador's is distinct from democratic transitions in South America on a number of scores, not least of which is the role of the military. In the first place, El Salvador is not a case of *re*democratization. Although during the 1920s the country experienced a period of political relaxation, it was largely confined to urban areas. Moreover, given the limited suffrage at the time, it can hardly be regarded as a democratic interlude. The absence of any democratic "point of reference" contributed to the high degree of uncertainty regarding the military's behavior during El Salvador's transition.

Secondly, during the 1980s, the transition process was shaped by the context of the civil war. The demands of the war resulted in an increased militarization of state and society, complicating subsequent efforts to establish civilian control over the military and making demilitarization an essential element in achieving lasting peace and democracy. In fact, it was only as a result of an internationally mediated and monitored peace agreement that a genuine process of democratization and national reconciliation was possible in El Salvador.

Finally, unlike other Latin American cases, international actors played a central role in the unfolding events in El Salvador. Throughout the 1980s, the Reagan administration's preference for a military solution to the conflict sharply limited possibilities for a negotiated outcome. U.S. military assistance and training, while assuring the survival of the Salvadoran government, was insufficient to guarantee a military victory over the FMLN. Moreover, U.S. assistance failed to fundamentally transform the Salvadoran armed forces, one of the stated goals of U.S. policy. After 1989, the United Nations was instrumental in brokering a negotiated settlement to the conflict and overseeing the implementation of a series of sweeping reforms dictated by the peace accords.

Given the differences between El Salvador and other Latin American cases, a theoretically informed case study approach can provide a sounder basis for future comparative analysis. We adopt a consciously historical-structural perspective, viewing particular historical and structural legacies of prolonged military rule as constituting constraints or opportunities for transforming civil-military relations. Although this approach is especially useful for studying the Central American cases, it also may be of use in analyzing the role of the military in other Latin American cases. Moreover, the Salvadoran case, while unique, can provide important lessons regarding the possibilities for military reform and restructuring in other war-torn societies.

Differing Approaches to Studying the Military

Much of the literature on civil-military relations in the developing world has concerned itself with the issue of military intervention in politics and, more recently, military disengagement. To explain military intervention some authors draw heavily on factors external to the military such as a country's level of socioeconomic development, the nature of its political institutions, and the behavior of its civilian elites. For example, proponents of modernization theory employing cross-national statistical analysis have pointed to correlations between indicators of development and the degree of military intervention in politics.[4] O'Donnell, while turning modernization theory on its head, emphasized the relationship between a particular stage of development—the exhaustion of import-substituting industrialization—and the rise of bureaucratic authoritarian regimes in Latin America.[5]

Huntington argued that "the most important causes of military intervention in politics are not military but political and reflect not the social and organizational characteristics of the military establishment but the political and institutional structure of society."[6] And finally, Stepan and Linz stressed the importance of elite behavior, especially the shortcomings of incumbent civilian elites, in explaining military interventions in Latin America during the 1960s and 1970s.[7]

Other authors have focused more on factors internal to the military, including the degree of professionalization of the officer corps, military doctrine and ideology, the social origins of officers, and foreign military training. Whereas Huntington believed that the greater the level of professionalization of the officer corps the less likelihood of military intervention in politics,[8] other authors claimed the reverse to be true in developing countries.[9] Some authors pointed to changes in military doctrine and ideology during the 1960s to account for Latin American militaries' greater willingness to intervene in their countries' political life.[10] Stepan emphasized both professionalization and military doctrine in his study of the 1964 coup in Brazil, arguing that "technical and professional specialization of the military in conjunction with doctrines and ideologies of internal security will tend to lead toward military role expansion and 'managerialism' in the political sphere."[11]

The importance of the social origins of officer corps generated debate among scholars of civil-military relations during the 1960s and 1970s. José Nun argued that Latin American militaries tended to represent middle-class interests because of the largely middle-class origin of the officer corps.[12] Similarly, Huntington viewed the military as the "advance guard of the middle class" in the context of "oligarchical praetorianism," spearheading "its breakthrough into the political arena."[13] Finally, some authors pointed to the importance of foreign military training and assistance, especially U.S. assistance, in shaping the military's political behavior.[14]

During the 1980s scholars shifted their attention to the conditions under which military "disengagement" from politics might occur and whether or not disengagement would lead to long-term military "neutrality."[15] Most authors focused on the same kinds of factors, both internal and external to the military, used in earlier studies of military intervention. For example, in an edited volume on military disengagement, Danopoulos argues that "both societal and institutional dimensions determine whether and to what degree the armed forces will leave power, when they will do it, and how they will do so."[16] On a societal level, he finds a positive correlation between "high levels of socio-economic development and the degree to which the military are disposed to leave the levers of authority."[17] On an institutional level, he argues that the military's disposition to disengage is influenced by four factors: (1) the nature of the intervention and subsequent rule, (2) performance in office, (3) professional military concerns, and (4) the availability of acceptable alternatives. Similarly, in his study of military disengagement in Latin America and Africa, Welch adopts a framework that incorporates factors internal to the armed forces—including role perceptions, funding and internal management, and mission and deployment—and broader societal factors, such as levels of internal strife, economic trends, and leadership.[18]

Finer notes that while disengagement of the short-term variety is quite common in developing countries, long-term disengagement, or military neutrality, is rare indeed. According to Finer, the "preconditions for neutrality are, in short, that the successor regime must be one that *neither needs the military nor is needed by it.*"[19] Although he sees the latter precondition possible in developing countries, "the former is not likely to be realized."[20] Finer concludes from his analysis that long-term neutrality is only likely in industrialized societies with a "developed" political culture.

Following Stepan's initial attempt to study the role of the military in democratic transitions in the Southern Cone, several studies on civil-military relations and democratization in Latin America have appeared. Although most adopt a framework that combines societal factors with a focus on the military institution, recent studies are limited by their lack of historical perspective and the scant attention paid to the Central American cases.[21]

The paucity of literature on Central American militaries is particularly disturbing. Despite the central role militaries have played in shaping the politics of the region, there are few systematic studies of the military available.[22] For obvious reasons, in the past Central American scholars have been unable or unwilling to study the armed forces. Not surprisingly, the military has been viewed as something of a mysterious black box, with few willing to risk peeking inside. Although the changing political landscape may offer new opportunities for researching a traditionally forbidden subject, as of yet there are few Central American scholars willing to step forward.[23]

The literature on the Salvadoran armed forces is particularly poor. Historical accounts of the military are either dated[24] or overly apologetic.[25] More recent treatments of the military, both journalistic and academic, focus almost exclusively on the 1980s. The more "academic" discussions are generally quite superficial in their analysis and are not based on extensive firsthand research.[26] Of the journalistic accounts, the most enlightening is Millman's, which documents military corruption and provides important insight into internal military politics.[27] Finally, there is a handful of studies that examine the Salvadoran military's role in the United States' counterinsurgency program.[28]

MILITARY POWER AND THE STATE

Most theorists of the state recognize "the central role of the coercive apparatus in modern, especially authoritarian states."[29] Some scholars of the military go so far as to argue that "the creation of a permanent army is the foundation of state sovereignty."[30] Given the military's fundamental role in guaranteeing the state's political domination in society, we concur with Stepan in that "we accord the military some independent theoretical status as an actor, instead of merely subsuming them in larger categories such as the 'state,' or even in regime categories such as 'bureaucratic-authoritarianism.'"[31] Unlike Poulantzas, whose structural determinism "conceptually removes the military from the exercise of power," we assume that the military will develop over time its own set of political and institutional interests that may or may not coincide with those of the state and of economically dominant groups.[32] This is not to suggest that the military's relative autonomy is without limits; rather, like any complex organization, the military will develop and seek to advance its own interests and prerogatives.

One important limitation on the military's autonomy arises from its very nature. The armed forces' raison d'être is to defend the state. "As a defensive apparatus, by its nature the military defends what exists and thus in the face of social disintegration, it constitutes a last recourse for the continuation of the system."[33] However, being a "defensive apparatus," it is extremely limited in its ability to create an alternative to the existing system. Thus, when the military stages a coup d'etat "against the state," it is usually to defend the state from itself and not to replace it with something else.[34]

The military's autonomy is also subject to structural constraints. In other words, the military's scope of action is limited by both domestic and transnational structures of power. For example, as the economy comes to rely less and less on labor-repressive agriculture, the need for a centralized system of social control administered by the military may diminish. This can lead states to reign in the military's independent scope of activity. Those states with broad-based social legitimation are more likely to succeed in limiting the political space occupied by the military than those with low levels of legitimacy. And finally, transnational structures of power also can limit a military's autonomous realm of action. Transnational actors like the United States, motivated by geopolitical and economic interests, can contribute to the military's role expansion or contraction through training and assistance programs. Likewise, the nature of a country's insertion into the international economy can constrain the range of options available to state policy makers on a whole range of issues, including the military.

If we accept the armed forces' relative autonomy vis-à-vis the state and society, and that they are likely to develop their own interests over time, as well as the capacity to advance these interests, then studies of civil-military relations should not limit themselves to the issue of how armed forces are related to governments. It is our contention that to understand the military's political role in a given polity, it is necessary to study the nature of the military's political power in its various dimensions. In other words, the military's political power is not limited to its relationship with government, which is only one dimension of military power. Given its monopoly on violence, the military can exercise political power whether or not it occupies the government. Instead of using the terms *intervention* and *disengagement,* we prefer to use the concepts of *militarization* and *demilitarization* in studying the military's evolving political role. While militarization and demilitarization presuppose intervention and disengagement, respectively, they imply much more.

Militarization refers to "the overwhelming of the state apparatus as a whole by the armed forces—in essence the 'colonization' of the majority of state and state-related structures (at the apex of the pyramid) by the military."[35] The process of militarization "may be open and explicit but may also take more indirect, 'subterranean' forms in which the armed forces do not occupy the front line in the political sense."[36] For example, even when the armed forces return to the barracks after a period of military rule, they still may be able to protect or even expand their entrenchment in postauthoritarian political structures. In such cases, the military can continue to exercise "a tutelary presence from which to influence the political process."[37]

Militarization is not only limited to the state level; it also can occur at the micro level of everyday life. Although militarization does not always occur simultaneously at both levels, it is mutually reinforcing. For example, the military's domination of the state apparatus provides it with resources that can facilitate its colonization of everyday life (or what Habermas refers to as the "colonization of the lifeworld"[38]). Likewise, the military's exercise of social control at the micro level can provide it with a "loyal" political clientele that ensures its continued control of the state. Militarization generally occurs at the micro level when the state is incapable of achieving hegemony in the Gramscian sense—i.e., it is unable to generate societal consensus. In such instances, the armed forces use coercion to guarantee the state's political domination. The military's colonization of everyday life also can be related to military security doctrines that "regard the monitoring of domestic social, economic and political spheres, in which subversion 'lurks,' as part of its own professional incumbency."[39] Finally, militarization at the micro level often takes place in economies where the primary mode of production is labor-repressive agriculture. To fulfill the labor requirements of the agro-export sector, the military and police are called upon to regiment the labor supply.

In all of these cases, the military may establish a centralized system of social control, whereby the armed forces expand their penetration of formerly autonomous networks of associational life at the local level. The instruments of control usually consist of the security and intelligence branches of the armed forces but can also include local police forces, the army's reserve system, civic action units, civil defense patrols, and paramilitary organizations linked to the armed forces. Nevertheless, it is important to remember that the military's "colonization" of everyday life, whether in response to some perceived security threat or as necessitated by the economic requirements of the agro-export sector, rarely goes uncontested. As Habermas argues, social movements may arise that challenge these assaults on the "lifeworld," resulting in serious legitimacy conflicts.[40]

Demilitarization, on the other hand, refers to the armed forces' "decolonization" of the state apparatus and of everyday life, not simply a return to the barracks. Demilitarization at the state level consists of sharply reducing the military's traditional institutional prerogatives or "reserved domains" and eliminating its ability to exercise "tutelary power" over the political process.[41] At the micro level, demilitarization refers to the progressive dismantling of those institutions central to the military's system of social control. As with militarization, demilitarization is a matter of degree and can suffer setbacks and reversals. Moreover, the extent and nature of militarization can shape the prospects for future demilitarization.

Central to our conception of militarization and demilitarization is the issue of military power—the sources of the military's power, how it uses its power, and the limits on that power.[42] Besides its monopoly on violence, we need to explore other sources of military power. For example, alliances with strategic elites, both domestic and transnational, can enhance the military's power, as can the military's cultivation of its own political clientele. Regarding the use of power, we need to ask whether the military uses its power to benefit some groups over others, or whether it attempts to forge consensus among competing groups. Does it use its power to serve its own political and institutional interests? How does the changing nature of the military's political power affect the way it exercises power? To what extent is the military's political power limited by international and domestic forces? And finally, how does internal factionalism within the military affect its political power?

By focusing more broadly on the nature of the military's political power and its historical relationship with the state and society, we can move beyond the limitations of much of the literature on civil-military relations. Such an approach is particularly appropriate, not just from a theoretical standpoint, but also from a more practical policy perspective. For example, it could be argued that in many Latin American countries the failure of civilian leaders to grasp the full extent of their military's political power contributed to ineffectual policies vis-à-vis the armed forces during the postauthoritarian period. In short, crafting an effective strategy of reform to overcome the military obstacles to democratic consolidation requires a clear understanding of the various dimensions of the armed forces' political power.

STRUCTURE OF THIS BOOK

The central argument of this book is that the extent and nature of militarization in El Salvador during the period 1931–1992 produced powerful obstacles that limited the possibilities for demilitarization in the wake of the peace accords. One constant feature of the Salvadoran military was its unwillingness to subject itself to civilian control or to give up its network of social control in the countryside. Although the twelve years of civil war affected the military's desire to govern directly, it did not convince the military of civilian politicians' ability to govern or to defend the state. The peace accords represented a historic opportunity to dramatically transform the military's political role; however, they did not address several key dimensions of the military's political power.

The first task is to analyze the nature of the Salvadoran military's political power before the 1979 coup, focusing on the armed forces' evolving relationship with the state and society. Of particular concern is the way in which the military consolidated its domination of the political sphere. It is our contention that the military's assumption of power in 1931 was the result of a gradual process of militarization rooted in the military's modernization and the growing stresses related to the agro-export model of development. Thus, although the 1932 uprising provided the necessary justification for further militarization, the process of militarization predated the 1932 uprising.

The military's political domination after 1932 also rested upon its relationship with key civilian groups and the United States, and a growing paramilitary network of control in the countryside. As the military consolidated its political power, it began to develop a separate set of political, institutional, and economic interests, which did not necessarily coincide with those of the coffee oligarchy. Whereas Rouquié argues that the "military are not 'the watchdogs of the oligarchy' or big capital, but the guardians of the state,"[43] we contend that initially they were, but that due to the general weakness of the state apparatus and the instability of the agro-export model, they increased their autonomy, gaining ascendance in the political sphere until they became synonymous with the preservation of the state. Thus, while the military sided with the coffee oligarchy more often than not, occasionally, as during the Osorio regime in the 1950s, the military was willing to introduce policies designed to weaken the oligarchy's economic dominance. In fact, throughout the period 1931–1979, there was a series of reformist coups, generally initiated by junior officers in alliance with civilian groups interested in reducing the coffee oligarchy's control over the economy. Nevertheless, despite the initial success of some of these reformist coups, coffee elites successfully resisted attempts to introduce more profound changes. In short, although the military developed its own set of interests, in no way could it fundamentally challenge the prevailing economic model.

Also limiting the scope of the military's reform initiatives were the very sources of its political power: its power derived from its institutional autonomy, its control of the state, and its rural power base. Although factions within the military were willing to enter into alliances with different political and social forces, not even the most reform-minded of officers were willing to contemplate the prospect of civilian control over the military or an end to its network of social control in rural areas. Instituting such reforms would have seriously eroded the military's ability to exercise tutelage over the political process.

The second task of the book is to consider the way in which the formal transfer of power to a civilian president during the 1980s affected the military's political power. Although one would expect a positive correlation between a formal transfer of power to civilian rule and a reduction in the military's political power, it is our hypothesis that during the 1980s the military was successful in consolidating its presence within the state, expanding its network of control in the countryside, and preserving its institutional and political autonomy.

This paradox can be best understood by analyzing the way in which the military's political power was influenced by four key factors: (1) the context of the civil war, (2) a series of political pacts between the military high command and civilian political leaders, (3) internal factionalism within the armed forces, and (4) U.S. military assistance. These factors reinforced traditional obstacles to achieving civilian control over the military. For example, the intensification of the armed conflict reinforced the military's perception that it was the only national institution capable of defending the state. Thus while the military no longer governed directly, its political power expanded in response to the demands of the war. A series of political pacts confirmed the military's expanded political role and U.S. assistance only served to legitimate this trend.

Although the Salvadoran military retained control over key political decisions during the 1980s, its political power was not unlimited. The military's growing dependence on U.S. assistance and internal divisions within the officer corps made it highly vulnerable to U.S. pressures. In return for continued U.S. assistance, the armed forces had to accept social and economic reforms opposed by coffee elites, demonstrate greater sensitivity toward human rights abuses, permit the election of a civilian government, and, ultimately, agree to a negotiated end to the war. And yet, despite U.S. and domestic pressures, the Salvadoran military exhibited an extraordinary capacity to resist more profound changes. This, of course, posed a formidable obstacle to demilitarization in the wake of the peace accords.

The third task of the book is to examine the extent to which the January 1992 peace accords created new opportunities for transforming the military's political role. Although the accords represented an attempt to change dramatically civil-military relations, leading to a relationship of civilian supremacy, there were a number of limitations in this endeavor. In assessing the opportunities for enhancing civilian supremacy, it is necessary first to identify key aspects of the military's political power not addressed by the accords. Secondly, an analysis of the implementation of the accords related to the military is essential. Particular attention is paid to the problematic aspects of the implementation efforts and the likelihood of resolving these in a manner that contributes to further demilitarization. Finally, given the likelihood that the military will resist direct challenges to what it considers fundamental or core interests, achieving civilian supremacy will require more than simply reducing the military's prerogatives. As Stepan argues, demilitarization encompasses a multiplicity of tasks in which civil society, political society, and the state all have a role to play.[44] What is needed is a *política militar*[45] that addresses all aspects of the military's traditional domination of the political sphere. Consequently, we go beyond simply assessing the prospects for democratizing civil-military relations to suggesting the broad outline for an alternative *política militar*.

A final task is to consider the extent to which the process of demilitarization in El Salvador can inform policy initiatives elsewhere in the region. The Salvadoran experience is particularly relevant to its Central American neighbors that have attempted military reforms in the wake of internal wars, but it also provides important lessons for policy makers involved in peace-

keeping operations in other war-torn societies. The Salvadoran case illus-
trates the significant role that both international and domestic actors can
play in the demilitarization process.

   This book attempts to fill an important void in the literature. First of all,
as discussed above, it offers an alternative approach to studying the role of
Central American militaries during transitions from authoritarian rule and
in the wake of internal conflicts. Not only does it take into account the dis-
tinctiveness of Central American transitions, but also incorporates a consciously historical perspective to understand the legacies of prolonged military rule. Secondly, it builds upon the work of Stepan and others, refocusing
our attention on the role of the military not just during the period of direct
military rule, but also during the transition from authoritarianism and the
consolidation of democracy. And finally, the study complements recent
work on civil-military relations and the problem of democracy by contributing to the formulation of an explicit strategy for enhancing civilian control
of the military.

THE 1931 COUP AND THE CONSOLIDATION
OF MILITARY RULE

THE MILITARY AND POLITICS PRIOR TO 1931

THE SALVADORAN military assumed direct control of the national government on 2 December 1931, after a mostly bloodless coup against President Arturo Araujo, a civilian reformist politician elected just eleven months earlier. The military's assumption of direct governmental control was not particularly exceptional by Latin American standards during the initial and most difficult years of the Great Depression. It certainly was not unique in the Central American case, where after 1930 military officers occupied in short order the presidential office in Guatemala, Honduras, and Nicaragua, in addition to El Salvador. What is exceptional about the 1931 coup in El Salvador is that it marks the beginning of over half a century of uninterrupted political domination by the Salvadoran military. There are few other cases in Latin America that are comparable to this experience: the Somoza dictatorship in Nicaragua (from 1936 to 1979), the Stroessner regime in Paraguay (1948–1992), and the Guatemalan military since 1954 come to mind regardless of the significant differences in the social and political evolution of each country and the role of their respective military institutions.

El Salvador's political history after 1930 is marked by some of the most evident outbreaks of social strife anywhere in the Central American region, which alone goes a long way in explaining the permanence (and consequences) of direct military rule. However, already during the nineteenth century, as was the case in the rest of Central America, the force of arms was instrumental in achieving and holding public office. *Caudillos* and their armies, organized around liberal and conservative ideologies, battled for control of the government after the proclamation of independence from Spain in 1821. Not until the 1870s did a semblance of stability emerge as coffee production took hold and the landholding elites became concerned with establishing political order and constitutional legality. Still, no government was replaced peacefully by another until the first years of the twentieth century, and not until after 1911 were civilians to occupy uninterruptedly the presidency of the republic.

Interestingly, it was the civilian government of Manuel Enrique Araujo (1911–1913) that proceeded to organize a modern professional military structure in El Salvador. Among other things, his government established two officer rolls to differentiate those who had risen through the ranks through field experience and those who had formal training in the recently established Escuela Politécnica. The deployment of academy-trained officers proceeded thereafter.[1] A second innovation of the Araujo regime was the creation of the Guardia Nacional, the rural police force that remained in existence until the 1992 peace accords eliminated the military's role in public security. The Guardia Nacional was founded and directed initially by Spanish officers under contract by the Salvadoran government.

From 1911 until 1931, civilian politicians occupied the presidency and headed all the government's ministries while the military and the Guardia Nacional grew in size and territorial presence. Thus, the simultaneous development of political competition among civilian groups representing different factions of the coffee oligarchy and the increasing strength and modernization of the military organization laid the ground for the political crisis that was resolved finally through the 1931 military coup.

Political competition from 1913 to 1931 was characterized by varying degrees of violence, especially during local and national elections. After president Araujo's assassination in 1913, control of the national government fell into the hands of individuals belonging to the Meléndez and the Quiñónez families, who were related by marriage and powerful in their own right as producers of sugar and coffee.[2] Their political dominance was opposed by other individuals and families who organized political parties and clubs with little or no ideological content but who promised social and economic improvement as a means to garner votes on election day. Such messages echoed the aspirations of an incipient labor movement that by the early 1920s was the most active in all of Central America.[3]

However, the main characteristic of political competition prior to 1930 seems to have been the increasing levels of political mobilization that were promoted and tolerated by the political elites. The governments of Jorge Meléndez and Alfonso Quiñónez Molina (1919–1927) sought the support of rural communities in the more populated western parts of the country, as well as the support of urban labor organizations.[4] But to ensure their victory at the polls, they resorted also to violence, including the formation of the so-called "Ligas Rojas," a network of popular organizations under the control of the government that functioned until 1922; the Ligas were employed as shock troops during election campaigns and provided political intelligence otherwise. Certain groups were attracted to the Ligas because they also offered a channel of communication to the country's leadership; for example, Indian communities in the west of El Salvador saw the Ligas as a means of countering the growing influence of Ladinos in their villages.[5]

In comparison to political activities under the civilian governments, the role of the military as an independent force in politics prior to 1931 was quite limited and provided few overt evidences of the military's decision to take over and retain control of the country's governmental institutions. Outside of a couple of minor incidents involving a revolt of cadets at the military school in 1922 and an attempted coup in 1927, the military's role under the Meléndez-Quiñónez presidencies was subservient to the authority of the state.[6] However, while militarization at the level of the state was quite limited, a significant military presence remained in some parts of the country from the days at the turn of the century when conflict with neighboring countries (especially Guatemala) was of concern to the national government and the military establishment. The military also provided some police services before and after the deployment of the Guardia Nacional in the rural areas beginning in 1912. Finally, the government used the military on occasions to repress the opposition, as happened especially during periods of electoral activity.

The military establishment during the 1920s was divided into two main groupings: the regular army, made up of conscripts who served for one year, and the rural reserve units, made up of ex-soldiers who were on call until the age of fifty. The regular army was organized around eleven infantry regiments, stationed in the main cities and towns of the republic, and one regiment each of artillery, machine guns, and cavalry (all stationed in San Salvador, the capital). There was an air force unit, too, but it was extremely small at the time. The Guardia Nacional was a hybrid institution, for it belonged formally to the military and could be mobilized to repel foreign aggression, but its main duties were rural policing.[7]

What stands out very clearly during these years is the extent of militarization in the rural areas. In addition to the rural duties of the Guardia Nacional, the regular army was made up mostly (if not entirely) of rural conscripts, for many of whom the army represented the first and only formal training they were ever to receive. In the army they were taught reading, writing, and arithmetic, as well as the idea "that they had a fatherland to whom they owed loyalty."[8]

After their tour of duty, the conscripts returned to their villages and resumed their lives as peasant farmers or rural laborers, but their military service had not ended: they became part of the reserve force and some were called upon to serve actively in the so-called *patrullas cantonales* or *escoltas militares*. These units were engaged in rural policing but were under the direct authority of local military officers (the *comandantes locales*) and were charged with keeping the peace, providing support to municipal and judicial authorities, and informing their superiors of any unusual activities in the surroundings. In more general terms, the *patrullas cantonales* were part of a system of rural political control that relied on the selective co-optation of individuals of the peasant class; this co-optation not only strengthened the national state's presence but also contributed to the weakening of communal ties as peasants confronted peasants in the struggle over land, debt, and assorted privileges.[9]

How pervasive was the "colonization" of everyday life in the rural areas of El Salvador? There is little available data at present with which to work. In 1892, the military reserve forces totaled nearly sixty thousand men but these were not active in rural policing activities; they were, strictly speaking, soldiers in the reserve who could be called up for duty in an emergency. At most, they attended training sessions on Sunday mornings.[10] However, by the 1920s the evidence available suggests that paramilitary structures in the rural areas were much more developed and pervasive.

A document for 1925 from the western department of Ahuachapán, which lists the entirety of members of the *escoltas militares* and their *comandantes,* as well as the reserve troops, was sent to the departmental governor's office for purposes of exonerating them from the payment of the head tax *(impuesto de vialidad).*[11] Each *escolta* was made up of four *superiores (comandante primero, comandante segundo, sargento, cabo)* and from five to eight *soldados.* Thus, an *escolta* had anywhere from nine to twelve members. Some of the *soldados* were as young as seventeen and as old as fifty, but most were in their twenties, which suggests that they had just completed their military service.

In the entire department, there were seventy-six *escoltas* with a total of 2,080 members. According to the 1930 census, Ahuachapán had a population of about eighty thousand. If one half were men and half of these in turn were under eighteen years of age, then the total adult male population would have been about twenty thousand. Thus, about one out of every ten adult males in Ahuachapán was part of an active paramilitary structure. Assuming there was some degree of turnover, the proportion of adult males who were involved in the *escoltas* at some point in their early manhood would have been considerable, all at no cost to the state (except, of course, those head taxes that were not collected). If the 1,265 soldiers in the reserves are added to the soldiers in the *escoltas,* a total of 3,345 *ahuachapanecos* were under some form of direct military control in 1926; that is, one out of every six adult males.

While additional research must be undertaken, the impression is that the Salvadoran countryside, especially coffee-growing areas, had come largely under military control or surveillance by 1930. The Guardia Nacional together with the *comandantes locales* and their *escoltas militares,* plus a considerable number of troops in reserve, constituted a parallel power structure that could easily challenge other local and national authorities, such as the *alcaldes,* the urban police, the state's ministries, and even the president of the republic himself.

However, it should be clear that this paramilitary structure was not a strong force in terms of firepower. All military weapons (rifles, machine guns, cannons) were under the control of the regular army in its barracks and fortresses, whereas the soldiers in the *escoltas* had to make do with machetes and an occasional shotgun, handgun, or hunting rifle. Nor was there any threat of external war that might have required a general mobilization. Instead, the importance of the paramilitary structure had to do with the social control it exercised in rural areas and the socialization of its members through literacy and instruction in values that enhanced a sense of belonging and obedience to the nation state.

The role of the armed forces and its paramilitary structures became even more critical with the election of Pío Romero Bosque as president (1927–1931). Romero Bosque had been minister of war under the previous administration of Alfonso Quiñónez Molina, but his initial decisions as president were geared at breaking with the previous regimes, especially in regard to electoral guarantees and civil rights in general. He suspended the state of siege *(estado de sitio)* under which the country had lived for some years and criticized openly the violations of civil rights that had occurred under the Meléndez-Quiñónez regimes. Such a shift in position had much to do with recent social and political developments, including the rise of organized labor and increased peasant and communal activism, combined with an increasingly radical discourse on the part of middle-class intellectuals.[12]

The politically charged atmosphere in El Salvador increased dramatically with the onset of the economic depression in 1929. As government revenues collapsed, public employee salaries went unpaid; in the rural areas, coffee was not harvested because the market price did not even cover production costs; and important foreign debt obligations that had been acquired in the expansive 1920s began to soak up the shrinking dollar reserves to the detriment of imports of consumer and capital goods. By 1930, new political alignments in preparation for presidential elections in December reflected the disenchantment of large masses of the electorate with the old parties, factions, and leaders.

Before the economic crisis hit, President Romero had initiated a number of measures to benefit the working class, including the formal recognition of labor organizations and the regulation of working hours. However, these measures did not apply to rural laborers, a pattern that would be repeated over the following decades.[13] While urban working-class discontent certainly was growing, in the rural areas much more explosive tendencies were at work. In the western parts of the country, native communities were becoming radicalized under the influence of the recently founded Communist Party, as well as the appeal of mainstream politicians who were out for votes.

The one politician who struck an effective chord was Arturo Araujo, a wealthy landowner who took up the cause of the poor and dispossessed: as a candidate for the presidency he promised land distribution and employment without spelling out how such measures could be accomplished in the middle of a severe economic crisis. He also received the support of many Indian villages in the western departments that felt they had been abandoned by the governments of Quiñónez and Romero in their struggle against non-Indian (Ladino) groups for control of their municipalities. And to be on the safe side, he chose as his running mate a military officer who had political ambitions of his own, General Maximiliano Hernández Martínez.[14] By appealing to the urban working and middle classes, as well as peasants and Indian communities, Araujo was able to win a little under half the votes in the election held on 11–13 January 1931 and was inaugurated as president shortly thereafter.

THE 1931 COUP AND THE REVOLT OF 1932

Araujo remained in office for only nine months. In the very depths of the economic depression, there was little that his government could do to prevent the deterioration of government services, much less honor his electoral promises of social and economic recovery. Of particular concern were the government's inability to pay its employees on time, which forced growing numbers of people into debt, and growing unemployment in the rural areas. As the months went by, the government did nothing and those who had voted for Araujo became convinced that he was not serious about his electoral promises.[15]

The military in 1931 was not indifferent to the worsening social and political climate. Even before the presidential elections of January 1931, there was concern that groups within the military were planning a coup d'etat. Araujo's choice of General Hernández Martínez as his vice-presidential candidate probably sought to appease or intimidate *golpistas* within the military who were concerned over the Romero government's inability to deal effectively with the economic crisis.[16] In the end, however, it did not work: Araujo was overthrown on 2 December in a relatively quick (although disorganized) coup carried out by officers and soldiers stationed in a couple of San Salvador barracks. General Hernández Martínez, who in addition to being vice president also was minister of war, apparently was not involved in the planning and execution of the coup; in fact, he was held prisoner for a short time in the artillery barracks before being released and appointed to finish Araujo's term in office. U.S. Minister C. B. Curtis had a much more visible and active presence in the development of the coup as he ferried officers around from one barrack to another in order to reach a consensus on the formation of a military junta.[17] This junta *(directorio militar)* was made up of twelve officers, of which three had the rank of colonel, two were captains, and seven were lieutenants. Three days after the coup, the junta turned over the government to General Hernández Martínez and ceased to function on 11 December.

Thus, the overthrow of Araujo was the immediate product of a discontented military and, especially, of its junior officers stationed in San Salvador. The proclamation that the junta issued on 3 December says nothing about their reasons for taking over the government other than that Araujo "had resigned" (which was not true). Their motives probably had to do with very mundane matters: the fact that they had received no salaries nor funds to feed the troops for nearly nine months and that they had to request credit from local merchants in order to survive.[18]

Of much more import was the decision of the military to settle into the government for the long term. Hernández Martínez was constitutionally entitled to finish out Araujo's term but the government he headed made no pretense of favoring civilian politicians and their followers. From the very beginning the presence of military types was evident in government posts, from the key ministries (war, interior) to departmental governorships.[19] Nor did civilian political leaders organize in support of Araujo or oppose the new regime in the weeks following the coup. Instead, the new government allowed elections for municipal councils to be held on 3–5 January 1932.

The main immediate concern of the new regime was the issue of international recognition. As a product of the violent overthrow of the previous government, the Hernández Martínez regime did not merit recognition by the other Central American countries, which as signatories of the 1923 Washington Treaties were bound to withhold recognition until constitutional government had been reinstituted, or by the United States, which although not a signatory to the treaties agreed to abide by them. But the new Salvadoran regime considered itself perfectly constitutional, since Hernández Martínez, as Araujo's vice-president, was simply completing Araujo's term.[20] Furthermore, the new government had rapidly gained the support of the country's landholding elite, which feared social instability if the government were to collapse.

The pressure that Washington brought to bear on Hernández Martínez to resign proved completely irrelevant in the face of the massive peasant uprising that began on 23 January 1932 in the western portions of the country. Thousands of peasants picked up their machetes and marched on the principal cities and towns of western El Salvador, taking and holding some of them for a few hours or days until the regular army moved in and restored government authority. In the days immediately after the uprising, the rural areas were subject to severe repression as the military and civilian vigilantes executed anyone suspected of participating in the rebellion or aiding the rebels.[21]

The rebellion had both a short- and long-term impact. In the short term, the rebellion served to strengthen Hernández Martínez's hold on the government by uniting the military and the large landholding interests behind him. It also softened U.S. insistence on his resignation before diplomatic recognition could be extended to El Salvador.[22] In the long term, the revolt defined the regime's policies for the next decade and provided the military with an explicit new role, that of defender of property and privilege. In particular, it provided the regime with a strongly anticommunist discourse that pleased the country's economic interests and terrorized almost everybody else into a position of submission and discipline.

THE RATIONALE FOR DICTATORSHIP

The 1932 uprising at no moment threatened to overturn the status quo. In strictly military terms, the peasants had no manner of countering the army's machine guns. Nor did they have any unified command structure that would have allowed them to pool their forces and carry out more selective (and effective) attacks on government forces. The Communist Party, according to the most recent information available in the archives of the

Comintern in Moscow, was totally unprepared to lead the rebellion but became a useful whipping horse, nonetheless.[23] In the end, the rebellion was put down in a few days and the country began a new stage in its history: that of uninterrupted military rule for the next half-century.

The rebellion, then, represents both the end of a very incipient democracy in El Salvador and the beginning of a series of authoritarian regimes that justified their existence precisely on the need for strong government under military guidance to prevent further social explosions. However, these authoritarian regimes were not exclusively reactionary or even conservative: instead, they existed in a state of continuous tension between those lines of thought that would try to prevent crisis by promoting change of varying degrees and those who would seek to prevent even expressions of the need for change, although both coincided on the need for military control of the state.

From the first days of the Hernández Martínez regime, these tensions were evident. One telling position can be found in the year-end report *(memoria)* before the legislative assembly of the newly appointed minister of government, General Salvador Castaneda Castro. Castaneda's interpretation of the events of 1932 places the blame for the insurrection on both the role of agitators (i.e., the Communist Party) and the existence of a skewed social system that generated hatred and resentment within the proletariat.[24] Only a new government, untainted by the unprincipled wheelings and dealings *(politiquería)* of regimes past, would be in a position to address the grave social problems of El Salvador that Castaneda defined in terms of two groups that lived within its territory, one whose mindset reflected twentieth-century thinking and another that still lived in a state of mental backwardness. He said that the great challenge for such a government was precisely to incorporate those (the "immense majority") who lived in the past and place them on the same footing with the modern groups in society. In sum, he said, what was needed was a regime of "renovation and evolution," committed to change but within reasonable limits and without harming the interests of those who already had a stake in society. According to him, the government of Hernández Martínez was precisely what the country needed: born within the "military class," it was "an essentially civilian and constitutional regime" concerned primarily with raising the living standards of the majority of Salvadorans.

To achieve these necessary changes in society, according to Castaneda, three basic conditions had to be met: discipline and the elimination of all political intrigue, sufficient resources to finance specific measures, and reforms of the country's legislation. In general, Castaneda's thinking was typical of an apologist for authoritarian forms of government who believed that social and economic change was necessary but who had little faith in the people's ability to improve their own lot. For example, he said that it was not enough to raise peasants' wages, because experience showed that they then work fewer days and end up drinking more alcohol. Still, he said, there was nothing as effective as an improvement in the lot of the people's lives to deter the spread of communism.[25] To that effect, the government of Hernández Martínez would initiate the construction of low-cost housing for urban workers and the distribution, through rental or sale, of state-owned land to peasants, all of this financed through special taxes on consumption under the name of *mejoramiento social* (social improvement).

The discourse in favor of redressing social grievances was balanced by Castaneda with calls for increasing political controls over the population to prevent expressions or actions of dissent, as well as to assure that the distribution of plots of land and low-cost housing not benefit "those who do not deserve them." Such controls, which helped establish the government's credentials with the country's coffee elite, were established partly through the introduction of mandatory identity papers (the so-called *cédula de vecindad*) that every adult was required to get from her or his municipality. This measure, introduced in June 1932, was a direct response to the peasant uprising and justified by Castaneda as a means of guaranteeing the security of all "peaceful and laborious" individuals against the elements of "anarchy and disorder."[26]

But there was also a more exclusive set of identity papers that could be purchased for one hundred *colones* (fifty dollars at the current exchange rate): the *cédula patriótica de defensa social*. The purpose of these documents was to raise one million *colones* for the Fondo de Mejoramiento Social and to provide the bearer with a more powerful identity card in accordance with her or his status. Castaneda specifically mentioned the rich as the target group for the *cédula patriótica*, as the funds raised would go for programs that aimed precisely at preventing attacks on property, a matter of interest to the "capitalist and well-to-do classes." But the middle class also could participate, since many of its members were supportive of the government's policies that addressed the "social problem"; for them, the government offered a plan to pay for the *cédula patriótica* in monthly installments.[27] Ownership of a *cédula patriótica* also allowed the bearer to request and receive a permit to carry weapons.

In the aftermath of the failed revolt, then, there emerged a new organization of society based on specific class and property privileges that addressed the continued threat of communist subversion. Society was organized along lines that identified the individual either as a friend or an enemy of the regime, as evidenced in the identity papers that she or he carried. Within this simplified concept of society, there was no room for major discussion or debate, both because most opposition had been cowed into nonexistence by the repression following the peasant insurrection and because the media was loath to engage in political debates of any substance.[28]

The Organization of Military and Paramilitary Structures

General Castaneda said that the Hernández Martínez regime was as "civilian and constitutional" as any previous one, with the only difference that a few military types were involved in its operation.[29] In fact, the armed forces were the backbone of the new regime and their discipline an example for the rest of society. The regime's concern with discipline had to do with its reiterated commitment to internal peace and order, which were necessary for the normal functioning of all productive and social activities, as expressed by President Hernández Martínez and his ministers during the more than twelve years that the regime was in power.[30]

Order and peace would be maintained by a watchful population and effective police forces of various types, the first to provide the government with intelligence on suspicious activities and the second to control or eliminate those involved. As a first measure, the paramilitary organization in the rural areas was reorganized and strengthened by the incorporation of more individuals into the *patrullas cantonales* and *escoltas militares*.[31] Unfortunately, there is very little information on the size and distribution of these rural patrols, which, as with the size of the regular armed forces, was handled as a military secret. Only for 1946, two years after the fall of Hernández Martínez, is there reference to the size of the "escoltas militares de barrio y cantón," which according to the minister of defense then added up to a nationwide total of 47,560.[32] El Salvador's population then was about one million, of which a quarter were adult males, which suggests that one out of every five adult males was active in the system of rural patrols. This proportion is similar to that for 1926 in the department of Ahuachapán, when the system was still in its infancy.

Although little can be said about the size or presence of the rural patrols, their importance was an enormous, if not vital source of military power. On the one hand, they operated at little or no cost to the government because the *patrulleros* received no remuneration.[33] On the other hand, they presumably were reliable allies of the military establishment since all their members had served in the army before and remained under the control of the *comandantes locales,* who were formally within the military structure of command. In this manner, the military established a structure of control and discipline that extended from the president of the republic himself to the humblest campesino.

This combined structure of military and paramilitary organizations was founded not only on a shared obedience to authority but also on an effective transmission of shared values. The recruit who entered the barracks for a one-year tour of duty was subject immediately to military training combined with schooling in the basics of arithmetic, reading, and writing, as well as notions of patriotism and duty.[34] Since the great majority of recruits came from the rural areas, the barracks was the only schooling they would receive in all their lives and served, in addition, to integrate them fully into the service of the state. It even is conceivable that the military much preferred unschooled recruits that then could be molded into exactly the type of citizen required by the regime.[35]

For many a male in the rural population, then, life included a very close and constant relationship with the military. At seventeen or eighteen, he was drafted and served as an infantry soldier. After his term of duty, he returned to his village to serve in the *escoltas militares* until around thirty years of age, at which time he became a member of the military reserves until the age of fifty. As a member of the *escoltas,* he had to invest time and effort without pay but there were obvious compensations: direct access to government authorities, higher social status, and special employment opportunities.[36]

In the course of the 1932 peasant rebellion, another paramilitary structure was created and later legalized: the Guardia Cívica. Members of the Guardia Cívica were recruited primarily from members of the elite and the middle class, although anyone with the "right credentials" could belong to this organization.[37] During the rebellion, members of the Guardia Cívica assisted the regular army in repelling attacks by insurgent peasants and in identifying and eliminating those suspected of participating in the uprising. Subsequently, they remained active in patrol duties similar to those of the *escoltas militares.*

An umbrella organization for the Guardia Cívica, the Asociación Cívica Salvadoreña (ACS) was created shortly after the rebellion to assist the military in the maintenance of public order, instruct the country's citizens on their civic duties and obedience to authority, and instill respect for property, work, and family.[38] The "Supreme Council" of the ACS included top military officers and members of the country's elite, with similar criteria applying to the departmental and local leadership structures of the ACS (made up of military commanders and "honorable individuals" of the community). The local organizations of the ACS were instructed specifically "to seek the rapprochement of the different social groups in order to maintain harmony between them."

The Guardia Cívica and the ACS were granted public recognition by the regime on 5 November 1932 during a parade, when the archbishop of San Salvador handed them their insignia and President Hernández Martínez was proclaimed "supreme chief" of the ACS. Subsequent legislation placed the ACS on the same footing as a state institution: those who criticized the ACS or its members would be treated as "enemies of peace and public tranquillity."[39]

About a year after the insurrection, the Guardia Cívica had ceased largely to function in its role of patrolling the urban and rural areas. Its members now engaged in occasional parades and met to discuss issues of common interest.[40] But the military establishment that the Guardia Cívica had supported continued to exercise its authority over the country, much like it had been doing since the beginning of the century but now with an openly political role. The military, including the Guardia Nacional, its one security force at the time, became the guarantor of the fundamental institutions of the state and an "unbreachable barrier" in the face of adversity.[41]

The regular army remained modest in size during the regime of Hernández Martínez: three thousand soldiers "to man the forts, ports, and military depots."[42] Nor did it have large amounts of weapons; the machine gun was its principal offensive weapon, it had no motorized equipment to speak of, and its air force was mostly unprepared for combat. Even if it had wanted to, the precarious economic conditions of the 1930s limited the purchases of military hardware. During the 1930s and early 1940s the officer corps experienced some reductions in size (see table 2.1). Particularly radical was a cut in the number of retired and reserve officers in 1942 as a result of instructions issued to all retired and reserve officers demanding that they present official documentation if they wished to retain their status. Since most apparently were not "regular" officers to begin with, they were scratched from the lists.[43]

Its cadets trained at the military school for three and then four years but the courses they took were mostly equivalent to what a civilian student would study in a public or private school.[44] However, the outbreak of war in Europe increased United States concern about military preparedness in El Salvador, as well as the influence of Italian and German diplomats and military officers in the Salvadoran armed forces. Hernández Martínez had named a German general, Eberhardt Bohnstedt, to head the military school in 1938. Under pressure from Washington, Hernández Martínez requested his resignation just two years later. In 1941, a U.S. colonel became director of the academy and the U.S. legation became fully staffed with military at-

TABLE 2.1
Officer Corps of the Salvadoran Military

	1914	1920	1925	1930	1933	1936	1939	1942	1950
Active	1,100	475	358	317	349	380	370	372	355
Reserves	3,115	2,990	2,879	2,784	3,441	3,453	3,445	912	848
Retired					669	757	721		
Guardia officers					36	53	53		
Air force officers						5	8		

Source: El Salvador Ministerio de Defensa Nacional, *Anuario Militar* (San Salvador: Imprenta Nacional) for corresponding years. Reserve and retired officers were grouped as of 1939. The separate Guardia Nacional officer list was eliminated in 1936, as was that for the air force in 1939.

taches who assessed El Salvador's military needs. When El Salvador declared war on the Axis shortly after the United States did, it received a loan of $1.64 million in weapons.[45]

In sum, the military was not designed to fight a conventional war against foreign enemies but to defeat, instead, internal enemies of the state. After 1931, it also began to gain experience in the direct administration of the state apparatus. In addition to the principal government ministries of war (defense) and government (interior), the regime of Hernández Martínez appointed mostly military officers to the departmental governorships; together with the departmental military commanders, military officers exercised overwhelming control over public administration and what few political activities were permitted.[46] When a new constitution was written and ratified in 1939, even the traditional autonomy of the municipal councils was canceled to a great extent as a result of the president's authority to appoint mayors directly; only the council members would be elected by the "neighbors" of each town.[47]

POLITICAL ACTIVITIES UNDER THE HERNÁNDEZ MARTÍNEZ REGIME

El Salvador never ceased to have a republican and democratic form of government under the Hernández Martínez regime. Up until 1939, the country's political life was governed by the Constitution of 1885, a liberal document that still holds the record for longevity in El Salvador's history. And the constitution that replaced it in 1939 defined the form of government as "republican, democratic, and representative." However, the *practice* of republican and democratic forms of government was quite something else.

The Hernández Martínez regime came into existence precisely as a reaction to liberal, electoral democracy. The peasant rebellion of 1932 only hammered in that point and made order and discipline the regime's bywords. While electoral events continued to occur as mandated by the constitution and various by-laws, the regime viewed organized political activity as a threat to the country's economic and social stability. It is not even possible to determine how certain political events developed because the press did not report them and official statements are extremely spare. For example, popular elections for president of the republic were held on 13, 14, and 15 January 1935, but no results were posted.[48] Nor were any results published for the elections for deputies to the National Assembly (legislature) in January 1936. The only available reference to an electoral turnout is for the constituent assembly election in 1939 when 210,810 voters cast their ballots, a number nearly equivalent to the total electoral body according to the government.[49]

Hernández Martínez was reelected in 1939 and again in 1944, but on both occasions it was the legislative branch that did the honors. In the first case, the sitting constituent assembly decided to reappoint Hernández Martínez for a third term to guarantee the country's tranquillity and in response to "the sovereign will of the people, expressed clearly, definitely, and precisely in the records of the plebiscite that were annexed to the results of the elections held on 23, 24, and 25 October of last year [for constituent assembly] and of the town meetings *[cabildos abiertos]* held previously in the entire country."[50] In the second case, just three months before his overthrow, a second constituent assembly decided unanimously to give Hernández Martínez a fourth term (until December 1949), explaining its decision in terms of the advantages of continuity in government and the challenge represented by the post–world war era. It also stated that the government of Hernández Martínez represented a "truly democratic" order of things.[51]

The reelections of Hernández Martínez and the renewal of the legislative assembly and municipal councils went completely unopposed. With the exception of some opposition activities reported by the government, the years of the *martinato* seem to have transpired under the most complete sense of peace and tranquillity imaginable.[52] In addition to the memories of 1932, which hung like a cloud over the nation, the threat of political persecution for those not partisan to or tolerant of the regime was underlined by a state of siege that lasted from January 1932 until March 1935, and again from December 1941 until the overthrow of the dictator, with a limitation on constitutional rights in the interim.[53] The state of siege allowed the police and Guardia Nacional to arrest people and search homes without warrants, to control the contents of all forms of correspondence, and to limit expressions of public views.

The states of siege were complemented by specific laws and constitutional provisions that limited personal and collective rights. Part of this legislation had been inherited from the regime of Pío Romero Bosque, including the prohibition of "communist activities," reforms of the penal code that defined the nature of "illicit meetings," and a code for the celebration of public meetings and demonstrations.[54] Subsequently, the Constitution of 1939 recognized freedom of expression and press but prohibited the circulation of material that "tends to the dissolution of Salvadoran society or the moral breakdown of its customs"; a series of amendments to the constitution passed in 1944 included one that prohibited outright any organization contrary to democratic principles.[55] Informal agreements also were reached between the regime and the owners of newspapers to limit reporting "on internal politics . . . and religious issues that do nothing else but injure the deeply-rooted sentiments of the people." Also off limits were "anti-social ideas" and all ideas "contrary to our democratic system, whose tolerance at other times produced . . . deep wounds in the Salvadoran family, that have with difficulty been stanched."[56]

Within this restrictive legal and institutional environment, the only organizations that could, in practice, enter the field of politics were those that had the direct blessing of the regime. As it happens, that meant only one: the official party, the Partido Nacional "Pro-Patria." This organization played a key role in organizing the vote for the 1935 presidential election, the only popular election that Hernández Martínez entered after becoming president. Even though he ran unopposed, the party organization seems to have made a big effort to register voters in its lists and prepare them for voting day.

Data is not available at this time to present a nationwide panorama of the party's activities prior to the 1935 election, but select documentation from the western department of Sonsonate provides some insight into the workings of this organization. In the first place, the Pro-Patria organization was integrated into the government bureaucracy; its local activists received instructions from government ministers in the capital, which instructed them on how to register and organize their membership.[57] Secondly, party proselytism centered primarily on the registration of members in the party rolls to commit them to vote for the official candidate on election day, in addition to the distribution of party identification documents to those so registered; on the basis of the available evidence, there seems to have been very little ideological content to Pro-Patria's campaign.[58] And thirdly, attendance at the polls was a carefully planned and monitored affair in which voters were not left on their own. For example, the president of the Sonsonate party committee wrote to the national headquarters to explain how they would deliver the vote: "We have thought to entertain the crowd with movies in the evening and invite them then to meet at a predetermined place at three in the morning, where we will hand out coffee, tamales, and bread; there they will be duly organized to arrive at the voting booths at the prescribed time, all of this in agreement with the authorities."[59]

When the regime got around to passing an electoral law in 1939, it did little to promote the exercise of democratic rights. While the vote was obligatory of all adult males, women who wished to vote had to demonstrate that they had completed the first three years of elementary schooling. Voting itself was not secret; instead, voters would present themselves before the electoral officials and declare in a "loud voice" their political preferences, afterward signing their name on a list or requesting another to do so if they themselves were illiterate.[60]

Political activities, then, were highly controlled and limited only to electoral events. Part of the result expected by the regime from these preordained electoral results was a degree of legitimacy that would enable Hernández Martínez to claim that he headed a truly representative government; this was an important consideration, especially in the arena of foreign recognition. But the registration of supporters for the cause of Pro-Patria and the voting procedures at the polls also enabled the regime to exercise additional social and political control over the population. When the *patrullas cantonales, escoltas militares,* and Guardia Cívica are added to the system of military service and reserve forces and these, in turn, to the registration lists of Pro-Patria and the polling places, the result is an impressive system of incorporation and oversight of the population that left hardly any room for the exercise of civil and political rights expected in a democracy.

THE END OF THE DICTATORSHIP

During the first half of 1944, a number of countries in Central America were shaken by an upsurge of disgust with dictatorial forms of government. In two of these, Guatemala and El Salvador, the government was overthrown but only in Guatemala did a more open and democratic regime take its place. In El Salvador, Hernández Martínez was forced to resign his post and for a few months it seemed that a coalition of democratic, civilian-led forces might have the upper hand. In the end, the military retained control of the government and reinstituted a variant of the *martinato* that lasted for another four years.

Still, the events of 1944 that led to the resignation of Hernández Martínez are of great importance because they offer an opportunity to analyze the relationship between a number of democratic social forces, long suppressed by the military regime, and the armed forces, which were their main suppressors. Both were strongly influenced by the international situation, in which the imminent defeat of the totalitarian powers of the Axis raised the question of how great a commitment to democracy might be expected from the Central American regimes. In El Salvador, at least, the commitment was more formal than real, but the concessions that were extracted from the military for a few months during 1944 were the result of a hard-won battle that began some years before the events of April and May 1944.

The first open expressions of rejection toward the Hernández Martínez regime came from within its own ranks when in 1939 a number of high public officials resigned in protest over the president's plans to promulgate a new constitution. The ministers of foreign affairs and public works and the vice ministers of defense, government, and education all left the government, an important blow to a regime that was trying to give itself a new face of constitutional legality.[61] The new constitution included a very clear prohibition of presidential reelection that many took at face value. However, when Hernández Martínez decided in early 1944 to amend the constitution to permit his reelection, it was not long before both civilian and military groups were seeking ways to overthrow the government.

Forceful resistance to the regime initially came from within the military, including officers who had graduated from the military school since 1930. Some of them, who called themselves the Juventud Militar, issued typewritten fliers in February 1944 attacking Hernández Martínez for violating the constitution and preventing an open discussion of his government's excesses; they were especially critical of the president's desire to remain in office beyond the end of his term.[62] On 2 April, a group of officers and some civilians attempted a military putsch in San Salvador by taking over two infantry regiments and the air force. The government responded with force, sending in loyal battalions to put down the rebellion; about one hundred people were killed in the fighting in the streets of the capital, most of them civilians who were caught in the crossfire.[63] The government arrested a good number of the military and civilian conspirators and ordered the execution of twenty-one officers after a hasty trial. Not all were shot but the divisions within the military establishment were no longer a secret.[64]

The president's hold over the military did not crumble suddenly. A full month of civilian resistance to the regime, led initially by groups of university students, was required to pressure Hernández Martínez to resign. By the first days of May, opposition to the president was sufficiently widespread to spark a general strike to demand Hernández Martínez's resignation. Shops and public services closed their doors, while Hernández Martínez tried to rally support behind his regime. He addressed the nation by radio on 5 May, thanking the military for remaining loyal and praising the city's workers for not supporting the uprising. He also explained that the entire country was at peace and at work, that only in the capital were the subversives trying to create panic among the people. He ended by calling for the professional and clerical workers to return to work so that shops and banks could continue to provide the humble folk with the services they required. In that manner, he said, social harmony would be restored and the country would achieve prosperity.[65]

The president also sought to persuade the country that the military was behind him. A manifesto signed on 6 May by 196 officers of infantry, artillery, air force, and police units in San Salvador stressed the military's unity on behalf of public order and the defense of "sovereign rights" but criticized those "ambitious politicians who disregard the constitution's provisions in order to satisfy their own passion for personal interest, while damaging the interests of the community."[66]

Still, the pressure on Hernández Martínez was too great for him to remain in office. Three days after the military officers' manifesto in support of his government, Hernández Martínez resigned the presidency and turned it over to his trusted minister of defense, General Andres I. Menéndez, who became the provisional president of the republic.

The Failed Democratic Opening

As of 9 May, El Salvador entered into a six-month period of heightened political activity as a variety of political groups prepared for the presidential elections scheduled for early 1945. During these months, an opening toward a democratic form of government seemed possible but in the end failed due to the disorganized nature of the opposition and the military's concern that events were spinning out of its control.

The civilian opposition to Hernández Martínez that came to the surface during April and May of 1944 had been nurtured in the discourse of the struggle against fascism and totalitarianism of the Allied powers. As such, it was a largely urban, middle-class opposition that perceived a basic contradiction in El Salvador's political system: a military dictator who had occupied the executive office for over a dozen years and had been reelected to office by a pliant legislative body that, in turn, had been elected unopposed. The military, that had provided the institutional support for the regime of Hernández Martínez, was an accomplice, too.

However, Hernández Martínez's resignation and the installation of the new president, General Menéndez, convinced the opposition that a fresh beginning was possible without an overhaul of the different branches of government. Thus, the officer corps of the armed forces was left untouched and the legislative assembly that had voted on Hernández Martínez's constitutional reforms and reelection was left in place. What did change was the amount of political space allowed to the political forces (including the opposition to Hernández Martínez) to make their case, seek out supporters, and organize their cadres for the upcoming election. But that space could be closed as easily as it was opened.

In general, two main political forces emerged during the five months of political opening: the movement led by Arturo Romero, a medical doctor, which included most of the opponents of the dictatorship of Hernández Martínez, and the forces that sought to reimpose a government similar to that just overthrown, including a good number of military officers. The majority of officers, still recovering from the fighting in April, remained on the sidelines for a while and let the political forces have it out, a practice that was to be repeated during other coups in the future.

The civilian forces led by Romero that had worked to overthrow Hernández Martínez appealed especially to the military, since they realized that its role was vital to achieve an electoral victory as well as to remain in office once elected. They claimed that the military had fought for freedom and was now one with the people. They also insisted that they were not communists but democrats committed to the establishment of basic civic rights and the progressive betterment of the people's conditions.[67] The party around which they organized, the Partido Unión Demócrata (PUD), stood for a fairly conventional program of social reform, including social security, minimum wage, literacy campaigns, and expanded state-supported primary education. However, the PUD made hardly any mention of rural issues, which it addressed only in terms of increased mechanization of agriculture, improvement in the living conditions of the peasantry, and agrarian legislation (without spelling it out). It did specifically make a commitment to improve the living conditions in military barracks and provide training opportunities for officers, both within the country and abroad.[68]

The opponents of the Romeristas accused them of being communists in sheep's clothing intent on taking over the state and establishing a Stalinist dictatorship. They criticized the increased activity of labor unions, from which they expected the next surge of communist subversion that "will envelop in its nets all those naive and simple people who, unfortunately, will suffer the same fate as in 1932." They reminded the voters that communists everywhere had burned churches, assassinated priests, and attacked the military (communists were the "sworn enemies" of the military).[69]

Accusations and counteraccusations in fliers and public meetings all came to an end on 21 October, when the military decided to remove General Menéndez from the presidency. The timing of the coup was no coincidence. The previous day in neighboring Guatemala, a group of young reformist officers had staged a successful coup promising sweeping democratic reforms. Whereas Menéndez seemed disposed to allow free elections to occur, Colonel Osmín Aguirre y Salinas, who replaced him, was well-known for his conservative point of view. He had served as a member of the *directorio militar* of 1931 and as chief of police under the provisional government of General Menéndez. In his first message to the nation on 21 October, Aguirre began by pointing out that "anarchistic" movements of recent days had kept the country in a state of anxiety and divisiveness. Although he promised to respect electoral freedoms, he also insisted on the need for peace and security to rid the country of the "specter . . . of class struggle." By bringing into his government individuals of a variety of political persuasions, he reasoned, the people would be represented according to "the purest democratic principles."[70]

In fact, Aguirre's coup d'etat put an end to El Salvador's democratic opening initiated just a little under six months before. A few days later, Arturo Romero and other opposition leaders were sent into exile in Guatemala. A call for a general strike and even an attempted invasion from Guatemala by Romero's supporters were insufficient to force Aguirre from office.[71] When elections were held in January the field for president had been narrowed down to one candidate, General Salvador Castaneda Castro, one of Hernández Martínez's earliest collaborators and minister of the interior in 1932 and 1933. Even though Castaneda Castro had been retired from the military by Hernández Martínez, he still represented the continuation of the military regime of years past, albeit enveloped in a discourse of democratic practices and values.[72] Under his direction, the government of El Salvador would continue to exclude political groups that were not con sidered convenient to the interests of the state, although the rhetoric of his regime was quite similar to that of the civilian reformist groups that followed Romero.[73]

CONCLUSION

In a matter of thirteen years, the role of the armed forces of El Salvador had changed radically. Up until 1930, the military had played a subsidiary role to civilian politicians and economic elites. This does not mean that the military was unimportant but that its autonomy was defined by the existing political system and its functions limited by the existing political culture. In 1930, the minister of war was a civilian to whom the armed forces answered in matters of organization and operations. Similarly, the military's budget was discussed by the legislature and publicly known. But already under the Araujo presidency, General Hernández Martínez was appointed minister of war in especially trying social and political circumstances that led eventually to the coup d'etat of December 1931. Moreover, the armed forces' paramilitary presence in the rural areas was quite pervasive prior to the coup. In other words, the process of militarization was well underway before Hernández Martínez assumed the reins of power.

The new government of Hernández Martínez did not formulate and execute its policies only in response to the economic crisis of the 1930s. The social protest evident under the Araujo presidency and the peasant rebellion of January 1932 were much more traumatic in that they convinced a good number of military officers that social pressures within the country could not be handled by democratic means. Instead, a paramount concern of the military was the maintenance of "perfect order," that is, a political system in which no crisis was allowed to happen, in which no anomalous behavior was permitted, and in which repressive measures were the answer to practically all forms of social and political dissent. Put in simple terms, the Hernández Martínez regime attempted to replicate the discipline of the barracks in the entire country, a discipline with which the entire officer corps and a good number of members of the *escoltas militares* were already familiar.

The military really had little choice. If democratic forms had been respected, the result would have been some program of reforms to decompress social and political pressures, but that was no guarantee against revolution or disorder. The existence of the military would have been strongly questioned, too, as it was identified most clearly with the old regime. Thus, a form of government that did not allow the imponderables of democracy

to surface was best for those already in positions of authority. This was an especially important concern in a society where the room for political ma-
neuvering was very limited given the severe maldistribution and concentration of wealth and power.

Since the Hernández Martínez regime did not undertake any significant
reordering of wealth and power, its principal function was reduced to guaranteeing the existing social structure. The reiterated use of terms such as
order, discipline, tranquillity, anarchy, and *lawlessness* defined the regime's priorities and concerns much more than specific policies of social and economic development. *Democracy* only came into use near the end of the
1930s, when the regime became aware that its interests lay in a close relationship with the United States and a rejection of the overtures of the Axis
powers, Germany and Italy. Furthermore, democracy was not understood by
the military leaders as the practice of open debate and contested elections
but as a matter of "public opinion" and "popular support" as perceived by
the military leaders themselves.[74]

As in the other Central American countries governed by military officers, the opposition that the Hernández Martínez regime and its immediate
successors had to face was largely urban and mostly middle class. This opposition could become quite vociferous but its real political weight was limited, as it realized itself when it appealed to the military for support and understanding during the unstable times of 1944. As long as the most
powerful part of the military remained united behind the military president, there was little danger of an overthrow of the government. In fact,
Hernández Martínez's resignation did not alter the preeminent position of
the military as the supreme institution of the state or the role of the rural
paramilitary organization that by 1944 was integrated fully into the structure of power.

Nor were all civilian-led political forces and factions opposed to the military regimes. Hernández Martínez and his successors in the presidency had
no trouble filling the most important positions in government with civilians.
The legislative assembly was nearly all civilian, as were most of the ministers
in the cabinet and the entire state bureaucracy (teachers, clerks, accoun-
tants, scribes). The judicial branch was run by civilians. The most sensitive
posts were reserved naturally for the military: the presidency, the key political ministries (defense, government/interior), and the departmental governorships. Still, Minister of Government Castaneda Castro was not entirely
off the mark when he described the Hernández Martínez regime in 1933 as
"essentially civilian" with a little help from the military.

In such circumstances, the civilian opposition to the military governments was reduced to espousing moderate, reformist policies that sought to return the military to the barracks while ignoring some of the more fundamental social and economic problems that had led to the severe crisis of 1932. In turn, some of the military's younger officers would pick up the reformist discourse and make it their own, seeking out alliances with those same civilians who had opposed the Hernández Martínez, Aguirre y Salinas, and Castaneda Castro regimes. The revolution of 1948, discussed in the next chapter, constituted precisely a realignment of political forces, in which the military continued to play the central role.

THE NEW ARMED FORCES OF THE REVOLUTIONARY GOVERNMENT

THE 1948 COUP: ANOTHER BEGINNING

THE MILITARY leaders that overthrew president Arturo Araujo in December 1931 called themselves the "military youth" *(juventud militar),* thereby suggesting that a new generation of military officers had come to the fore, intent on providing fresh leadership to a country staggering under the weight of a severe economic and social crisis. The peasant rebellion a month later certainly helped to justify the need for a military government, at least in the minds of the officers themselves. The political calm imposed by the twelve years of the Hernández Martínez regime reinforced the military's perception that it had done its duty to preserve the state.

However, the young officers that initiated the *martinato* were shunted aside from positions of leadership only a few days after the overthrow of President Araujo. Their hold on power was short-lived and their political influence thereafter quite minimal. The events that preceded Hernández Martínez's resignation in 1944 suggest that younger officers again played an important role in military politics but, as in December 1931, they were quickly overpowered by their more conservative seniors, who continued to run the country very much like the previous regime had done. These historical precedents were not lost on the young officers who undertook the 1948 coup against President Castaneda Castro.

As Salvadoran coups go, the one in 1948 was rather a fluke. There was no evident economic crisis nor grassroots movement destabilizing the government. The military establishment continued to enjoy the privileges and stature awarded it by the regime of Hernández Martínez and its immediate successors. The country's business class perceived the beginning of a new era of development based on the recipes of international organizations that championed hydroelectric power generation and technologically advanced agriculture as answers to a variety of social ills.[1] For a small and resource-poor country, these recipes made eminent sense. Why, then, the 1948 coup?

In the absence of manifest social or economic instability, the causes can be attributed to political processes that had been ongoing within the military for some time. One of these was the frustration of younger officers with the persistent hold on power of the older generals, most of them lacking in formal military training.[2] Another was the younger officers' realization that social and economic change was accelerating in Central America and that sooner or later the Salvadoran government would have to reckon with it.[3] And finally, a small number of professional military officers who had trained abroad became impatient with what they perceived as a cautious, unimaginative attitude toward reform among their senior commanders.

Already in June 1945, just a few months after General Castaneda Castro had assumed office, a group of younger officers attempted a coup against his government. In the aftermath, a number of the plotters were exiled, including Major Oscar Osorio, a key figure in the 1948 coup, who was packed off to Mexico. As has been pointed out, Castaneda Castro, mindful of the consequences of Hernández Martínez's harsh punishment of the insurgent officers in April 1944, did not dare to judge and punish the conspirators of June 1945, a concession to military plotters that continued under the governments of the next decades.[4]

Castaneda Castro's solution to the 1945 coup attempt only postponed open opposition to his regime within the armed forces. The officers involved in the plot continued to keep in touch, waiting for an opportunity to make another attempt, which came near the end of 1948. The trigger on this occasion was precisely the same as in 1944: the sitting president's intention of continuing in office beyond the prescribed term. As it happens, Castaneda Castro had made statements about the critical situation in the world and the need for continued military vigilance "to conserve and strengthen the democratic system" in the face of "enemies of different aspect but of an equally terrible character."[5]

As his four-year term in office neared its end, Castaneda Castro tried a sudden maneuver to enable him to continue as president a couple of years more. He called the members of the legislature into session on 13 December 1948 and had them put together a convoluted decree that called for elections within three days for a constituent assembly to prolong his period in office until early 1951.[6] The very next day, in the afternoon, shooting broke out in downtown San Salvador between regular troops under the orders of rebellious officers and police forces loyal to the president. In a matter of hours, after intense negotiations in which the diplomatic corps played an intermediary role, Castaneda Castro resigned his office and was taken prisoner.[7] At this moment, many of the senior officers and their civilian allies who were the visible heads of the old regime were retired and some even were imprisoned and tried for a variety of offenses. For all practical purposes, the *martinato* was over.

The day after the coup, a rally in support of the coup leaders was held in the main plaza in downtown San Salvador. One of the rebel officers, Lieutenant Colonel Manuel de Jesús Córdova, announced the formation of a new government headed by a Revolutionary Council of Government (Consejo de Gobierno Revolucionario—CGR). He also addressed the reasons behind the coup, among which he underlined Castaneda's violation of the constitutional norm prohibiting presidential reelection, the dissatisfaction within the armed forces over unfair disciplinary measures, and the practice of military spying on the officers themselves. He announced, furthermore, that the CGR was intent on creating "a new system of government" based on the military's defense of "the rights of the people." To that effect, Córdova called for an understanding "on the basis of reciprocal concessions between the people and the army."[8]

Many of the eight thousand in attendance at the meeting in the plaza were university students, who lent their support to the new government when they realized that the young officers appeared serious about making a break with the past. The student newspaper, *Opinión Estudiantil*, which had been banned under the previous regime, was allowed to circulate again. News also broke that both ex-Presidents Castaneda Castro and Aguirre were in jail, accused of disregard of constitutional provisions and illicit enrichment and corruption. A few days later, the CGR published a decree ordering the trial of twenty-four officials (six military officers and eighteen civilians) of the Castaneda regime accused of corruption. Another decree by the junta repealed the constitution, product of legislatures "that met without any legitimate mandate," and made a case for a new constitution "adapted to the new political, social, and economic conditions under which the nation's life was evolving."[9]

These measures seem to have generated some popular support. Two weeks after the coup, a "day of national rejoicing" was celebrated at the cathedral in San Salvador, where soldiers and university students stood guard around the members of the CGR. The archbishop asked those present to back the new government and promised that the clergy would support "the claims of the Salvadoran people." Reynaldo Galindo Pohl, a civilian member of the CGR and one of the student leaders who participated in the coup, promised to restore the rights of the people, clean up public administration, and "set the foundations of a democratic system in accordance with the structure of the state and the conscience of the people."[10] In March of the next year, another particularly interesting public event took place at the national university. On this occasion, Major Osorio handed the CGR's guiding principles, the so-called "Fourteen Points," to the rector, who in turn openly expressed his support for the military and the program of the new government.[11]

The Fourteen Points, which were issued ten days after the coup, expressed the views of the junior officers and their civilian allies about the future they wanted to build. As such, it is a key document in understanding the contradictory nature of military politics in El Salvador. Four of the Fourteen Points speak about the need to build an effective democracy (including free and honest elections), three discuss a new constitutional and governmental order (including municipal autonomy, effective separation of the branches of government, and a reduction in the powers of the executive branch), and two address the need to improve the efficiency of the bureaucracy. But it is the two on the armed forces that are the most intriguing, since one insists on returning the military to its apolitical condition (before 1930?) and another calls for national unity so as to bring together "civilians and national army into an indestructible block."[12] The desire to carry out reforms in alliance with civilians and to return the military to its professional, apolitical role of "guardian of the freedoms and the sovereignty of the Republic" would create severe problems of disunity and instability in succeeding years, both within the armed forces as well as in groups of civilian politicians.

However, in the first years of the new government, popular support and economic conditions worked on behalf of the military rulers and their civilian allies. The international price of coffee rose to record heights during the first half of the 1950s and large-scale production of cotton along the coastal plain began after the construction of highways into hitherto inaccessible areas. Electrical generation, a precondition for the creation of new industries in the urban areas, increased dramatically with the operation of the first dam on the Lempa River, financed with a loan from the World Bank. In sum, the state assumed an activist role in promoting economic and social development, which the country's military rulers presented as their crowning achievement.

MILITARY REFORMISM

The government's commitment to economic and social development was not entirely new. A few months before its overthrow, the Castaneda regime made noises about drafting a labor code and creating a national social security system.[13] It also had begun initial studies for the construction of a hydroelectric dam on the Lempa River to generate the power required for industrialization. In general, it was clear to the Castaneda government that the country's future should be based on more than coffee and that international conditions were ripe for a diversification of the economic base. However, the new revolutionary regime enunciated a much clearer and more coherent policy of development, both in terms of legislation and specific programs of action.

Only four months after taking office, the CGR appointed a commission to propose government policies to stimulate employment, raise salaries, and increase productivity.[14] These goals would be possible only if new sources of energy were available to the country, which explains the government's concern about harnessing the hydroelectric potential of the Lempa River. Galindo Pohl, who by mid-1950 had resigned his post on the CGR to become president of the constituent assembly, stated the government's policy in no uncertain terms. He understood that El Salvador's "possibilities in agriculture are limited" but that industry is a viable alternative. However, industry requires large amounts of energy and the Lempa River "is the salvation of our country . . . Without the Lempa our economic future would be somber."[15]

In anticipation of industrial development, the CGR proceeded to enact labor legislation. In August 1950, a labor code was decreed by the CGR that set the basis for the social legislation of the following years. Its provisions reflected the controlled nature of social change envisioned by the country's new rulers. For example, the labor code explicitly excluded workers employed by rural enterprises and those engaged in seasonal work (such as sugar cane cutters and coffee pickers). People employed as domestic help also were forbidden to organize unions. Those who could organize, such as factory workers, were limited to protecting their social and economic rights but had to refrain from expressing political views or participating in party politics within the context of their unions, much less carrying out "subversive activities" or any "that go counter to the democratic regime."[16]

Such limitations on labor reflected the armed forces' decision to retain their traditional political role within the country's rural areas and to concede some leeway to the labor movement within the urban areas only. Those who did not abide by these limitations were treated harshly.[17] Those who did had an opportunity to enter into a labor aristocracy that benefitted from medical care and pension plans under the social security program and could buy a subsidized house from the government's housing agency.[18]

Another important element of the new government's social policy was public education. After presiding over the drafting of the new constitution, Reynaldo Galindo Pohl became minister of culture in 1951 and proceeded to strengthen the state's role in education. Public spending on education over the decade reached its highest levels both in absolute and proportional terms, rising from a little over US$2.8 million in 1949 to over US$12 million in 1959. The unity of soldiers and teachers was extolled as a pillar of the revolution, with teachers molding "the soul of the nation" and soldiers guaranteeing peace and order.[19]

However, the most radical of the reform measures, on paper at least, had to do with the creation of a new system for the selection of elected public officials. During the dictatorship of Hernández Martínez and its successor regimes, elections were considered an exercise in legitimation, an expression of popular will under the guiding presence of authorities that knew what was best for the people. The regime born of the 1948 coup understood that elections (and democracy) had a different function: to provide political alternatives to the people (within limits) and to assure that the popular will, as expressed in votes, was duly respected. As mentioned before, these concerns were included in the Fourteen Points issued by the CGR a few days after taking office and addressed indirectly when the CGR abolished the Constitution of 1939. By stating its intention of breaking radically with the past, the CGR was committing itself to the establishment of a democratic system that had been the byword of political reformers from 1944 onward.

A first step in that direction was the creation, by decree, of a transitory electoral law *(ley transitoria electoral)* issued at the beginning of 1950. Under the provisions of this law, a national electoral authority was established for the first time in the country's history: the Consejo Central de Elecciones (CCE). This body was made up of three permanent officials and three deputies; one of each appointed by the CGR and by the Supreme Court of Justice, which in turn appointed the remaining two. Since the justices of the Supreme Court had been appointed by the CGR, the composition of the CCE turned out to be entirely favorable to the government. The CCE appointed the fourteen departmental electoral councils, which in turn proposed the appointments of the municipal electoral councils to the CCE. The local electoral councils *(juntas receptoras de votos)*, which directly handled the voting procedures, were appointed by the municipal electoral councils. All electoral officials from the departmental level downward received salaries as employees of the state.[20]

In general, the authority that emerged in 1950 to handle elections for the legislative and executive branches was beholden to the government, from those appointed to the CCE to the lesser officials who drew state salaries. This arrangement, in itself, would have sufficed to produce electoral results favorable to the government. But the electoral law also established that all public political events (demonstrations, marches, meetings) required the departmental governor's permission before they could be held. It also retained the practice of assigning all legislative seats from a given department to the party winning a majority, thereby reducing the chances of pluralist representation in the legislative branch of government. Otherwise, the electoral law stipulated no exclusion of individuals or groups from the political process by making voting obligatory (and secret) for all individuals above eighteen years of age and by enfranchising women.

While nothing in the electoral law need have been an obstacle to a functioning party or electoral system, in August 1949 the CGR had already banned communist parties or groups, as well as parties with religious affiliation or that received economic aid from abroad.[21] By placing administrative obstacles on free party organization and action and defining who could be recognized as a party or not, the regime defined its concept of democracy in terms of exclusion of those whose presence was deemed inconvenient.

Still, the political reforms of the CGR did represent a significant change over electoral organization and practice of the past. In the first place, political parties were recognized as permanent fixtures of the political system and not just as conjunctural expressions of political opposition or personalistic movements. In the second place, the right to vote was enshrined as a basic right for everyone, independent of gender, social class, or educational qualifications. In the third place, electoral events were scheduled and held religiously as mandated by the country's laws and constitution. These important advances would be respected by all succeeding governments and altered only during late 1960 and early 1961 when coup and countercoup interrupted the "normal" operation of the system.

Full representative democracy, on the other hand, still remained a distant goal. While the electoral law explicitly excluded the military (and the clergy) from voting, it placed no limits on political participation by military officers in active service. Nor were limits placed on the material support that parties might receive from individuals, groups, or the state apparatus itself. In other words, the conditions for the existence of an "official" or government-supported party were still very much like those in the two preceding decades.

As was the case of previous governments that sought to legitimize their existence, the principal concern of the CGR was the writing and promulgation of a new constitution. To that effect, the CGR called for elections in March 1950 to choose simultaneously a constituent assembly and a president; the elected president would remain in office for five years, subject to the provisions of the future constitution, while the constituent assembly, after promulgating the new constitution, would function as the legislative body until the end of its term.[22] Osorio resigned from the CGR to become a candidate for president and a new party, the Partido Revolucionario de Unificación Democrática (PRUD), was organized to back Osorio's candidacy and to field a slate of candidates to the assembly.

A number of opposition parties formed to contest Osorio's candidacy but the opposition eventually boiled down to only one party, the Partido de Acción Renovadora (PAR), whose candidate for president turned out to be another military officer, Colonel José Asencio Menéndez. Nearly 650,000 people went to the polls after an uneventful election campaign that lasted a little under two months. The results gave PRUD and Osorio a comfortable majority of a little over 345,000 votes to approximately 266,000 for PAR (in addition to 36,256 votes declared void).[23] However, PAR did win a majority of votes in four departments, giving it fourteen deputies in the constituent assembly to thirty-eight for PRUD. PAR previously had accused PRUD of illegal campaign and voting practices but it did not present any formal charges of fraud once the results were announced.[24] As an initial exercise in electoral politics, the campaign and the election results held out promise for the future; however, this would be the only time in the 1950s that an opposition party would sit in the legislative branch of government.

The constituent assembly finished drafting and approved a new constitution for the country in August 1950. While ratifying the essentially democratic nature of the political system promised by the CGR, it contained ample provisions for social and economic justice, similar to those of the Mexican Constitution of 1917. Economic freedom was guaranteed insofar as it was consonant with the "social interest," and private property would be allowed "as a social function." Labor organizations and a system of social security for workers were mandated. However, article 158 specifically prohibited all propaganda "advocating anarchistic or anti-democratic doctrines."[25]

This provision, reiterated in the Constitution of 1961, allowed the government to handle groups on the Left, whether moderate or radical, with particular harshness and became one of the principal bones of contention of political conflict until the peace accords of 1992.

Osorio's presidency lost no time in accusing opponents of the regime of trying to subvert democracy. In March 1951, the government imposed a state of exception *(estado de sitio),* which Osorio explained was necessary to counter the activities of the "enemies" of Salvadoran democracy. He said these enemies were of two types: those who wished to regain privileges they enjoyed under the Constitution of 1886 by reimposing the social and economic conditions in existence prior to 1948; and those who wished to establish a communist state in El Salvador by pushing the country toward a crisis. The first were not identified by name but stood accused of raising money "among the blind" who refused to see that conditions of poverty and injustice led to social rebellion; Osorio was referring to the rich who rejected the government's policies of social betterment and economic reform. The second group was identified by name as the Communist Party of El Salvador, engaged in subverting military discipline, opposing reform measures that benefitted the working class, and provoking labor organizations into unreasonable actions to destabilize the economy.[26]

Osorio reiterated his warnings to the extremes on the Right and the Left *(reaccionarios y extremistas)* in a speech on the third anniversary of the 1948 coup in December 1951. He described the "men of the revolution" as individuals committed to the common good who would never pardon those "bad sons of the country" who had sold out to foreign interests or who worked on behalf of certain classes against the common interests of the nation. He reminded his listeners that El Salvador was living in a revolutionary period and that the revolution would take the trouble to remind those who still had not realized this. In sum, anyone who took advantage of the liberties granted by the revolution to subvert its program "would suffer the consequences."[27]

In September 1952, the Osorio government again decreed a state of exception, claiming that it was under attack by communists and reactionaries. Osorio's speech on that occasion was very similar to the one he gave in December 1951. Even though a group of rightists had just been jailed (and then freed) under suspicion of plotting to overthrow the government, his criticism was leveled primarily against the Left, which stood accused of introducing propaganda from abroad and preparing its cadres in the use of guns and terrorist bombs. He repeated his claim that the disloyal opposition on the Right, through its constant criticism of the government, aided and abetted the opposition from the radical Left.[28] Some safe houses of the Communist Party were raided and twelve hundred people subsequently were arrested under the presumption of belonging to the party.[29]

This rhetoric, combined with the occasional suspension of constitutional guarantees, quickly established the limits of Salvadoran democracy in the 1950s. A comprehensive statement of these limits took the form of a law "for the Defense of the Democratic and Constitutional Order," passed by the legislature in November 1952. After establishing that totalitarian doctrines, such as communism, nazism, fascism, and anarchism are contrary to democracy, it listed twenty specific activities against democracy subject to criminal prosecution and punishment.[30] Some of these acts are conventional enough (such as transport and assembly of explosives, attempt to overthrow the government or incite rebellion among the troops, and sabotage of public services, among others) but others could be construed in any way the authorities saw convenient. For example, it was forbidden to organize and support strikes "that might affect public order" or to broadcast information deemed inimical to the country's political and economic stability. It also was punishable to disrespect or slander the heads of the branches of government, deputies of the legislative assembly, cabinet ministers, "and any other high officials of the government." It even was a crime "to revile the name, flag, or emblems of the Nation."

After the 1950 election for a constituent assembly, opposition parties organized and campaigned but, because of constant harassment by the regime, mostly dropped out of electoral contests for legislative and municipal posts before balloting took place. For the legislative elections of May 1952, PRUD ran unopposed after opposition groups withdrew their candidates at the last moment, claiming that fraud would be committed; thus, PRUD got all of the over seven hundred thousand votes cast.[31] The 1954 legislative and municipal elections produced the same results.

It was not until 1956, when presidential elections were combined with legislative and municipal ones, that part of the opposition decided to stay in the race to the bitter end. As a result of criticism about holding presidential, legislative, and municipal elections at the same time, the legislative assembly reformed the election law so that the election for president was held on a different date from the others. In this manner, the people would have the possibility of splitting their preference.[32] This gave the opposition parties hope that they might get at least some seats in the legislature and they proceeded to choose candidates to oppose the PRUD.

Three military officers and one civilian emerged as opposition presidential candidates, all backed by parties of the Center or the Right. However, the central election council, in the hands of PRUD supporters, proceeded to disqualify each candidate until two remained.[33] When these two opposition candidates announced their withdrawal, charging government oppression and fraud, only the PRUD's candidate, Colonel José María Lemus, was left.[34] A high PRUD official explained the opposition's withdrawal was simply because they did not stand a chance against the PRUD, which had organized more than five thousand committees to get out the vote and which could claim, in his opinion, about 70 percent of the popular preference. He added that the opposition parties did not bother to organize because they did not believe in democracy.[35]

On election day, Colonel Lemus faced only token competition from two opposition parties, who called for abstention after their request to withdraw had been denied by the electoral council. Under such conditions, Colonel Lemus received nearly 678,000 votes out of over 723,000 cast. The elections for legislative assembly, held on 13 May, also were controlled tightly by the regime: journalists observed how electoral officials instructed people to vote for PRUD, how children were sent by their parents to vote for them, and how people voted in public. One electoral official told a journalist that "people did not have a clear idea of what they had to do . . . and for that reason they were told where to mark their ballots." Or as another remarked: "The voting procedures are under perfect control."[36] Not surprisingly, PRUD got over 550,000 votes to 34,000 for the one participating opposition party.[37]

The lopsided political advantage of the PRUD did not keep Lemus from calling for a more active and committed opposition when he spoke before the legislature in September 1957. But his analysis of the opposition's failure to do better at the polls said nothing about government manipulation of the electoral machinery and its exclusion of opposition groups via administrative measures. Instead, he claimed that it was the shortcomings of the opposition that were to blame for its poor showing: its parties lacked ideological consistency, its leaders did not look out for the country's best interests but sought only the spoils of office, and its programs contained only criticisms without offering alternative solutions. He, on the other hand, was the very model of moderation and equilibrium.[38] He reiterated similar positions in a speech a year later, when he underlined the importance of voting and denounced the opposition's calls for electoral abstention.[39] The fact is that opposition parties did not win a single seat in the legislature from 1952 all the way until 1964, even though they did organize and campaign in a halfhearted manner.

A number of fundamental contradictions underlay Salvadoran "democracy" as it was espoused and practiced in the 1950s. On the one hand, the group of military officers and civilians who took over the government in 1948 were committed to carrying out social and economic reforms that were not negotiable under the terms of the Fourteen Points of 1948. The reformist rhetoric was a constant of PRUD's campaign slogans, especially with reference to the condition of the rural population.[40] On the other hand, the reformist program of the PRUD government gradually took on the form of a crusade against international communism. During the years of the government of the CGR, it was the rightist opposition to the reformist program that caused most concern; little mention was made of communism or Soviet imperialism as enemies of the Salvadoran revolution. However, by early 1951, the Communist Party was singled out as a dangerous opponent whose disregard for democracy required the implementation of undemocratic countermeasures.[41]

The anticommunist rhetoric was fueled by the radicalization of the Guatemalan revolution and the growing estrangement between the armed forces of the two countries, not to mention the increasingly active presence of United States diplomats and military missions in the region. By mid-1952, Osorio was receiving telegrams from Guatemalan opposition groups who praised him for his anticommunist stance.[42] After the overthrow of the Arbenz regime in 1954, relations between the strongly anticommunist Guatemalan governments and those of the "Salvadoran revolution" remained close. The anticommunist crusade reached a high point in October 1960 when the Guatemalan president, General Miguel Ydígoras Fuentes, and Colonel Lemus signed a pact at a border post that committed both regimes to stop "communist infiltration."[43]

In addition to military reformism and anticommunism, there was a third obstacle to the development of a pluralist, representative democracy in El Salvador in the 1950s, namely, the social and cultural conditions under which the population had lived for at least a full generation. Since the 1931 coup d'etat, for most Salvadorans there had been no contact or experience whatsoever with democratic forms of political choice and participation. The events of 1944 and 1948 had touched and inspired mostly the small urban population, whereas the rural masses still were under the sway of powerful landed interests and the ever-present paramilitary structure.

Out of this two-faced social and political reality, there emerged a political system that also had two sides to it. In the rural areas, reformism and empowerment were strictly limited and severely controlled, as if the magnitude of rural social problems actually was beyond the capabilities of the regime to do anything about them. The regime did not even trust the good judgment of the rural masses in the struggle against revolutionary ideas because they were illiterate and ignorant of the issues.[44] In addition, 1932 was still fresh in the minds of the military leadership, many of whom had graduated from the military school right around 1930 and whose interpretation of reality was heavily influenced by the specter of rural insurgency, which they believed could be ignited by just a small spark.

In the urban areas, the threat of a radicalized opposition was kept under control by means of more flexible attitudes and practices. Social and economic reformism, expressed in the regime's support for social security and labor legislation, subsidized public housing, and cheap electricity, as well as its political alliances with select groups (for example, teachers, industrial laborers, and urban entrepreneurs), created political spaces in which much more political debate might take place. As long as good or excellent prices for coffee held in the world markets, the regime could afford to buy political support among the urban groups.

Finally, there was the issue of the opposition itself. Outside of the Left, which was systematically excluded and repressed, no viable alternative to the PRUD existed either on the moderate Left or the Right. The PRUD had filled the Center, pushed the Left completely out of the bounds of political participation, and threatened and cajoled the Right into meaningless electoral charades. By 1956, some Salvadorans were aware that military reformism left little or no room at all for a democratic opposition to grow. The university students, for one, were convinced that the struggle for democracy would be a long one.[45] But for the time being, the strength and unity of the armed forces sufficed to keep things in place.

The Armed Forces of the Revolutionary Government

The 1948 coup and the subsequent period of military reformism facilitated the armed forces' consolidation of political power. From a force that supported three military presidents from 1931 to 1948 in terms of the defense of constitutional order and social peace, the military after 1948 acquired an institutional political presence and became, as its ideologues were fond of saying, "the mailed fist of the people" (*el brazo armado del pueblo*).[46] Explicit provisions also were included in the Constitution of 1950 that made the armed forces responsible for obedience to the law, for public order, and even for guaranteeing that no sitting president try to seek reelection.[47]

The international environment also placed new demands on the Salvadoran military, particularly in response to United States concerns about the propagation of communism in the region. During a first phase, it was the reformist governments of Guatemala under Presidents Arévalo and Arbenz that involved the Salvadoran government and military in an international crisis. A second phase evolved out of the Cuban revolution of 1959 and subsequent United States policy to isolate and, if possible, overthrow the revolutionary regime. Both of these international issues strengthened the discourse of anticommunist officers within the armed forces and, together with the 1948 commitment to reform, complicated attempts to promote a more open political system in the country.

The military's contribution to social reform and improvement followed, in some respects, the tradition of earlier periods of its history. The role of the barracks molding loyal citizens through elementary education continued to be part of the military's raison d'être, and was included as a major achievement in practically every yearly report of the minister of defense to the legislative body.[48] However, under the governments of Osorio and Lemus the military was openly engaged in support of the public education system and national literacy campaigns. An alliance of sorts between soldiers and teachers was offered to the public as a key component of the 1948 revolution. The armed forces every year handed out medals and prizes to the outstanding teachers of the public school system as part of the overall effort being made in education.[49]

In addition to support for education, the military's role in the maintenance of public order and the struggle against crime was presented as an ongoing task of great importance. Public order was as important for the officers of the 1948 revolution as it was for those of the 1931 coup d'etat, given the military's traditional abhorrence of any outbreak of public disobedience and violence.[50] The military's continuing responsibility for public order required no particular changes in tactics of crowd control or intimidation of rural populations. The struggle against crime also was very much in keeping with the military's long-standing direction of the security forces, the Guardia Nacional and the Policía Nacional. The Guardia continued to be praised by the military hierarchy for its role in the fight against rural crime and as a military unit in times of national emergency; it also continued the practice of the Hernández Martínez years of hiring out *guardias* to provide protection to landowners and businessmen for a fee.

In the case of the National Police, there was one attempt at modernizing this force into a more professional institution through a technical assistance agreement signed with the United States government in August 1957. The agreement provided for a strengthening of lines of authority within the force, the creation of an efficient filing system, standardized procedures for reporting crimes, the establishment of criteria for the selection of personnel, and the development of a training plan.[51] However, little seems to have come of this agreement because there was talk again in 1960, after President Lemus's overthrow, about the need to modernize the National Police.

The military's principal raison d'être, namely the defense of national sovereignty in the face of an invading army, was the least of its worries. Still, important efforts were made to improve the status and training of officers at a variety of levels, a reflection of the concerns of the leaders of the 1948 coup, whose own professional training began in the reopened military school of the late 1920s. Only four months after the coup, the CGR decreed a raise in salaries for "the professional members of the army."[52] In March 1950, a consumer cooperative for officers was opened in order to allow the members of the "military family" to achieve their "economic liberation." Plans also were devised and executed for the construction of houses for military officers.[53]

Officer training requirements were stiffened after 1950, as part of an overall attempt to professionalize the officer corps. Admission to the Military School, for example, was made more competitive. The Military School had been under the direction of United States officers since 1940, when Hernández Martínez fired the German general, Eberhardt Bohnstedt, from his post. United States officers remained in charge of the school until 1956, at which time Colonel Manuel de Jesús Córdova, one of the original junta members in 1948, was appointed to the position of director. In 1951, in addition, a military mission from Chile arrived in San Salvador to direct a newly founded general staff school *(escuela de guerra)* that has operated since. The Chilean mission remained until the beginning of 1958, when it turned over the direction of the school to Salvadoran officers.[54]

Of much greater long-term importance was the military assistance agreement signed between the United States and El Salvador in May 1953. This agreement included a U.S. military training mission to assist the Salvadoran armed forces in aspects such as artillery, infantry, and aviation.[55] For the Salvadoran government and military, the agreement signaled a new United States presence in the region that demanded of the Salvadorans a different relationship with the neighboring government and armed forces of Guatemala.[56] In April 1952, the Salvadoran armed forces still considered their Guatemalan colleagues as counterparts in a common struggle to achieve reform and development, but by mid-1954 the Salvadoran government and military brokered an agreement between the Guatemalan military and the rebel forces led by Colonel Carlos Castillo Armas that ended the reformist experiment in Guatemala.[57] When the Guatemalan minister of defense visited El Salvador in May 1957, a new friendship centered around anticommunism was evident, even though the official speeches referred to shared ideals that originated in the struggles of Francisco Morazán and Justo Rufino Barrios to achieve Central American unity during the nineteenth century.[58]

The U.S. presence not only contributed to the shift in the Salvadoran military's ideological stance on behalf of an anticommunist policy with international ramifications; it also consolidated a long association between the Pentagon and the Salvadoran military's high command. Beginning with the appointment of an American officer to head the military school in 1940 and continuing on with the sale of arms and military equipment during the years of World War II, U.S. military assistance during the 1950s shifted to the training of Salvadoran officers in United States military installations, both in North America and in Panama. Whereas in 1954 no Salvadoran officers received training at U.S. installations, in 1956 six had done so within the continental United States and fifteen at installations in the Canal Zone in Panama; in 1958 the corresponding numbers were six and twenty-six.[59] Very soon, the United States was training far more Salvadoran officers than the countries that traditionally had done so (such as Spain, Italy, France, and Mexico). Still, U.S. direct military aid was negligible during the 1950s; only in 1960 did the United States extend a small amount of military aid in the form of a grant to the Salvadoran armed forces.[60] The Salvadoran military still preferred to pay for its military purchases while it could; during the 1950s, there were sufficient funds in the government's regular budget to buy the munitions and light arms that the military most needed to maintain its effectiveness.

For the ranks, military service continued much as it had under the governments of Hernández Martínez and his immediate successors. Almost every recruit came from the rural areas and went through the same training scheme as his predecessors, including a dose of schooling in literacy and numbers.[61] After a tour of duty of one year, the soldier was discharged and became part of the reserves, subject to serve in the *patrullas cantonales*. The ex-soldier also had to attend weekend meetings where he was instructed on issues of discipline, obedience, loyalty, love of fatherland, and "the dire consequences of communist doctrines." There were some rewards, of course: the office in charge of the military's reserves, the so-called *servicio territorial*, took interest in the personal problems of the ex-soldiers and provided medical and economic assistance in those cases of "indispensable need."[62] For a poor peasant and his family, the military's support could mean access to a loan, the possibility of holding on to a small piece of land, or some assistance in case of illness or to help educate a son or daughter.

There are no figures on the size of the paramilitary structure during the years of military reformism. However, if the 3,500 individuals recruited in 1955 are used as a yearly base figure for the entire decade, by 1960 there would have been 35,000 ex-recruits liable for service in the reserves and the *patrullas cantonales*.[63] To this total must be added those who served before 1950, so that the total for 1960 should at least be similar to that for 1946, when according to the then-minister of defense it stood at a little over 47,500.[64] Whatever their precise number, the paramilitary organization continued to play a key role in the control of rural areas and in the electoral events that gave the PRUD such an advantage at the polls.

The extensive militarization of the countryside did not prepare the armed forces for the crisis that erupted in the urban centers in 1960, notwithstanding the primarily urban thrust of the government's reformist policies. In fact, after 1932 all open opposition to the government had erupted in the urban areas, primarily in the capital, San Salvador, from where it spread to other cities and towns. Thus, a close look at the events of late 1960 and early 1961 is vital for an understanding of the military's occasionally ambivalent role within the Salvadoran political system.

The Political Crisis of 1960

The presidency of Colonel José María Lemus began with some conciliatory gestures after a contentious election campaign in which he ended up as the only candidate. After decreeing an amnesty for all political exiles, he annulled the Law for the Defense of Democracy that had given the regime wide powers to prosecute almost anyone for antigovernment statements and activities. But a critical economic situation developed at the end of 1957 as a result of the rapid decline of the international price of coffee, which the government had little way of counteracting. Between 1957 and 1960, El Salvador experienced a 34 percent drop in the value of its principal export. Given that coffee exports accounted for close to 90 percent of total export earnings, and that the government remained heavily dependent on export taxes, government revenue remained flat during this period.[65] Just as excellent prices for the country's principal export crop had allowed the government of Colonel Osorio to undertake ambitious programs of public works and social security, Lemus was forced to juggle the budget in order to bring expenditures into line with falling income. Of particular concern to his government was the economic impact on the working class and the attitude of businessmen in the face of growing social tensions.[66] He even called a meeting of one hundred of the leading entrepreneurs in December 1958 to discuss the economic situation and suggest possible solutions; he reiterated his concern for the peasantry and asked the businessmen to maintain the salary levels of the peasant workers who brought in the coffee crop in order to avoid "social ferment."[67]

However, the social ferment he was so concerned about erupted not in the countryside but in San Salvador, precisely around very similar issues to those that had inspired the opposition to Hernández Martínez in 1944. As the legislative elections of 1960 came into view, new parties formed and old ones sought realignments in the hope of forcing the government to concede more political spaces. The Left organized around the Partido Revolucionario Abril y Mayo (PRAM), named precisely after the events of April and May 1944 that forced Hernández Martínez from office, while a splinter group of the PRUD led by ex-President Osorio formed the PRUDA (PRUD Auténtico) and the Partido de Acción Renovadora (PAR) geared up for yet another electoral effort.[68]

Particularly troublesome for the government were the university students. Their annual farcical parade made fun of regime figures in none too kind terms; the one held in May 1959 prompted President Lemus to order the government's prosecutors to file charges against those responsible for the "vulgar" event.[69] For the government, the students also were a problem because they gravitated increasingly toward left-wing politics, especially after the triumph of the Cuban revolution in January 1959.

In response to the perceived growth and increasing aggressiveness of the opposition, and particularly of the Left, the regime began to close the limited political space that was available for political debate and organization. In November 1959, a new electoral law was passed unanimously by the legislative assembly; it made it more difficult to register new parties by requiring more signatures and flatly outlawed parties of anarchistic or communistic tendencies. President Lemus promulgated the law the following month amid street demonstrations organized by students and opposition party leaders. In response, he warned of the growing communist threat in the upcoming legislative elections.[70]

The results of these elections, held in April 1960, were true to form: all seats in the legislative assembly were won by PRUD. However, interesting developments occurred at the municipal level, where PAR won control of the municipal council of San Salvador, the capital, as well as a number of neighboring municipalities.[71] This electoral victory by PAR set the pattern for the following decade, when the regime decided that controlling voting results in San Salvador was too difficult or costly and allowed opposition activities to proceed with relatively little hindrance. But in 1960, this limited political opening came too late to defuse the opposition's frustration with electoral fraud and the gamut of political intimidation that had allowed PRUD to keep a stranglehold on the electoral process.[72]

By August, the government had suspended constitutional guarantees in response to a plot that it claimed to have uncovered. All the while, street demonstrations against the government, conservative newspapers, and the United States embassy grew in number, which prompted the legislative assembly to pass a law that allowed the police to break up any meeting that might lead to a public disturbance.[73] The following month, the police invaded the campus of the national university and proceeded to beat up students and university authorities (including the "rector" or president). By then it was apparent to diverse military commanders that the government was losing control of the situation.

A group of officers loyal to ex-President Osorio staged a coup d'etat on 26 October 1960, not unlike 1944, when students and middle-class professionals led the struggle against the Hernández Martínez regime in alliance with reformist military officers. However, the international environment was markedly different in 1960, with Central America caught up in the United States' concerns about a spreading Cuban revolution and radicalized student and labor groups throughout all of Latin America. In turn, one of the central concerns of the junta that replaced President Lemus was precisely the moment and the conditions under which the United States would extend diplomatic recognition, an important precondition for any government that sought to remain in power for any length of time.

The new government's composition paralleled that of the 1948 junta: three military officers and three civilians with close ties to the national university.[74] By inviting these three civilians to join the junta, it seems clear that the military officers who organized the overthrow were aware of the need to placate demands by students and middle-class groups whose main complaint about the Lemus regime was its blatant manipulation of electoral events.[75] The junta explained its decision to take over the government precisely in response to Lemus's trampling of the constitution and his repression of the citizenry, which had led in turn to the loss of "the principle of authority"; it insisted on its commitment to respect the Constitution of 1950 to the letter and proceeded to free a number of individuals who had been arrested for political reasons. Most importantly, the junta announced that it would organize elections in which all political parties could participate. Until then, the junta would exercise complete legislative and executive powers, having discharged all deputies from their posts in the legislative assembly and having replaced all the justices of the supreme court.[76]

From that moment on, the junta's main concern was the organization and holding of elections. To that effect, it announced the election of a legislative assembly that would draft a new electoral law, under which a president would be elected popularly to start a term in office in September 1962.[77] A week after the coup, it reiterated its commitment to electoral democracy and to the existing social and economic structures as outlined by the Constitution of 1950, explaining that "no substantial reforms would be attempted that are incompatible with the provisional character of the new regime."[78]

In fact, the junta ended up wasting time and political capital on disclaimers about supposed leftist infiltration among some of the new cabinet members, on proposals to carry out revolutionary measures (such as those beginning in Cuba under the regime of Fidel Castro), and plans to reform the armed forces. The very fact that the junta insisted on absolutely free elections that excluded no one and in which the government would favor no particular political grouping was in itself tantamount to a political revolution after decades of systematic exclusion of the Left and of most opposition parties.[79] The support expressed to the junta by certain groups, such as the university student association and a leftist labor federation, must have worried the political Right.[80] And even though the junta denied it was thinking of any substantial reform program, its few policy decisions and declared intentions hinted at the creation of a political system in which traditional power holders would have to share the direction of the state with other groups.

The junta's commitment to free and open elections began to take shape by early December 1960 when it repealed the previous electoral law and canceled all political parties. It also named an interim electoral commission charged with convening a congress to produce a new electoral law.[81] The congress was to begin its work by mid-January 1961, and finally convened on 23 January, one day before the junta was overthrown by another military coup. But other measures provided sufficient proof about the junta's decision to open up the political system, including the decision to allow the return to the country of all political exiles and to authorize the formation of new political parties.[82]

A new request by PRAM, the leftist political party, to achieve legal status was approved by the new Supreme Court, which ordered the electoral commission to proceed to legalize PRAM's existence. PRAM thereafter began to operate in San Salvador and even sent a delegation to Havana for the second anniversary celebration of the Cuban revolution.[83] The Christian Democratic Party came into existence in November as a reformist party of urban professionals and intellectuals committed to electoral democracy and proportional representation, the replacement of class struggle by class cooperation, the formation of a large middle class, and the unionization of workers (both in the cities and the countryside).[84]

The PAR, the only opposition party that carried over from the Osorio and Lemus days, expressed its support for the junta's policies and praised the armed forces for their role in the restoration of public freedoms.[85] The PRUD announced that its cadres were intact, that it would continue to support "progressive capitalists" and the working class, and that it had nothing to do with "the past events that perturbed the political order."[86] Even part of the business class joined in the political process by founding its own party, the Partido Social Demócrata (PSD), which announced a program of social betterment and effective political participation for all, including the expropriation of unused agricultural lands, fiscal reform, and increased spending on education.[87]

Increased freedom for political parties required changing the institutional environment within which the parties operated. By mid-December the junta announced that the National Police was to be reorganized to make it more professional. According to initial statements, the police force was to be decentralized and demilitarized; for example, the criminal investigations department would be placed directly under the state prosecutor's office. Training of the police was to be entrusted to Chilean *carabineros,* whose officers would even occupy executive posts for a time, while Italian advisors would train the traffic police and criminal investigators.[88] The Treasury Police, initially created to chase bootleggers and smugglers, was to be removed from the hands of the military entirely and placed under the Ministry of Finance.[89] It is interesting to note that no changes were planned or announced for the Guardia Nacional, the most important of the security forces, once again underlining the unwillingness of even the most reform-minded officers to dismantle the armed forces' paramilitary structure in the rural areas.

In any case, the thrust of the junta's proposals suggested a new role for the military, more in line with a professional function centered on national defense. Colonel Yánez Urías, a member of the junta, explained that the junta was preparing a set of laws to disengage the military from political matters and thereby assure its apolitical, professional existence.[90] However, one of the civilian members of the junta, Ricardo Falla Cáceres, before an audience of graduating cadets of the military school, insisted on the need for soldiers and civilians to remain united "to save the republic" and reminded his listeners of the constitutional mandate that entrusted the military with maintaining public order and obedience to the law, in addition to the defense of national sovereignty.[91] Both Colonel Yánez Urías and Mr. Falla Cáceres understood that the armed forces still exercised an overwhelming quota of power within the state; the problem was how to persuade most of the officers that it was in their best interests to seek a new arrangement in their relation with civilian political forces and the implementation of state policies.

The junta's emphasis on elections and freedom for the organization and operation of political parties did not prevent it from attempting some administrative and fiscal reform measures. It removed all members of the municipal councils because, in its opinion, most had been elected fraudulently; forty-eight mayors were removed outright while the situation of others would be studied more carefully before any decision was reached.[92] As an example of its desire to act responsibly and transparently, the junta also reduced the amount of secret expenditures of the presidential office (the so-called *partidas secretas*) by over 70 percent and increased the budget for education and culture by 20 percent.[93] A much more significant measure involved a change in the payment of taxes by coffee growers and exporters. Under laws passed in the early 1950s, coffee growers and exporters were exempt from the payment of income taxes; instead, exporters paid a flat tax on every sack of coffee exported. But the junta argued that this system was unfair, because exporters simply passed on the export tax to the producers, so that nobody ended up paying income taxes and the exporters paid no tax at all. Thus, the junta decreed that thereafter exporters would have to pay income taxes on their profits, in addition to the flat export tax.[94]

These measures, together with the opening of political spaces to accommodate the Left, generated immediate reactions from conservative businessmen, owners of newspapers, and military officers, as well as United States diplomats, concerned that events unfolding in revolutionary Cuba were a prelude to similar situations elsewhere in Latin America if strong countermeasures were not taken. The United States underlined its opposition by refusing to recognize the junta. As a result, the junta stood accused of harboring leftists in the cabinet and of dividing the military, not to mention exhibiting "pro-Cuban" inclinations.[95] In turn, this forced the junta to make frequent disclaimers of what it was *not* and what it was *not* going to do.[96] It even authorized air force airplanes to shower the countryside with leaflets warning the peasantry of the dangers of communism.[97]

Less than a month after coming to power, the junta announced that it had stopped a plot directed by "regressive " individuals, both military and civilians, who were in touch with certain diplomats, but no names were given at the time. However, on 18 November the president of the Chamber of Commerce was jailed under suspicion of conspiring to overthrow the government; although he was released the very next day for lack of incriminating evidence, considerable damage had been done to the junta's image among those concerned about antibusiness elements within the government's supporters.[98] Upon his release, the president of the chamber stated that he most likely had been "a victim of a communist tactic" that sought to divide the military, the church, the free press, and the private sector; in his opinion, "the battle for El Salvador had begun."[99]

The junta responded with statements by its members and advertisements in the newspapers disclaiming any intention of undermining private property or changing "the social and economic structure of the state." It did commit itself to measures that furthered social justice and freedom, as well those that eliminated "unjust privileges," but none of these, in its opinion, meant communism.[100] Perhaps the clearest statement of the junta's politics was expressed by junta member René Fortín Magaña during the opening ceremonies of the congress that was to discuss a new electoral law: "instead of driving the adversary into the depths of the catacombs, we must accept the challenge of the totalitarian doctrines and confront ideas with ideas persuaded as we are that this is the only acceptable way in defense of democracy."[101]

The very next day, on 25 January 1961, the junta was overthrown in a bloodless coup organized by military officers and civilians with a different approach to democracy, political participation, and the role of the armed forces in general. In a little over three months, the country had swung from a regime that prohibited and repressed political expressions that it deemed unconstitutional to one that advocated (in principle) complete freedom of expression and organization. For some, the change was excessive; for others, it was insufficient. As had happened in 1944 and 1948, the military decided for everyone and placed the country on a new course that lasted until 1979.

CONCLUSION

In one of the most exclusive residential areas of San Salvador there stands a monument dedicated to "the revolution." The monument is referred to popularly as "the naked one" because on its curved structure is the figure of an unclothed man, arms uplifted as if in celebration of freedom from oppression. The monument, built during the early 1950s to commemorate the political process initiated after the coup d'etat of December 1948, was carefully maintained by the governments of Osorio and Lemus but after 1960 it was left to deteriorate: garbage accumulates on the ground, the "eternal" flame went out years ago, and the anniversary celebrations of the revolution are now history. Its very location is ironic: a symbol of revolution surrounded by the homes of the well-to-do who had little in common with the objectives of the military reformers of 1948. The fact that the monument still stands during times when many others dedicated to revolution have fallen all over the world is suggestive: the revolution of 1948 was so innocuous that it neither threatened nor enthused anybody outside of its most immediate ideologues and leaders. Viewed in this manner, the monument is an apotheosis to a revolution that came and went without much ado, a sort of nonrevolution.

However, the importance of the governments born of the 1948 coup in the development of Salvadoran democracy should not be underestimated. During the 1950s, significant changes occurred in the rhetoric and practice of politics in El Salvador. In the first place, the regimes that grew out of the 1948 coup brought to the fore a new generation of officers. Trained in the Salvadoran military academy and schooled abroad in some cases, they espoused a populist and democratic rhetoric that appealed to urban groups while rejecting any arrangement with the Left. They called their movement a "revolution" and identified their role as that of "the mailed fist of the people." This was an important change when contrasted with the seventeen years of military rule under Hernández Martínez, Meléndez, Aguirre, and Castaneda Castro, committed as they were to the maintenance of a traditional social and political order. For the military and civilian leaders of 1948, reform was necessary to keep El Salvador abreast of its immediate neighbors who, in the cases of Guatemala and Costa Rica, were in the process of advancing their own reformist initiatives.[102]

In the second place, the military reformers of 1948 introduced the country to an electoral and party system that departed markedly from that of the 1930s and 1940s, when only the official (government) party was allowed to exist. To administer this new party system, an electoral authority was created, supposedly independent of the state or any party in particular, that would ensure the honesty of electoral events. That the electoral authority was not truly impartial (in contrast to the one created in Costa Rica around the same time) does not render the junta's initiative meaningless. The confrontation between military factions during the events of 1960–1961 indicates that important forces during the regimes of Osorio and Lemus were committed, in fact, to the creation of a largely unfettered system of party politics. The failure of this initiative is attributable as much to those military factions that did not believe in an open political system as to those civilians in positions of economic power who feared the consequences of a working, representative democracy. Nor should the hegemony of the PRUD be attributed only to fraud and corruption; the PRUD probably benefitted as much from the disorganization of the opposition as from its control of electoral and political activities. Furthermore, the ideological posture of the opposition generally was to the right of the regime, reflecting certain elite sectors' objections to the reformist policies of the PRUD. Therefore, the PRUD was able to claim a role as the only "revolutionary" group in the country, by openly describing the poverty and injustice suffered by the majority of the population while claiming to undertake the necessary reforms to change the situation.[103]

Third, a constitutional foundation was set in 1950 that lasted for over thirty years. Among its most outstanding innovations was an enlarged role for the state in social welfare, education, and economic development. As the state's most powerful institution, the military became wedded to these constitutional provisions and defended them forcefully. In fact, the military's reason for being became so tightly meshed with the social and economic reforms envisioned in the constitution that any criticism of the reforms was construed as criticism of the military itself. The restrictions on political expression and action in the Constitution of 1950 should be seen in this light, as well as the limited openings for urban labor and opposition political parties.

Juxtaposed with these innovations were important elements inherited from years past that made politics under the governments of Osorio and Lemus very similar to that under Hernández Martínez and his immediate successors. For one, the existence of an "official" party in the form of the PRUD represented a clear continuity with the Pro-Patria organization that championed the leadership of General Hernández Martínez. Although under the Hernández Martínez regime no other party organizations were allowed to form, the political opening of the 1948 revolution did not translate into significant participation or representation by opposition groups. For the ordinary citizen, the PRUD of the 1950s probably looked and acted very much like the Pro-Patria of the 1930s and 1940s, the period when the young officers of the 1948 coup had come of age within the military. The experience abroad of some of these officers also influenced their outlook on pluralist politics and "official" parties; for example, Oscar Osorio had received training in Italy (from 1938 to 1940) and in Mexico (after his involvement in the 1945 coup attempt), neither of which had functioning representative democracies at the time.

Another key holdover from the old regime was the military's control of the security forces. From its inception, the Guardia Nacional had been under the direction of military officers, as was the National Police. This concentration of police power under the Ministry of Defense did little to foster an environment for democratic debate and dissent, especially when the president of the republic was a military officer, too. A reform of the police undertaken during the Lemus presidency with support from the United

States did not eliminate its rough procedures for controlling crowds and dealing with dissidents. After Lemus's overthrow in the aftermath of the severe repression unleashed against university students and other protesters, the junta attempted to separate the police from the military's control and professionalize it through training by outside advisors. However, the junta said nothing about the Guardia Nacional, which was far more powerful in terms of firepower and territorial presence than the National Police.

Finally, there was the paramilitary structure in the rural areas. At no moment did the Lemus and Osorio regimes consider curbing the presence or the role of the *patrullas cantonales* and *escoltas militares.* Not only were these bodies an integral part of the military organization but their support was indispensable for effective control of the rural areas and for the electoral drives of the PRUD. Thus, not even the junta that came to office in October 1960 was prepared to question the existence of these rural paramilitary units. Their existence since the 1920s had turned them into a permanent fixture of the rural political scene; in a sense, the paramilitary organization functioned as the permanent political party of the armed forces, mutating under different names to adapt to the changing times.

By 1960, the political system inaugurated with so much enthusiasm and hope twelve years before had reached a crisis point. The juntas born of the coups d'etat of October 1960 and January 1961 attempted to defuse the crisis, the first by announcing its intention of opening up the political system but postponing any substantial social and economic reforms, the second by reimposing a restrictive political system under military leadership but implementing a number of reform measures. Some of these reform measures moved the country toward more representative political practices but, as seen in the next chapter, the principal concern of the leadership was economic and social development under the aegis of national security, the military's byword for a continued and decisive political presence.

THE ERA OF NATIONAL CONCILIATION

UNDER THE SHADOW OF THE CUBAN REVOLUTION

THE OCTOBER junta had been singled out by its critics for supposedly harboring communists in high positions of government and tolerating the activities of leftist political groupings that would have been outlawed under previous regimes. Undoubtedly, the October junta's rhetoric and avowed intentions marked a significant departure from traditional military discourse in El Salvador that was met with skepticism by its critics and even disbelief by some of its supporters.

Although the junta strongly rejected any tilt toward the left, its position was complicated by the increasing concern of conservative groups in El Salvador and policy makers in the U.S. about the impact of the Cuban revolution in the Central American region. The United States withheld recognition for five weeks, during which time the junta's emissaries visited Washington and Central American capitals to allay fears about Cuban infiltration and the activities of the Salvadoran Left. When Washington finally extended recognition, the junta had expended precious political capital in its own defense and had encouraged its opponents to remove it by force.

By the time the countercoup took place on 25 January 1961, the October junta was very much alone. Some demonstrators marched down the streets of San Salvador in support of the junta but were dispersed violently by the security forces. The subsequent establishment of martial law in the country and the arrest and exile of leading figures of the deposed government ended all resistance in a matter of a few days.[1] But the new government's greatest asset was the wide support it enjoyed among officers, many of whom were concerned about the junta's plans regarding the future role of the armed forces. As such, the January coup represented a forceful return of the military to the political arena, imbued with a sense of mission similar to that of 1948.

Most of the coup leaders were majors and captains who looked to Colonel Julio Rivera (then but thirty-nine years old) for guidance and leadership.[2] Rivera, who became a member of the new junta, the Directorio Cívico Militar, had been appointed director of the general staff school (Escuela de Comando y Estado Mayor) by the deposed junta; the other military member of the *directorio,* Colonel Anibal Portillo, also had been appointed by the junta as head of the general staff. Three civilians joined the *directorio:* Antonio Rodríguez Porth, a prominent lawyer and ideologue of the Salvadoran Right; Feliciano Avelar, a lawyer; and Jose Francisco Valiente, a medical doctor. The makeup of the *directorio* and its initial statements pointed to a government committed to socially regressive policies and authoritarian politics, which turned out to be only partly correct.

The first order of business for the new government of the armed forces was an explanation for the January coup, which appeared in the form of a communiqué to the nation at large. Most of the explanation had to do with the October junta's supposed inability to return the country to legality and order; instead, the junta had allowed "the development and propagation . . . of forces and doctrines alien to democracy." In addition, "regressive forces of despotism" were behind the October coup d'etat. The resulting confusion among the population, said the communiqué, could only lead to chaos, which both communists and followers of ex-President Oscar Osorio (the "regressive forces") would take advantage of to attack the country's "democratic institutions." But most important, the October coup and resulting junta were the product of a "small group of officers, without the support or the knowledge of the Armed Forces." Still, the armed forces felt responsible for the state of things and, thus, were "compelled" to take control of the situation.[3]

This initial communiqué was followed ten days later by a proclamation of the armed forces, signed by 438 active officers of military detachments, barracks, and diverse military installations. While it reiterated some of the explanations of the first communiqué, it added on statements of what was to become standard military thinking about national security during the heyday of the Cuban revolution. Most importantly, the new regime was committed to undertaking "initial measures destined to improve the living conditions of the people," including programs of public works and housing, tax reform, increased agricultural output, and universal social security coverage. The issue of land was broached indirectly in terms of "the review and planning of land use and ownership," the first time since the days of *mejo-ramiento social* under the Hernández Martínez regime that some sort of land distribution was contemplated. On the political side, new elections were to be held for a constituent assembly and municipalities in order to return the country to constitutional rule. All in all, the *directorio* concluded that social peace, security, and freedom could be attained by eradicating poverty and misery.[4]

These statements about the need to raise the standards of living of the Salvadoran population and achieve a more democratic political order had been issued many times in the past. Under the regime of Castaneda Castro, democracy and development were an important part of official rhetoric; Presidents Osorio and Lemus had reiterated their commitment to redressing social grievances and building a democratic political order. However, after 1961, development and democracy took on a more urgent tone, prompted at the international level by the Alliance for Progress and within El Salvador itself by the appearance of new political actors committed to reformist change. Development policies were closely tied to the creation of the Central American Common Market (CACM), while measures to open up the political system sought to defuse tensions by legalizing new parties and offering them real opportunities to participate in the decision-making process.

Social and economic reforms were a key concern of the *directorio* from its first days in office. In contrast to the October junta, which had stressed its unwillingness to devise any reform policy of any kind, the *directorio* made it clear from the very beginning that it would fight communism with "deeds."[5] The anticommunist and reformist rhetoric also addressed Washington's concern about the need for social and economic change to counter the perceived revolutionary threat from Cuba. In fact, President John Kennedy, just sworn into office, announced that the new government of El Salvador had been recognized by the United States on 15 February because it had made a commitment to hold early elections and to work for social and economic progress.[6]

In March, the *directorio* decreed increases in rural wages and reductions in the rents of rooms in "mesones," the infamous tenements of the urban poor (when they weren't forced to sleep out in the streets).[7] The following month, the *directorio* proceeded to nationalize the central bank, which had been created during the first years of the regime of Hernández Martínez as a public corporation but which had been administered by individuals who represented the principal private banks. It also established foreign currency control measures to prevent capital flight. These measures provoked the resignation of José Antonio Rodríguez Porth and José Francisco Valiente, the two more conservative civilian members of the *directorio,* and brought its membership down to three.[8]

During the remainder of 1961, a few more reform measures were instituted, including a new income tax that raised rates among individuals with higher income and a further increase in rural workers' salaries.[9] Combined with the measures previously cited, the entire package did not constitute a radical departure from the social and economic policies of the Osorio and Lemus regimes, which also had espoused a gradualist approach to economic development and social improvement. Nevertheless, the measures generated heated opposition from agricultural and industrial interests that saw in them the beginning of more profound reforms that might affect land ownership and control of the banking system.[10] In fact, the next fifteen years were fraught with tensions between private sector groups concerned with protecting their interests and reformist military officers concerned with controlling the activities of the marxist Left and the spread of revolutionary ideas. For the military, the struggle could not be won exclusively on the battlefield but, as frequently mentioned in counterinsurgency theories, involved the hearts and minds of the people. To win hearts and minds, the *directorio* and successive regimes undertook not only social and economic reforms but also sought to widen political participation by allowing the formation of new parties and establishing mechanisms for their representation in legislative and municipal bodies.

Revamping the Political System

The downfall of the Lemus regime clearly was the result of urban protest, particularly of middle sectors disgruntled with electoral fraud and manipulation. The October junta had insisted on the issue of electoral reform as one of its key concerns; the *directorio* could not do otherwise, especially in light of U.S. concerns about the advancement of democratic electoral procedures that would address the issues of legitimacy and popular support. A new political organization, the Christian Democratic Party, that was seen by Washington as a viable alternative to military reformism, also entered the political arena. In sum, the new military leadership had to adapt to new conditions within the country and abroad while retaining control of the political process and keeping various military factions from openly quarreling with each other. This balancing act required greater amounts of concessions than previous regimes would have tolerated but did not exclude the use of repressive measures that had characterized the past.

Most of the political parties in the country that had participated in the negotiations with the October junta to produce a new electoral law were willing to continue to talk with the *directorio* about the same issue. Only the PRAM, with its marxist leanings, and the Social Democrats, which stood accused of harboring *osorista* elements, were not invited to join in the conversations.[11] Less than a week after the coup, a "Preelectoral Council" made up of representatives of the five recognized political parties began to draft a new electoral law. The Christian Democrats soon dropped out of this initiative, however, not without first expressing their position on desired changes to the law.[12]

In September 1961, the *directorio* promulgated the new electoral law, a document that reflects both changes and continuities in electoral practices. Voting for both men and women continued to be obligatory and political parties of a communist or anarchist tendency were forbidden outright. However, interesting innovations suggest that the *directorio* was concerned about the legitimacy of electoral events. For example, voting booths were to be devised so as to guarantee the secrecy of the ballot and ballot boxes were to be made of transparent material to avoid ballot stuffing. Those political parties participating in the election also would be allowed to check that voters were duly registered and to oversee the voting procedures in general. But political parties with international connections or those that received funding from abroad were forbidden, which by 1961 not only meant the Communist Party but also the recently founded Christian Democrats.[13]

This electoral law, which was to remain in effect until 1979, did not prevent fraudulent or irregular electoral practices from taking place. As it happens, the more obvious cases of voting booth fraud might be more difficult to commit but other loopholes continued to exist, such as the rejection of a candidate to office who faced a pending lawsuit (an easily arranged situation) or of an incomplete candidate list presented by a given political party.[14] But in 1961, the law offered opposition parties a better chance to contest elections successfully than in the past and, in general, was accepted by all of those in good standing.

Regardless of the *directorio*'s commitment to democracy and political rights, it was clear that certain political groups would have a difficult time surviving. The PRAM was targeted especially, since it was assumed that it had close contacts with the Cuban revolutionary government. Just two days after the January coup, the *directorio* announced that "abundant Communist propaganda from Cuba" had been entering the country and that prominent members of the previous government had espoused "pro-Castro" ideology.[15] Even before its promulgation, the *directorio* had indicated that the electoral law would determine which political parties would be allowed on the basis of their "democratic" nature. On a more positive note, the regime also announced that political exiles with no "communist antecedents" could return to the country; Colonel Rivera went so far as to announce that "political persecution" would cease but warned that drastic measures would be taken against those who tried to subvert public order.[16] In fact, the secretary general of PRAM, Roberto Carías, was arrested at the end of February and diplomatic relations with Cuba were finally severed in March.[17] And in July the government announced that it had uncovered a "communist" plot and jailed numerous individuals on charges of subversion.[18]

The exclusion of the Left was not as determining a factor in the evolution of the political system as was the creation of another "official party" in the tradition of the Pro-Patria party and the PRUD. Initially, the *directorio* had announced that it would remain in office only for the time needed to organize and hold free elections, and its minister of defense even had suggested that no official party would contest them.[19] But it was clear also that key officers did not consider the military's role as a simple spectator or even guardian of democratic procedures; instead, they continued to believe in a constitutional role for the military that transcended political parties or electoral practices. The very same minister of defense who downplayed the creation of an official party also reiterated the military's commitments to upholding social and economic rights enshrined in the constitution; he emphasized that the military's position on these issues also was a result of its "identification" with the cause of the people and that its role as the people's "mailed fist" continued as before.[20]

By September 1961, the military's true intentions became clear with the founding of the Partido de Conciliación Nacional (PCN), an organization closely linked to the *directorio* that inherited much of the PRUD's organization and following. Colonel Rivera resigned his position on the *directorio* to assume that of coordinator of the new party. The opposition protested that the *directorio*'s claims of electoral impartiality were now moot but could do nothing to prevent the formation of this new "official" party.[21] In fact, the military's role was true to the form developed after 1948: an initial commitment to electoral democracy followed by rules for political participation and government-sponsored parties that put the opposition at a disadvantage.

The new *partido oficial* stood at the center of the political spectrum not only in ideological terms but also as the key player in the competition for power. As its name indicates, the PCN claimed to represent all groups in society and to work for national unity and the elimination of factional strife, with the armed forces providing leadership and inspiration. Direct control of the PCN was effectively in the hands of a "general coordinator," always a military officer and, after 1962, the president of the republic. Civilian collaborators joined the party and provided an intellectual veneer to its policy statements and electoral pledges, as well as heading a number of ministries, but they never could aspire to the top position of "general coordinator" or seek the presidential candidacy.[22]

A civilian alternative to the PCN was the recently founded Christian Democratic Party (PDC, in its Spanish acronym). Its founding documents placed it somewhat to the left of center in the Salvadoran political spectrum, although its policy statements tended to be sufficiently vague so as to not frighten off potential voters who wished primarily to move away from military domination of the political system.[23] It insisted on its role as a "third force," a viable alternative that stressed values and spiritual regeneration in the face of totalitarian communism and materialistic capitalism. Over the years, it would become an important contender in the struggle for control of the government. Its challenge was perceived as especially serious by right-wing, anticommunist groups among civilians and military officers, because its reformist rhetoric could not be discounted easily as marxist-inspired.[24] In fact, it was the only party that over the years posed a real electoral alternative to the PCN.

A few other opposition parties were active in the 1960s, but they garnered few votes in comparison to the PDC. The Partido de Acción Renovadora (PAR), the main opposition grouping of the 1950s, took on a leftist stance after 1965, when it came under a new leadership that talked about land reform via expropriation, a more independent foreign policy, and a variety of state-sponsored social welfare programs. The PAR was proscribed after the 1967 presidential election and its position occupied by the Movimiento Nacional Revolucionario (MNR), a small social-democratic organization. The Partido Popular Salvadoreño (PPS), founded in 1965, stood to the right of the PCN and received support from coffee-growing interests in the western portions of the country.[25]

In fact, there was never a dearth of political parties waiting to compete for votes with the PCN. The elections for a constituent assembly scheduled for mid-December 1961 were contested by five parties (PCN, PRUD, PAR, PDC, and the Social Democrats, plus a couple of other very small groups). The PSD, PDC, and PAR formed a coalition called the Unión de Partidos Democráticos that pledged to work for free elections, proportional representation, an amnesty for exiles, and civil service stability.[26] As expected, the results gave the PCN a lopsided advantage in the popular vote (over 205,000 to about 88,000 for the opposition) and all fifty-four deputies in the constituent assembly. Although there were some complaints of fraud and violence, there was no significant evidence of imposition in favor of the PCN by the armed forces, at least in the more populous urban areas. What was evident was a high level of voter apathy: only 43 percent of registered voters bothered to deposit their ballots on election day.[27]

Total control of the legislature by the PCN allowed for the drafting of a new constitution in a little over two weeks. The Constitution of 1962, which remained in effect until 1982, was really a copy of the 1950 document with some minor changes, including a reduction of the presidential period from six to five years. Otherwise, the new legislature recognized the de facto decrees of both the October junta and the *directorio* and appointed a civilian, Rodolfo Cordón, to the presidency for six months until the popularly elected president could take over on July 1.[28] In sum, the elements of continuity with the regimes born of the 1948 coup were far greater than the changes and discontinuities resulting from the coups of October and January.

The campaign that led up to the presidential election held in April 1962 underscored the elements of continuity, especially regarding the role of the armed forces as the principal political force and arbiter of state policies. When Colonel Rivera resigned from the *directorio* in September to head the organization of the new Partido de Conciliación Nacional, nobody was fooled by claims of electoral impartiality and transparency. In fact, most of the statements and complaints of the opposition political parties had to do with the continuing role of the armed forces in politics. The Social Democrats announced early on that they were not going to participate in the elections at all because the continued presence of the armed forces in the political process made it impossible to have free campaigning and honest voting.[29] The PDC, too, indicted the armed forces for continuing to control the country in the same dictatorial fashion as the regimes of the PRUD; it was especially critical of the support provided by the *directorio* to the candidacy of Colonel Rivera and the PCN and the intimidation and persecution of political opponents by the security forces. Under such conditions, said the PDC, it would not participate in the elections for president.[30]

The PAR, on the other hand, initially decided to participate if certain conditions were met, including the replacement of the heads of the security forces by officers not active in the campaign, the electoral supervision of the Organization of American States, and some form of government funding for the opposition parties to counterbalance the advantages of the official party. The PAR also called on the armed forces to respect their initial commitment to an orderly and honest electoral process.[31] But in the end, even the PAR decided to abstain from participating in the elections scheduled for 29 April after most of its conditions were rejected by the electoral council.[32]

Colonel Rivera's election proceeded unopposed, but he campaigned forcefully as if there were real opponents in the field. His message was a reiteration of the *directorio*'s policy of social justice and improvement, including references to his support for the social doctrine of the Catholic Church.[33] He dismissed the decision of the opposition parties to abstain as a sign of weakness in the face of the strength of the PCN and accused them of turning their backs on the people who supported them. He also attacked the greediness of "backward-minded oligarchic groups" and the "mad impulses of the left" that sought to reduce the Salvadoran population to abject slavery. The PCN, on the other hand, stood for equilibrium and justice and represented all sectors of Salvadoran society.[34] In general, the discourse of the military officer-turned-politician of the 1960s sounded very much like that of his comrades in arms of the previous decade.

The results of the election were also very much in line with those of the 1950s. Colonel Rivera's triumph was assured formally from the moment that the ballot boxes closed at six o'clock in the evening of 29 April. Local and foreign journalists covering the event reported that voting proceeded normally and that voters were not harassed by security forces.[35] In fact, no harassment was necessary to win the vote as evidenced by the high level of abstention: only a little more than four hundred thousand ballots were cast, of which about twenty thousand were blank (no mark whatsoever) and about twelve thousand were annulled, while all the rest were marked for Colonel Rivera. By comparison, during each of the two presidential elections of the 1950s, total votes cast surpassed six hundred thousand.

ELECTORAL POLITICS: 1964–1968

Even though the new party system that emerged after 1961 appeared to signal a continuation of the one-party rule typical of the 1950s, succeeding electoral events proved sufficiently plural to sustain the regime's claims that it was working to promote a real democracy. But given the anticommunist nature of the *directorio* and its successor governments, the political parties that were allowed to function after 1961 stood at the center and on the right of the political spectrum, much like during the 1950s. On the other hand, the political system also proved sufficiently manageable until 1972 to assure that no opposition party might pose a real challenge to the military's preponderant political role.

The challenge from the Left was addressed initially by a strong anticommunist law passed in September 1962, just three months after Colonel Rivera took office. The law included prison terms for those convicted of promoting, organizing, and aiding groups seeking to propagate communist doctrine, as well as those attempting to organize illegal strikes and communicating with communist organizations overseas. Arrests of suspected communists began immediately, many of whom were exiled to Costa Rica and Nicaragua.[36] The Salvadoran Ministry of the Interior also established working relationships with the other Central American regimes to control "communist infiltration"; special offices in each country exchanged information on the movement of individuals, transfers of money and weapons, and distribution of political literature and propaganda.[37] Simultaneously, the regime drew closer to conservative groups within the business and landowning class and appointed prominent entrepreneurs to posts in the government.[38]

The shift to the right of the Rivera regime was balanced by an important change in the political system: the passage of a new electoral law in June 1963 that opened the possibility for recognized opposition parties to win seats in the legislative assembly. As opposed to the winner-take-all provisions of the 1950s, the new law established a system of proportional representation whereby deputies from each department were apportioned according to the number of votes received by each party. However, representation in the municipal councils continued under the terms of the winner-take-all procedures of the past.[39] Even though, as the Christian Democrats made clear, other extralegal practices would have to be stopped if truly honest elections were to be held, the new law was sufficiently attractive to ensure that opposition parties participated in future electoral events.

The first test of the new electoral procedures took place during the legislative elections of March 1964. Since 1952, no opposition deputies had sat in the legislature and only once had the opposition bothered to field candidates (in the December 1961 elections for a constitutional assembly). By November 1963, three parties had been registered to participate: the PCN, the Christian Democrats (PDC), and the Partido de Acción Renovadora (PAR). The Partido Revolucionario Abril y Mayo (PRAM) was denied registration under the anticommunist provisions of existing legislation, while the PDC and PAR stated their lack of faith in government guarantees of honest elections. The PDC specifically demanded that the government confine the Guardia Nacional and the Treasury Police during the electoral process but received no guarantees from the government.[40]

Still, the regime was able to claim success when over one million voters registered to elect fifty-two legislators and hundreds of representatives to 261 municipalities across the country. Although abstentionism remained high (less than a third of those registered bothered to vote), the election proceeded uneventfully and produced results that gave the opposition a degree of hope that the country was finally moving toward a more pluralist and representative form of government. The PCN retained control of the legislative assembly with thirty-two deputies (as well as winning 224 of the 261 municipalities), but the voters elected fourteen deputies from the PDC, as well as six from the PAR. More significantly, the rising star of the Christian Democrats, José Napoleón Duarte, was elected mayor of the capital city, San

Salvador, the first stepping-stone in his future rise to national prominence. Duarte himself acknowledged that, for the first time since 1931, elections had been held in El Salvador without pressures brought to bear on the electorate by the military.[41]

The opposition's relative success in the 1964 elections should not be exaggerated. It did well in urban areas (especially in San Salvador), where an historic constituency of political opposition had existed since the movement in 1944 to oust the Hernández Martínez dictatorship. But the opposition's resources and organization in 1964 did not allow it to field candidates in all locations: although the Christian Democrats entered candidates to the national legislature in all fourteen departments, they did so in only 150 municipalities, while the PAR contested legislative seats in only eleven departments and presented candidates for seventy municipalities.[42] The limited resources of the opposition combined with the strong presence of PCN in rural areas, where most of the population still lived, was to mark electoral practice and results for the rest of the decade.

The regime's success in holding pluralist elections in 1964 was repeated two years later. President Rivera had already announced that the 1966 legislative and municipal election would be held within an environment of "maximum efficiency and impartiality" and stressed that constitutional guarantees had not been suspended at any moment under his government.[43] With the same three parties running, the vote produced results very similar to those in 1964: thirty-two deputies for the PCN, fifteen for the PDC, and six for the PAR. The Christian Democrats easily retained their hold of the mayoral office of San Salvador and thus stood prepared to launch a strong attempt for the presidency in the 1967 elections.[44]

The 1967 presidential elections were a novelty for many Salvadorans: for the first time since 1950, a presidential election was contested by more than one candidate. The PCN selected Rivera's minister of the interior, Colonel Fidel Sánchez Hernández, as its presidential candidate, while the Christian Democrats chose a prominent lawyer and businessman, Abraham Rodríguez, and the PAR put forth Fabio Castillo, a member of the short-lived October junta of 1960–61. In addition to offering the electorate an option of candidates, the 1967 vote also presented Salvadorans with substantially different programs of government, including for the first time the issue of land ownership. The PAR, which during the 1950s had espoused a commitment to furthering political freedoms and the construction of a working democracy, swung leftward under the leadership of Dr. Castillo and now spoke of the need to undertake profound land reform, an issue that had been at the heart of the Alliance for Progress but paid only lip service by the governments of the PCN. The Christian Democrats, too, had included land reform as part of their program of government, although not in such a preeminent position as the PAR.[45]

The land issue was not new, of course. However, since 1932 it had been abolished from political discourse or, in the best of cases, relegated to lists of good intentions by the governments of the PRUD and the PCN, which were much more interested in involving the state in industrial and social development in urban areas while leaving traditional landholding elites in control of agricultural production. But by the 1960s, the issue of land had come to the fore again, as a result of profound changes in export agriculture that had begun in the 1950s when El Salvador's last agricultural frontier, the coastal plain, was opened up for the production of cotton.[46] Cotton production disrupted traditional patterns of land use and displaced thousands of peasants from land on which they had grown basic grains. The number of peasants without access to land under any form of tenure increased markedly, prompting a rise in emigration to urban areas and to neighboring Honduras and enlarging the rural wage-labor force.[47] This growing population of displaced and dispossessed workers and their families listened readily to political leaders who addressed their grievances under the promise of land reform and the right to organize rural unions, two issues that military reformers had rejected outright since 1948.

The emergence of the land issue made for a tense political campaign in 1967. The candidate of the PCN, Colonel Sánchez Hernández, promised to follow the policies of the Rivera government of "evolution with liberty" and reminded voters that the alternative to the PCN was communism. The PAR, on the other hand, provoked great nervousness among some landowners, who organized an unsuccessful campaign to have the PAR removed from the ballots and even fielded their own candidate under a newly organized party, the Partido Popular Salvadoreño (PPS). The results of the election gave Colonel Sánchez Hernández a comfortable majority of approximately 233,000 votes, to a little under 180,000 for all the opposition parties, with an abstention rate of around 60 percent.[48]

Although the 1967 elections suggested that the PCN retained its rural political base and the advantages of an incumbent "official" party, the next legislative and municipal elections in 1968 made it clear that in an environment relatively free of legal impediments the opposition was at the verge of breaking through to majority status. Even though the candidates of the PAR were denied the right to register, the regime did allow the newly formed social democratic party, the Movimiento Nacional Revolucionario (MNR) to run, as well as the right wing PPS. Together with the PDC, which got nineteen deputies, the opposition elected a total of twenty-five deputies to the legislative assembly against the PCN's twenty-seven.[49] With this kind of majority, the PCN could pass most legislation except that concerning foreign loans and aid agreements, which required a two-thirds majority for approval. On occasion, then, the PCN was forced to negotiate with its legislative opposition, a novelty for the Salvadoran political system.

Even more serious for the PCN was the spectacular advance that the opposition, especially the PDC, made in the urban areas, where it took control of eighty of the municipal councils, including most of the important towns and cities.[50] Control of municipal government did not translate into significant increases of political power, given that municipalities handled limited funds and undertook few tasks (such as birth, marriage, and death records, oversight of markets and slaughterhouses, and small-scale public works). Furthermore, municipal budgets were authorized by the central government, which also provided them with supplementary funding. However, in addition to the political exposure that went along with public office, it was much easier for an opposition party to undertake political organizing within a municipality that it controlled.

With legislative and municipal elections scheduled again for 1970 and presidential, legislative, and municipal elections for 1972, the increasingly successful performance of the opposition during the 1960s gave it hope that the military could be persuaded to relinquish direct control of the government without threatening its existence or institutional integrity. However, one important reality stood in the way of a genuine process of demilitarization: the continued existence of a vast paramilitary network in the rural areas that was bolstered in the 1960s by the introduction of civic action programs and the creation of the Organización Democrática Nacionalista (ORDEN).

MILITARIZATION IN THE COUNTRYSIDE

After the triumph of Fidel Castro's guerrilla forces over the regular army of the Cuban government in the last days of 1958, an overriding concern of military planners in Washington was the prevention of a similar occurrence elsewhere in the Western Hemisphere. In addition to the social and economic reforms envisioned by the Alliance for Progress, Latin American militaries, in conjunction with the armed forces of the United States, sought to improve both their military capabilities and their public image, particularly in rural areas where the threat of guerrilla warfare presumably was greatest.

During the 1960s, the effective strength of the Salvadoran armed forces was quite limited. The standing army had about 4,500 men organized in nine infantry regiments, one artillery regiment, and one tank regiment; annual recruitment into the armed forces stood at about 2,700 men. Under wartime conditions, twelve more infantry brigades could be recruited from the reserves, which numbered about 30,000 men. The air force had few aircraft and about 1,000 men, while the navy did not amount to more than a few coastal patrol boats. The Guardia Nacional, with about 2,500 men, continued to provide rural policing in the entire national territory.[51] All in all, military spending during the 1960s ranged between 12.4 percent and 10.4 percent of the national budget, while U.S. military assistance to El Salvador was the lowest of all Central American countries with the exception of Costa Rica and Panama.[52]

The limited military capability of the Salvadoran armed forces was offset by the advantage of nearly half a century of pervasive paramilitary organization in the countryside. Still, the threat posed by the Cuban revolution required measures to strengthen the military's presence in the rural areas. A key element in this preventive counterinsurgency program was civic action (acción cívica militar, in Spanish), which directly involved the armed forces in programs to improve the welfare of the rural poor and reinforce their allegiance to the national government. In 1963, a national directorate of civic action was created within the Ministry of Defense charged with coordinating the military's participation in programs of road construction and repair, distribution of food staples, medical attention, and assistance to rural schools (uniforms, student outings). A National Central Committee of civic action, as well as regional and local offices, staffed by officials of the ministries of health, education, agriculture, public works, defense, and interior, provided the program with additional support and resources.[53]

The true impact of civic action in terms of bringing rural populations closer to the government and neutralizing the discourse of leftist and opposition political groups is difficult to gauge. Available figures indicate that the total number of Salvadorans who received direct benefits from civic action was not very large. In 1966, for example, civic action assisted in the distribution of food under the Catholic Church's Cáritas program to a total of nearly 17,000 individuals, and 26,000 children received Christmas presents; in 1970–71, civic action gave out 10,000 pairs of shoes, 86,000 toys, and 10,000 pounds of used clothes, while its medical services filled over 8,600 prescriptions and pulled 676 teeth.[54] However, other programs and services for which there are no statistics suggest a wider coverage, such as the construction of roads and sports fields.[55]

Even if civic action programs did not contribute significantly to national development, they did provide the armed forces with an important public relations tool. The military broadcast its achievements through its own radio programs and distributed fliers in schools to increase student awareness and respect for flag, country, and "the family and moral traditions of our society."[56] In addition, the presence of troop units in specific locations provided the military with intelligence on local conditions, gave officers and troops the opportunity to come into contact with rural reality, and sought to improve the image of the military and the national government in the eyes of peasants and villagers.[57]

A more strictly political presence of the Salvadoran armed forces in the rural areas grew out of a decision to create the Organización Democrática Nacionalista, whose acronym in Spanish, ORDEN, stands precisely for order. ORDEN was founded during the presidency of Colonel Rivera at the initiative of the commander of the Guardia Nacional, General José Alberto Medrano, as an organization to counter leftist penetration of the rural areas. Medrano received support from the United States, which sent a team of Green Berets to train Salvadoran soldiers designated to work with ORDEN. By the end of the 1960s, its membership could have been as high as one hundred thousand.[58] No reference of ORDEN is found in official publications of the 1960s nor was its precise nature as a state or private organization made clear at the time.[59] However, it gained quickly in strength and numbers, working alongside the cadres of the PCN, the civic action programs, and the paramilitary structure of *patrullas cantonales* to ensure that the rural areas remain off limits to alternative political thinking and organization.[60]

Ever since 1932, the Salvadoran countryside had remained relatively calm, even though the country's population began to grow rapidly, doubling every twenty years by the 1960s, as did the concentration of landholdings. The pressure on agricultural land was alleviated somewhat by rural migration to the urban areas, prompted by the industrial growth that accompanied the creation of the Central American Common Market (CACM) in 1960. In addition, a large number of peasants migrated to neighboring Honduras, in search of available agricultural land or to find work on the banana plantations of the Caribbean,[61] as well as to Guatemala and Nicaragua on a seasonal basis to pick cotton and other crops.[62] But the unbalanced growth that the Central American countries experienced within the CACM brought the region to a crisis situation in 1969 and placed El Salvador at the very center of the problem. By 1970, El Salvador's future economic development was in doubt and its political system on the verge of breaking down.

WAR AND CRISIS

The issue of land, for so long ignored by El Salvador's military rulers and its coffee elite, erupted forcefully only two years after it had become an issue during the 1967 presidential election. Ironically, it was the land occupied by Salvadoran peasants in Honduras that triggered the crisis. The Honduran government, which was facing its own rural pressures from a unionized peasantry fighting off land encroachments by latifundia owners, enacted a land reform law that made no provision for the land rights of Salvadoran settlers. On the other hand, Honduran businessmen were demanding restrictions on Salvadoran imports that competed with their own products and generated a severe balance of payments problem.[63]

As the relations between the governments of the neighboring countries became strained, Salvadoran settlers returning to El Salvador spoke of being evicted and persecuted by Honduran gangs. A number of soccer matches leading up to the 1970 World Cup further inflamed popular feelings and resulted in stadium violence. On 14 July 1969, Salvadoran ground forces invaded Honduras along a wide front and the so-called "Soccer War" was on. The war lasted for a little over four days, during which the Salvadoran forces advanced a few miles into Honduran territory and captured one provincial town; the Honduran response involved its air force, which bombed and strafed port facilities and a refinery. International pressure, mostly from the United States, stopped the fighting in four days and produced a withdrawal of Salvadoran forces before the month was out, although it seems clear that neither side had the means or the desire to prolong the conflict.[64] On the Salvadoran side, six officers and eighty-four soldiers were killed and seven officers and 223 soldiers were injured.[65] Civilian casualties, both Salvadoran and Honduran, were estimated in the thousands.

For the armed forces of El Salvador, the war constituted a mixed blessing. In strictly military terms, the Salvadoran government was in no position to dictate terms to the Honduran regime; on the contrary, the flood of refugees returning to El Salvador threatened to destabilize a government with limited resources to attend to their demands for work and social assistance. But in a political sense, the regime of President Sánchez Hernández benefitted momentarily from an outpouring of popular support and national unity. Even before the fighting began, the main opposition political parties had joined up with the PCN and signed a declaration of "national unity" that committed them all to defend the human rights of their compatriots in Honduras.[66] For the first time in many years, all political forces in the country supported the national government in pursuit of a common goal.

What was that goal? On the very same day that the fighting began, President Sánchez Hernández described the conflict as one of "legitimate defense," under which the armed forces of El Salvador repelled acts of aggression along the border with Honduras.[67] Four days later, he underlined that the struggle of the Salvadoran people had only one objective: to guarantee the lives and the properties of Salvadorans in Honduras.[68] As this goal could be achieved only partially once the cease-fire had taken effect and the troops withdrawn from Honduran soil, he asked his countrymen to open their eyes instead to "the suffering of our own brothers here in our country" and expressed his hope "that national unity endure beyond victory, so that all together, with optimism and hope, we can find solutions to our problems."[69] More specifically, he spoke some days later of the need "to concern ourselves with that peasant mass which we must redeem, as a tribute to the blood that its youth spilled for the fatherland on the front lines."[70] Put in other terms, the effort of the peasant conscript on the field of battle could not go unrewarded.

The president had come full circle. From a concern for the plight of Salvadoran peasants in Honduras, he now addressed the underlying issue of Salvadoran politics: the need "to carry out without further delay the necessary changes," which he defined as educational, agrarian, and administrative (state) reforms.[71] In January 1970, the legislative assembly convened a national congress on agrarian reform, which President Sánchez Hernández addressed in no uncertain terms: land reform should be discussed frankly and openly and land reform could not be postponed any more. He also underlined the soundness of Salvadoran democracy as expressed in the free and open discussion of the country's problems.[72]

Talk about reforms and democracy, together with the perceived victory of the Salvadoran troops in the war against Honduras, gave the regime and the armed forces a shot in the arm. The triumphant military parade held upon the return of the troops was evidence of the national euphoria that surrounded the war effort; the regime's willingness to address the deep social and economic problems of the nation also suggests a sense of purpose and resolve unheard of in years past.[73] However, the government was clear on the need to proceed with caution. As Sánchez Hernández himself stated, land reform would proceed firmly but gradually, because "[the] task is so difficult and complex that it is not possible to carry it out under one single government."[74] Still, enormous expectations were raised by a political opening that had allowed the legal opposition a considerable presence within the legislature and municipal governments and a reformist rhetoric that acquired even greater urgency with the arrival of tens of thousands of destitute Salvadorans fleeing from Honduras.

The sense of national unity and support for the government was evidenced in the legislative and municipal elections held in March 1970. After a campaign that exploited nationalist sentiment, the PCN won nearly 60 percent of the votes cast, thereby taking thirty-two seats in the legislature to only fifteen for the PDC. It also won control of 254 of the 261 municipalities, even though the PDC retained its hold on the capital city.[75] But by the beginning of 1972, when elections were scheduled for all elected offices (presidency, legislature, municipalities), the tide had turned against the PCN. On the one hand, the government of Sánchez Hernández had not been able to deliver on its reform promises. In the area of education, the government's reforms had failed to address the issue of pay and working conditions for the country's expanding corp of school teachers, generating conflict with the teachers' union, including a number of crippling strikes. And the issue of land had been addressed in a very timid fashion under a law that regulated the use of irrigation water and that set limits on the amount of land that any one individual could own within an irrigation scheme.[76]

A FINAL CHANCE FOR DEMOCRACY

The regime approached the presidential elections of 1972 with an image problem. Its commitment to reform had alarmed the most recalcitrant groups within the landowning class; the political party they had formed to represent them some years back, the PPS, was joined by another right-wing group, the Frente Unido Democrático Independiente (FUDI), which represented the interests of large coffee producers in Ahuachapán. FUDI nominated General José Alberto Medrano, the founder of ORDEN and one of the more visible of the military leaders in the war against Honduras, as its presidential candidate. On the center and the left, the regime's promises of reform and respect for democratic freedoms were questioned openly and served to bring together the Christian Democrats, the Social Democrats (the MNR), and a new party on the left, the Unión Democrática Nacionalista (UDN), which was in reality a front for the Communist Party of El Salvador.[77] These three opposition parties formed the Unión Nacional Opositora (UNO) and elected José Napoleón Duarte as their presidential candidate, with Guillermo Manuel Ungo, of the MNR, as his vice-presidential running mate.

The PCN, in turn, chose Colonel Arturo Armando Molina as its candidate. Colonel Molina had served on the staff of President Sánchez Hernández but had received very little public exposure. The fact that the PCN faced a strong challenge on both the left and the right did not bode well for its chances on election day. Consequently, the regime began to tamper with the electoral system in order to guarantee the triumph of its presidential, legislative, and municipal candidates. First, the electoral council decided to hold the election for president two weeks before the scheduled date, when voting for all public offices was to have taken place. In this manner, if Molina failed to win an absolute majority, the legislative assembly would still be under the control of the PCN when it convened to choose the next president.[78]

Secondly, the legislative assembly introduced amendments to the electoral law in July 1971 aimed at hindering the operation of opposition parties. One important change raised the number of signatures required to register a new political party. Another change increased the fines and sanctions against parties that violated provisions of the electoral code; these increases threatened the most financially vulnerable parties with close ties to the popular classes. But most threatening to the opposition was the power wielded by the electoral council, beholden as always to the official party, to hand down judgment on these issues without the opposition having much of a chance to appeal.[79]

Thirdly, the electoral council maneuvered to make it difficult for opposition parties to name their representatives at all the voting booths. In the end, only the PCN had poll watchers at all 1,937 voting places, while the opposition was underrepresented in a good number of them. The opposition's requests to hold rallies and marches also were subjected to administrative foul-ups and outright rejection by the authorities. During the campaign the security forces carried out attacks on the opposition parties and even abducted a number of opposition sympathizers who were never heard from again.[80]

And finally, the regime carefully managed the vote count and the reporting of election returns. On the evening of 20 February, once the polls had closed, all radio and TV stations were ordered to transmit only the official statements put out by the electoral council. The initial results were favorable to the PCN, but by midnight the UNO began to catch up. Then, inexplicably, at four in the morning of 21 February, the electoral council stopped announcing updates entirely. At four in the afternoon of the same day, the electoral council suddenly announced that "unofficial results" gave the victory to the PCN candidate, Colonel Molina, by a margin of nearly twenty thousand votes over the runner up, José Napoleón Duarte of the UNO. But on the very next day, the departmental electoral council of San Salvador announced that the results issued by the national electoral council for the department were incorrect and that the real figure was nearly thirty thousand votes more in favor of the UNO. If this were the case, Duarte had won the election. Over the next four days, the PCN and the UNO issued contradictory results until the electoral council, on 25 February, issued the definitive results that gave Colonel Molina nearly ten thousand votes more than Duarte.[81]

There was still a minor technicality that needed to be resolved: Colonel

Molina had not won an absolute majority, since the opposition on the right, the PPS and the FUDI, had received over 14 percent of the vote. Thus, the election went to the legislative assembly, as mandated by the constitution in these cases; there, the PCN had a comfortable majority that quickly ratified Colonel Molina as the president-elect of El Salvador by a vote of 31 to 0. (The opposition had walked out of the hall beforehand.) Still, the inability of the candidate of the official party to gain an outright majority in the popular vote was unprecedented for the political system of El Salvador, where for the previous forty years the outcome of elections was known even before they were held.

Conclusion

The decade of the 1960s began with great expectations about the establishment of electoral practices that would allow for orderly and peaceful transfers of power from one administration to another, even from one party to another. Both the junta born of the October 1960 coup and the Directorio Cívico Militar of January 1961 expressed precise commitments to the establishment of competitive, honest elections. Later on, an observer might well have thought (as some did) that the movement toward effective electoral democracy was slow but irreversible, as indicated by the successively increased proportion of the popular vote achieved by the political opposition.[82]

The growing concern about economic development and social reforms espoused by leaders of the armed forces also suggested a maturing of the political system and a disposition to discuss any number of national problems. The very success of the Central American Common Market in stimulating production and trade under the aegis of the Alliance for Progress convinced many that the formula for development finally had been identified. But the decade ended in crisis, sparked by skewed growth within the Common Market and the resentment aimed at Salvadoran settlers by a variety of groups in Honduran society.

Salvadoran "democracy" had evolved fitfully under the restrictions and contradictions imposed by the regime, while the opposition tested the limits of activism that the regime was willing to tolerate. During the years of substantial economic growth before 1969, the regime was willing to tolerate almost any political grouping, with the exception of the marxist Left. Even the constitutional provision prohibiting the operation of parties with international ties, such as the Christian Democrats and the Social Democrats, was held in abeyance during the 1960s.[83] By 1968, opposition parties were close to gaining a majority in the legislative assembly and in 1972 they made a strong effort to win the presidency outright. The fact that over the years the opposition parties were predisposed increasingly to participate in the political system suggests that some hope existed for a meaningful transition to a working democracy.

However, there was nothing inevitable in this trend. In the first place, the military's commitment to democracy was peculiar to its own thinking and institutional interest. Ever since the 1948 coup, the military had insisted on its commitment to democracy; it had even maintained that its role in 1948 was precisely a reaction to the dictatorship of the previous regimes and that as "the mailed fist of the people" it acted in response to the popular will. But its officers defined democracy in terms that had little to do with liberal electoral practices. The minister of defense stated in 1961 that democracy was a system of government "based, fundamentally, on the equilibrium of the branches of government, their independence, and their powers of mutual oversight."[84] Furthermore, the military believed that the Salvadoran polity was threatened by grave dangers, such as illiteracy, class struggle, subversive doctrines, and "the spirit of factionalism," that required the presence of an ever alert armed forces. In fact, the keys to national development were order and peace and "a real national consensus," which the military claimed to back fully.[85] Democracy, it seems, had little to offer in this respect.

In the second place, the military never rejected, but with the one exception of the October 1960 junta, the clearly political role established for it in the constitutions of 1948 and 1962: guaranteeing public order, alterability in the presidency, and compliance with the law.[86] By 1967, the minister of defense could say that military officers had moved closer to civilians while disengaging from more direct association with the party politics of years past.[87] However, President Sánchez Hernández had no qualms about describing the military's role as "eminently political" in that it had responsibilities in the fields of foreign policy (defense of the nation's sovereignty) and citizen security (law and order); he did warn against military officers engaging in *party* politics, especially when they were enticed by "unscrupulous" individuals, and claimed that the Cuban army had been defeated by an irregular force because its officers had lost their "professional morality."[88]

In the third place, the relationship between military officers and civilians constituted a powerful impediment to the evolution of a working liberal democracy in El Salvador. In addition to the civilians (including many ex-soldiers) who participated in the various paramilitary organizations in the countryside and who provided a substantial part of the rural vote for the PCN, there was a sizable number of urbanites who were similarly beholden to the military for a job in the government bureaucracy or who saw in a military president a guarantee of social stability and defense of property.[89] This civilian base of support for the regimes of the PCN, protected and privileged to assure its loyalty, was loath to tolerate greater political freedoms that might imperil its standing come election time. The political intolerance that grew out of the alliance between civilians and military officers was heightened by the anticommunism of the times, which equated opposition to the regime with subversion and revolution.

And finally, the efforts that some Salvadorans made to expand and strengthen democracy in the 1960s received very little support from abroad. The United States, in particular, was much more concerned with security issues that Washington thought were best addressed by providing military training and supplies, thus bolstering the repressive aspects of the regime and largely ignoring its excesses.[90] The Alliance for Progress did contain elements of social reform that could have helped democratize Salvadoran society; some of these were discussed and announced quite openly but were implemented in a watered-down fashion and, in the case of land redistribution schemes, came too late to prevent the full-fledged social explosion of the 1970s.

By the beginning of the 1970s, then, the reformist experiment in El Salvador, directed by a series of military juntas and presidents, had run out of steam. Opposition political groups felt cheated and frustrated by the persistent use of fraud and intimidation at election time. Large numbers of rural inhabitants experienced increasing difficulties in finding work and land to feed their families; the massive peasant exodus from Honduras only complicated the problem. New political groups with moderately reformist programs, like the Christian and Social Democrats, challenged the PCN and pointedly championed civilian candidates for high office. The result was a strongly contested election in 1972 that the PCN lost in all likelihood in the ballot boxes but won anyway by dispensing with any pretenses of legality and fair play. From then on, politics was rapidly replaced by violence as the military first fought within its ranks to define its political role and, having resolved that, turned its attention to repressing a population that also had decided on increasingly violent actions to achieve its goals.

THE POLITICAL CRISIS OF THE 1970S

THE FRAUDULENT elections in February 1972 signaled the exhaustion of the military's reformist experiment. Opposition leaders' expectations that the political opening permitted under Presidents Rivera and Sánchez Hernández might lead to genuine political reform were dashed as the electoral council announced the official returns of the election. Legislative and municipal elections on 12 March only added to the opposition's frustrations. In the opposition's stronghold, San Salvador, the electoral council disqualified UNO's legislative slate, all but assuring the PCN of victory. Nevertheless, UNO organized a successful ballot-defacing campaign, whereby more than a majority of votes cast in San Salvador were null. However, instead of nullifying the elections as required by the electoral law, the electoral council ruled in favor of the governing party.[1]

Disillusionment over the military's traditional way of exercising political power was not limited to opposition parties. Within the armed forces there had been some opposition to Sánchez Hernández's imposition of Molina as the PCN's candidate. The level of discontent was serious enough to generate rumors of a coup and to necessitate a minor purge of some senior officers in December 1971.[2] The regime's electoral machinations only heightened the tensions within the officer corps. On 25 March 1972, two days after the electoral council's ruling, a group of rebel officers led by Colonel Benjamín Mejía launched a coup attempt to prevent Colonel Molina from assuming the presidency. Before the coup was suppressed, the rebels succeeded in taking control of two major military installations in the capital—the Zapote (artillery) and San Carlos barracks (infantry)—and capturing President Sánchez Hernández. It took the combined support of the security forces, the air force, and troop detachments from San Miguel and Chalatenango to finally put down the revolt. Despite its initial success, the rebellion failed to generate sufficient support among units outside of the capital. The level of casualties was the highest since the 1944 coup attempt, with over one hundred dead and more than two hundred wounded.[3]

Although the coup attempt most likely reflected officers' discontent with the imposition of Molina and the fraudulent nature of the 1972 elections, it is not at all clear how far rebel officers intended to go in changing the status quo. The coup was organized without consulting leaders from the UNO coalition. Duarte, the apparent victor of the February elections, made an eleventh-hour radio appeal to drum up popular support for the revolt, but his involvement appears to have been marginal. In fact, in the proclamation announcing the formation of a civil-military junta, none of the UNO leaders were mentioned. Moreover, one of the civilian leaders of the coup later claimed that if the coup had been successful, "Duarte would not have occupied the presidency."[4] Quite possibly, then, the rebel officers only questioned the way in which the military under Sánchez Hernández exercised political power, and not whether in fact the military *should* exercise power.[5]

THE BUILDING CRISIS

Although the literature on the period of the 1970s is quite extensive, most accounts are largely descriptive and do not shed much light on the factors contributing to the unfolding crisis. A few authors have put forward historically informed explanations, focusing on both structural and conjunctural factors. Baloyra, for example, views the crisis as dating back to 1932.[6] He argues that the "crisis of oligarchic domination" was rooted in the particular form of agro-export development that evolved in El Salvador, which was based on a system of coerced labor. Although the oligarchy was incapable of resolving the crisis during the 1930s, the military's assumption of power did not signal the oligarchy's total collapse. On the contrary, the military proved itself incapable of filling the political vacuum created by the crisis, as the oligarchy retained its ability to block any attempts to seriously undermine its economic dominance. This resulted in a crisis of hegemony, whereby successive military governments relied more on exclusion than consensus to achieve political domination. Military experiments with reform between 1948 and 1972 failed to produce the necessary societal consensus to resolve the crisis. In other words, the military could "control but not effectively lead society."[7]

We agree with Baloyra and others[8] that the crisis that erupted during the late 1970s was ultimately rooted in the particular nature of the agro-export model. Historically, agro-export production depended on a large, cheap, seasonal labor supply drawn from landless and land-poor peasants. The exploitive relations of production in the countryside necessitated a coercive apparatus capable of regimenting the labor supply. Such a model of development imposed several limitations on the political sphere. First of all, any serious agrarian reform program was out of the question, since it would reduce dramatically the available supply of cheap seasonal labor. Secondly, any attempts to promote industrial development would have to be subservient to the agro-export sector. In short, the very policies needed to reverse the increasing pauperization of the peasantry were not a viable option for the country's military rulers.

Besides the constraints imposed by the agro-export model, also limiting the scope of the military's reform initiatives was the contradictory nature of its political power. Because much of the military's power derived from its institutional autonomy, its control of the state, and its rural power base, not even the most reform-minded officers were willing to contemplate the prospect of genuine civilian control over the military or an end to its network of social control in the countryside. Such meaningful political reform would have seriously eroded the military's capacity to exercise tutelage over the political process.

Over time, the inherent contradictions of the model of agro-export development in El Salvador produced serious obstacles to the military's continued political domination. The process of accelerating land concentration associated with the expansion of coffee production was exacerbated by the introduction of nontraditional crops (cotton, sugar, and beef cattle) after World War II. While coffee remained the leading export, by 1970 cotton and sugar accounted for close to 30 percent of total extraregional exports.[9] The rapid expansion of cotton, cattle, and sugar production contributed to the growing number of landless and land-poor. The Pacific lowlands, where much of the cotton and beef cattle production was concentrated, had become a last refuge for peasants displaced by the expansion of coffee production in the highlands. Some peasants squatted on hacienda lands while others worked as *colonos* or sharecroppers. With the expansion of cotton production, however, land values shot up in this region. Landowners were no longer interested in sharecropping arrangements since they could rent out their land to the new class of cotton entrepreneurs. Consequently, a growing number of peasants no longer had access to land.[10]

As Dunkerley points out, since the nontraditional crops "generated neither a permanent nor a seasonal labor demand sufficient to provide the peasant economy with some form of generalized balance for the loss of land," many peasants were forced to migrate.[11] In addition to increasing rural-urban migration, more and more Salvadorans crossed into Honduras in search of land. On the eve of the Soccer War in 1969, some 300,000 Salvadorans were thought to have migrated to Honduras. The expulsion of 130,000 Salvadorans by the Honduran government in the aftermath of the war only added to the building land pressures.[12] Between 1961 and 1975, the landless population grew from 11.8 to 40.9 percent of rural families.[13]

The process of industrialization during the 1960s and 1970s, stimulated by El Salvador's integration into the Central American Common Market (CACM) in 1961, did not provide adequate alternatives to the growing influx of migrants to the urban areas. As Bulmer-Thomas points out, the model of industrialization implemented in El Salvador and elsewhere in Central America was a "hybrid model . . . grafted on to the traditional export-led model without challenging the hegemony of the export agriculturalists."[14] Much of the finance for new industries came from abroad and was biased toward capital-intensive *maquila*-type industries. Not surprisingly, the process of industrialization created a relatively small number of jobs and offered few opportunities for backward linkages that might have stimulated new industries.[15]

Although the military's system of social control had proved effective in maintaining "social peace" in the country, during the 1970s the increasingly precarious economic conditions for the majority of the rural population and the inadequacies of the urban economy presented a serious problem for the military. Taking advantage of the political opening initiated by President Rivera in the 1960s, a new set of political actors, including sectors of the Catholic Church, student organizers, political party activists, and development workers, contributed to a process of growing popular mobilization and organization in opposition to the regime.[16] A telling sign was the 1972 election. Unlike past elections, most of the opposition parties joined to form a broad coalition front to challenge the PCN. As we saw, caught off guard by the extent of disaffection with the regime, the military resorted to widespread fraud to guarantee the "election" of its candidate, Colonel Arturo Armando Molina.

In the rural areas, the growth of peasant organizations established during the 1960s (FECCAS—Federación Cristiana de Campesinos Salvadoreños, and UCS—Unión Comunal Salvadoreña) and the creation of new ones during the seventies (UTC—Unión de Trabajadores del Campo) presented the military with a formidable challenge. While the countryside had changed, the military had not. The traditional methods, coercion combined with meager handouts, were no longer adequate to guarantee control over peasants whose life conditions had become increasingly precarious and who were ever more willing to take direct action. Nevertheless, the military continued to view the rural population as it had during the 1940s and

1950s: as a mass of gullible and fearful peasants who would provide the raw material from which the military could derive, and mold, a never-ending supply of obedient soldiers and reservists, and through whom they could control the rest.[17] This solution made sense as long as El Salvador was able to "export" its agrarian problem to other areas. However, in the wake of the Soccer War, the Honduran safety valve was no longer available to ease building tensions in the countryside. Thus, as the 1970s progressed, the military's control over the countryside began to unravel.

As opposition increased, the armed forces began to strengthen and expand their military and paramilitary structures. Under the auspices of the United States Public Safety Program (1957–1974), the armed forces made significant progress in improving the technical capability of the security forces and in developing a modern intelligence system under centralized control.[18] The creation of ORDEN in the early 1960s greatly enhanced the military's intelligence-gathering capacity and control over the rural population. During the 1970s, the military began organizing reserve battalions that were attached to the various infantry brigades and military posts. Each battalion numbered from two to three thousand men. In addition, a training school for commandos was set up in the department of Morazán.[19] New equipment and weapons were purchased, not—as the defense minister put it—to make war, but to keep the armed forces in a state of readiness to defend the nation's interests.[20] Finally, the ranks of the *escoltas militares* were expanded due to, in the words of the minister of defense, the "increase in population," but, more likely, they were expanded in response to the increasing peasant mobilization in the form of land seizures, demonstrations, and union organizing.[21]

Efforts during the 1960s and 1970s to beef up the armed forces' internal security system were no more than a refinement of cruder methods of control and failed to stem the growing peasant mobilization. What was needed to maintain "social peace" in the countryside was not a more refined system of control but an agrarian reform program that enabled landless and land-poor peasants to overcome their increasing pauperization.

The growing popular mobilization was not limited to the countryside. Urban areas witnessed the dramatic growth of the trade union movement, which increased from a total of eighty unions with a membership of just over twenty-four thousand in 1966 to 127 unions with a membership of over sixty-four thousand in 1975. More importantly, independent trade unions were much more successful than government-controlled unions in recruiting new members. Whereas in 1971 the progovernment Confederación General de Sindicatos contained 42 percent of unionized workers, in 1976 its share was down to 19 percent.[22] The majority of urban dwellers did not receive a regular wage. They populated the mushrooming shantytowns of Mejicanos, Cuscatancingo, and Ayutuxtepeque on the outskirts of San Salvador. Living in squalid conditions, most eked out a living in the growing informal sector of the economy. Although only a small percentage of the shantytown dwellers were unionized, the subhuman conditions in the shantytowns facilitated increased levels of popular mobilization. Thus, throughout the 1970s, growing numbers of shantytown dwellers joined Christian base communities, neighborhood associations, and other urban-based popular movements. As repression against these organizations increased, many activists looked to the burgeoning guerrilla movements as the only alternative.[23]

In the context of growing peasant mobilization in the countryside and labor unrest in the cities, the military tried its hand at reform. In June 1976 the Molina government announced a program of mild land reform, the so-called *transformación agraria*. The plan targeted some fifty-nine thousand hectares of land largely devoted to cotton and cattle in the San Miguel and Usulután departments, which were to be divided among twelve thousand peasant families. Landowners were given the option of either selling their property or having it expropriated by the state. In the case of expropriations, the landowners were to be fully compensated with funds provided by USAID. Despite the provisions for full compensation, and the fact that most of the land targeted was state-owned, conservative landowning interests viewed the land reform as setting a dangerous precedent. They launched a fierce public relations campaign intended to block the plan and began taking their capital out of the country. Opposition also came from within the military, including the minister of defense, General Carlos Humberto Romero, who was the oligarchy's favorite to succeed Molina.[24] Lacking any significant popular support to counter opposition to the reform plan, in late 1976 Molina agreed to a "compromise" that effectively emasculated the program.[25]

Molina's failure to implement the proposed land reform highlighted both the limits of the military's political power and its complex and sometimes tense relationship with the oligarchy. Although it was timid in scope, conservative sectors of the oligarchy interpreted the reform as a challenge to their economic dominance. Several years earlier they had made clear their opposition to land reform when Sánchez Hernández had toyed with the idea.[26] In fact, the relationship with the military became so strained during the Sánchez Hernández government that hard-line factions of the oligarchy put up their own candidate, the former director of the National Guard, Jose "Chele" Medrano, in the 1972 elections. By the time of the 1977 elections, conservative landowning interests were able to impose upon the country the last of a series of military presidents and an opponent of agrarian reform, General Romero.

Having failed at reform, the only alternative left to the military was to step up repression. Romero appeared to be the right man for the job. As minister of defense he had been responsible for the July 1975 massacre of students demonstrating against the government's lavish spending on the "Miss Universe" pageant to be held in San Salvador. At least thirty-seven students were killed when National Guardsmen opened fire on the demonstrators, with many more wounded or "disappeared."[27] Romero also presided over the expansion of ORDEN, which led to increased levels of repression in the countryside. The intensification of repression, in fact, began even before Romero's inauguration. Only days after his election, an opposition demonstration denouncing the electoral fraud was violently suppressed by a combined force of army, National Guard, Treasury, and Customs Police units. Troops fired on the demonstrators, leaving several dead and wounded.[28] In the following weeks, progressive sectors of the Catholic Church were targeted for repression. On 12 March, Father Rutilio Grande, the Jesuit parish priest of Aguilares, was gunned down on his way to Mass. On 12 May, a second priest, Father Alfonso Navarro, was assassinated in his parish of Miramonte.

During Romero's government the repression reached new heights. Whereas under the Molina government the army and security forces were linked to thirty-seven politically motivated assassinations and sixty-nine disappearances, under Romero these numbers jumped to 461 and 131 respectively.[29] On 25 November 1977, Romero enacted the draconian Law for the Defense and Guarantee of Public Order, effectively giving the army and security forces carte blanche to wage their war against the popular organizations. During 1978 alone, the Catholic Church's legal office, Socorro Jurídico, estimated fifty-seven killings per month carried out by government forces and death squads.[30] The escalating repression did not go unanswered by armed groups on the Left. Guerrilla organizations staged a wave of kidnappings and assassinations of prominent business and political leaders. The spiral of violence, in particular the attacks on Catholic clergy and religious, drew international attention to the deteriorating human rights situation in the country.

Increased pressure by the Carter administration did contribute to some softening in Romero's position. In January 1979, Romero replaced the director of the National Guard, General Ramón Alvarenga, who was well-known for his involvement in human rights abuses. Then in March, he repealed the public security law. However, the increased flexibility on the part of the Romero government did not last long. During the spring of 1979, the growing labor unrest and activities of popular organizations triggered a harsh response from the government. According to Socorro Jurídico, 142 civilians were killed by government forces during the month of May. The repression remained at these levels through September.[31]

The solution chosen by Romero led the military down the path of increasing confrontation, one for which it was not really prepared. During the 1960s and early 1970s, military spending, as a percentage of the total government budget, had declined (see table 5.1). Not even the war with Honduras had served to increase the military budget to any significant degree in the years immediately following. And the figures on recruitment and training of new soldiers for the regular army were even lower than in the 1950s: 2,247 for July 1976–June 1977.[32] It seems, then, that despite the military's control of the state, the army remained relatively weak.

One possible explanation for this failure to beef up the army through increased recruitment might have to do with the declining confidence in the reliability of the regular army as a buffer against popular insurrection. While budget figures give only part of the picture, it is worth noting that be-

TABLE 5.1

Total Budgetary Outlays and Military Spending, 1961–1976 (in thousand colones)

Year	Total	Military	% Military
1961	173,433	21,561	12.4
1962	173,824	21,691	12.5
1963	176,979	21,333	12.1
1964	183,744	21,716	11.8
1965	201,324	22,416	11.1
1966	232,109	24,241	10.4
1967	236,644	25,881	10.9
1968	234,393	25,450	10.9
1969	291,892	28,223	9.6
1970	303,342	27,420	9.0
1971	356,074	33,020	9.2
1972	383,710	36,138	9.4
1973	449,961	38,778	8.6
1974	594,504	50,273	8.4
1975	709,609	52,271	7.3
1976	1,028,077	66,805	6.4

Sources: El Salvador Dirección General de Estadísticas y Censos, *Anuario Estadístico;* and El Salvador Ministerio de Planificación y Coordinación del Desarrollo Económico y Social, *Indicadores Económicas y Sociales.* The rapid rise in government spending after 1975 is a reflection of the coffee boom that generated additional income from export duties.

ginning in the 1960s the amount spent on all security forces began to increase as a percentage of total military spending (see table 5.2). Whereas during the 1950s spending on the security forces averaged between 20 and 25 percent of total defense expenditures, during the 1960s and 1970s it averaged between 28 and 38 percent. This resulted in an overall increase in the numbers of National Guard, National Police, and Treasury Police even before the fighting broke out in 1981 (see table 5.3).

As the cycle of violence continued unabated, it seemed as if the country had come full circle: in 1979 the country had returned to its same position as in 1932. The military then attempted, one last time, to undertake the "solution" it had employed in 1944, 1948, and 1960–61: namely, an institutional coup d'etat by reformist officers claiming to represent a clean break with the past. To fully understand the decision of reformist officers to stage a coup in October 1979, it is necessary to look at developments within the military institution leading up to the coup.

Rumblings Within the Military

Growing discontent during the 1970s was especially evident among younger officers. Although many junior officers had received more extensive training than some of their commanding officers, the opportunities for assuming leadership positions were limited because of the slow turnover at

TABLE 5.2
Budgetary Outlays for Regular Army and Security Forces (in thousand colones)

Year	Regular Army		Security Forces	
1951	11,860	(79.2%)	3,108	(20.8%)
1954	19,326	(78.6%)	5,261	(21.4%)
1958	18,148	(75.5%)	5,877	(24.5%)
1961	15,490	(71.8%)	6,071	(28.2%)
1967	15,698	(60.7%)	10,183	(39.3%)
1968	15,353	(60.3%)	10,097	(39.7%)
1971	21,474	(65.0%)	11,546	(35.0%)
1973	27,066	(69.8%)	11,712	(30.2%)
1975	37,490	(71.7%)	14,781	(28.3%)
1977	66,184	(70.7%)	27,482	(29.3%)
1979	129,224	(69.9%)	55,760	(30.1%)

Sources: El Salvador Dirección General de Estadísticas y Censos, *Anuario Estadístico;* and El Salvador Ministerio de Planificación y Coordinación del Desarrollo Económico y Social, *Indicadores Económicas y Sociales.* The rapid rise in government spending after 1975 is a reflection of the coffee boom that generated additional income from export duties.

the highest ranks. For example, President Molina had served as President Sánchez Hernández's private secretary, who had served as President Rivera's minister of interior. Molina would choose his minister of defense, Carlos Humberto Romero, to succeed him in the presidency. Moreover, both Rivera and Molina chose officers from earlier *tandas* (graduating classes) to succeed them as president.[33] As a result, entire *tandas* were excluded from the "spoils" of top commands within the military.

The lack of opportunities for younger, highly trained officers may explain in part the tendency beginning in the 1960s to move more and more officers into positions in government and public administration. For example, during the sixties military officers were appointed to serve on ANTEL's (Administración Nacional de Telecomunicaciones) board of directors, and to head up the Dirección General de Estadística y Censos.[34] During Molina's government, the number of military officers appointed to head up public institutions increased dramatically. In fact, several officers who came to play a key role in the coup had been appointed by Molina to positions at the helm of key state institutions prior to being promoted to the rank of colonel.[35] Despite having acquired significant administrative experience directing public institutions, Molina's successor, Gen. Romero, snubbed them, drawing instead from more senior *tandas* to fill key commands within the armed forces (see below).

One young officer, Maj. Alvaro Salazar Brenes, who played a key role in the 1979 coup, retired from the armed forces in June 1978 in the belief that the military's system of political domination was no longer viable. Having piloted both Molina and Romero during their election campaigns and served as an assistant to Sánchez Hernández, he had witnessed firsthand the abuses of power by the country's military rulers. Between June and August 1978, another dozen disillusioned junior officers joined him in retirement.[36]

Table 5.3
Estimated Troop Strength of the Salvadoran Military

Year	Army	Navy	Air Force	Total	Security Forces
1978	6,000	130	1,000	7,130	3,000
1979	6,500	130	300	6,930	3,000
1980	7,000	100	150	7,250	5,000
1981	9,000	100	750	9,850	7,000
1982	14,900	100	1,000	16,000	9,000

Source: International Institute for Strategic Studies, *The Military Balance, 1978–1994* (London: 1994).

A similar case of growing disenchantment can be found in Cap. Francisco Emilio Mena Sandoval's personal account of the 1979 coup. Mena Sandoval relates how as a young officer he participated in the fraud carried out by the governing party during the 1972 elections. Stationed at the Third Brigade in San Miguel, he and a group of younger officers were told by their commanding officer that the country was in danger of falling into the hands of communists and were duly instructed to "reverse the results" in San Miguel and neighboring municipalities. According to Mena Sandoval, who did not participate in the failed coup attempt following the elections, the experience of contributing to an electoral fraud led many of his fellow officers to reflect upon the proper political role of the armed forces.[37]

The growing disenchantment among some junior officers also was related to their exposure to new thinking about the need for structural reforms and the role of the military in national development. During the 1970s, officer training courses at the Escuela de Comando y Estado Mayor General included a special focus on social, economic, and political problems, and their military implications.[38] Agrarian reform was an especially salient issue during this period. For example, in 1973 a group of fifty-four officers—two colonels, twenty-one lieutenant colonels, fourteen majors, fifteen captains, and two lieutenants—participated in a series of seminars on agrarian reform. The topics included: (1) the concept of development and agrarian reform, (2) the agrarian reality and its repercussions for national development, (3) the justifications for an agrarian reform, and (4) the agrarian reform process. Addressing the seminar, President Molina emphasized the need for structural transformations and the role of the armed forces in bringing these about.[39]

A number of junior officers also studied at the Universidad Centroamericana (UCA). For example, Maj. Alvaro Salazar Brenes, who was one of the coup leaders, studied political science there during the midseventies. In fact, the rector at the time, who would later serve on the first junta, Román Mayorga, tried to cultivate relationships with junior officers, lending them books and inviting them to participate in informal discussions of the *realidad nacional.* His efforts no doubt reflected the Jesuits' belief that reforms would only come about if a key sector of the armed forces was on board. Not surprisingly, the junior officers who led the coup would rely heavily on the Jesuits' input in formulating the second *proclama,* and the first junta's cabinet would include several members with close links to the UCA.

The Molina government's capitulation to the oligarchy on the question of agrarian reform must have had an impact on those officers who had become convinced of the need for structural reforms. As discussed, Molina himself went out on a limb in support of an agrarian reform program, despite lacking the support of most senior officers. The selection of Romero as the military's candidate for the 1977 elections, besides closing off opportunities for a new generation of officers, reinforced the perception that the military was powerless in the face of oligarchic opposition. Romero was known for his opposition to the reform and was clearly the oligarchy's preferred candidate. These events must have led some officers to reexamine the military's traditional relationship with landed interests and to embrace agrarian reform as the only way to reduce the oligarchy's economic and political power.

The imposition of Romero's candidacy generated significant discontent within the officer corps. In March 1976, Romero, then minister of defense, conducted a minipurge of the senior ranks to consolidate his position prior to the selection of the PCN's candidate. It appears that Molina favored either Colonels José Guillermo García or Carlos Eugenio Vides Casanova to succeed him. Both had served in key public administration positions during the Molina government and formed part of what came to be known as the Equipo Molina (see below). Representing the 1956 and 1957 *tandas,* their election would have brought into top command positions a whole new generation of officers, since those *tandas* between them and Molina would have been automatically retired. Instead, Romero, who was a member of the 1948 *tanda,* would draw heavily from the 1955 *tanda,* thereby excluding more junior officers from top positions.[40]

Finally, the impact of the Sandinista revolution in Nicaragua in July 1979 cannot be understated. One participant in the October coup referred to it as *el impulso inicial* (the initial impulse), while another coup leader characterized the coup as a "preventative" step to avoid a revolutionary takeover in El Salvador. Both agreed that the Sandinista revolution convinced officers of the severity of the threat in El Salvador and the importance of not committing the same errors as had Somoza.[41] Reformist officers viewed events in Nicaragua as proof that structural reforms were necessary to head off a radical revolution.[42] Just like Somoza, Romero's overtures to opposition groups were too little too late. More conservative officers, on the other hand, while accepting that some reforms might be necessary, drew a different lesson from the Nicaraguan revolution. They viewed Somoza's overthrow as resulting from his lack of resolve in dealing with popular organizations linked to the armed Left. By not dealing more harshly with popular organizations, Romero likewise had contributed to an increasingly chaotic situation. Despite these differences regarding the necessary balance between reform and repression, both reformist and conservative officers shared a common institutional concern in the wake of the Sandinista revolution. They were determined to avoid suffering the same fate as the Nicaraguan National Guard. They must guarantee the armed forces' institutional survival at all costs.

The Road to the Coup

As the level of political conflict grew during 1979, various groups within the armed forces began plotting against Romero. One group of hard-line officers, including the subsecretary of defense, Col. Eduardo Iraheta, recently retired director of the National Guard, Col. Ramón Alvarenga, and assistant director of ANSESAL (Agencia Nacional de Seguridad Salvadoreña), Maj. Roberto D'Aubuisson, were known to be planning a coup during the spring of 1979. These officers were connected to the security forces and intelligence apparatus and enjoyed the backing of prominent right-wing families. They viewed Romero's willingness to accommodate the Carter administration's concerns about human rights as playing into the hands of the armed Left. Particularly outrageous to them was Romero's decision in January 1979 to replace Alvarenga as head of the National Guard, well known for his involvement in widespread human rights abuses, in an effort to placate the Carter administration.[43]

A second group of disgruntled officers, the Equipo Molina, included those who had served in key administrative and governmental positions during the Molina government. Col. José Guillermo García had served as President of ANTEL under Molina and was considered one of the his possible successors to succeed him. Col. Carlos Eugenio Vides Casanova had served as president of INSAFI, Col. Rafael Flores Lima had been secretary of information for the presidency, and Col. Jaime Abdul Gutiérrez had been a manager at ANTEL under García.[44] These officers represented three *tandas*—1956, 1957, and 1958—that had waited their turn to assume top leadership positions within the armed forces and government and yet were denied this opportunity with the election of Gen. Romero. Romero, who belonged to the 1948 *tanda*, relied heavily on officers from the 1955 *tanda* to fill key positions.[45] Although more independent from the oligarchy than the Iraheta-Alvarenga group, they shared its concern of saving the military institution at all costs.[46] However, unlike the hardliners, García et al. were willing to contemplate some reforms in order to preserve the military's political domination.

By the fall of 1979, it became clear that neither of these groups had any chance of ousting Romero without the support of a key group of junior officers. As discussed above, this group of young officers, which came to be known as the Movimiento de la Juventud Militar (MJM), had grown in-

creasingly disillusioned with the lack of opportunities within the military institution, the widespread corruption among government officials and top
military commanders, and the military's complicity in fraudulent elections
in 1972 and again in 1977. Their commitment to structural reforms and a
significant restructuring of the military institution was galvanized by the
Sandinista triumph in Nicaragua. Unlike previous coup attempts that were
generally limited to a few major army units in the capital, this time the reformist movement won support among junior officers throughout the country.[47]

   To guarantee success, the MJM needed the support of a handful of key
senior officers. This was seen as necessary not only to provide some institutional continuity but also to secure U.S. support. There is some doubt as to
who initiated the contacts. Accounts of the coup based largely on interviews
with coup organizers Lt. Col. René Guerra y Guerra[48] and Col. Gutiérrez
suggest that they sought out the support of junior officers, whereas accounts
by junior officers like Mena Sandoval present a contrary view.[49] Whatever
the case, by August 1979 an alliance was forged between the MJM and
Gutiérrez and Guerra y Guerra. The coordinating group consisted of
Gutiérrez (*maestranza*—repair shop), Guerra y Guerra (*maestranza*), retired
Maj. Salazar Brenes (air force), Cap. Mena Sandoval (*maestranza*), and Cap.
Román Barrera (artillery). In September, the organizers contacted both
García and Vides Casanova, who refused to sign on but did nothing to stand
in their way. Gutiérrez, in fact, provided an important link between the MJM
and conservative senior officers. Because of this relationship, several authors believe that Gutiérrez and García had been plotting all along and
simply used the MJM as a springboard into power.[50]

   The coup organizers also sought out Col. Adolfo Majano a few weeks
prior to the coup. Majano, who was subdirector of the Escuela Militar at the
time, was well known and respected by junior officers. He was seen as an
honest, incorruptible officer who put the interests of the institution before
personal ambitions. When representatives of the MJM met on October 6 to
elect the military members of the junta, Majano received the unanimous
support of those present. The delegates also elected Guerra y Guerra to
serve on the junta.

   Gutiérrez, who had not received any votes, argued that a new election
should be held, given that not all the delegates had been present to cast
their votes. The next day another meeting was organized, this time with all
the representatives in attendance. Guerra y Guerra failed to win majority
support and Gutiérrez was elected in his place.[51] The significance of the vote
cannot be overstated. Not only did it exacerbate the political/personal feud
between Guerra y Guerra and Gutiérrez, but it also guaranteed conservative

senior officers like García and Vides an important foothold in the future junta. After all, it was Gutiérrez who would appoint García as minister of defense over the objections of junior officers. And it was García who would marginalize those junior officers who formed the core of the MJM.

The coup organizers' efforts to cultivate civilian allies prior to the coup were extremely limited. According to Guerra y Guerra's account of the coup, a small civilian coordinating group was formed, consisting of his two brothers, Hugo and Rodrigo Guerra; Guillermo Quiñónez, a medical doctor; Guillermo Díaz Salazar, a Jesuit economist; Ricardo Navarro, a professor at the UCA; and Carlos Moreno, the manager of the Electricity Generating Authority.[52] There were also frequent contacts with the rector of the UCA, Román Mayorga, and the archbishop of San Salvador, Msgr. Oscar Arnulfo Romero. Romero was consulted often during the final preparations for the coup. The organizers waited until after the coup, however, to open a dialogue with political opposition leaders. According to one officer who participated in the coup, although the officers had conversations with a handful of opposition leaders, they concluded that the civilian opposition was principally concerned about receiving its "quota of power."[53] Not surprisingly, some opposition leaders viewed the coup as having been carried out behind their backs.

Although the coup organizers could afford to ignore civilian opposition leaders, they could not ignore the U.S. embassy. The exact nature of the Carter administration's involvement in the 1979 coup is still the subject of some debate. Most students of the coup agree that while the administration did not participate directly in planning the coup, its displeasure with the Romero regime must have convinced rebellious officers that the Carter administration would not stand in their way.[54] Following Somoza's fall in Nicaragua, the Romero regime had become a growing liability to the Carter administration, not only because of its notorious human rights record but also its apparent inability to stave off an increasingly militant popular movement. Not about to allow "another Nicaragua," administration officials turned up the heat on Romero. In the months prior to the coup, high-ranking State Department officials paid a series of unpublicized visits to San Salvador, urging Romero to move forward the date of the 1982 elections and to reduce the level of repression against opposition groups. Moreover, on 11 September, Assistant Secretary of State for Latin American Affairs Viron Vaky told the House Subcommittee on Inter-American Affairs that El Salvador was on the brink of revolution.[55]

It is unclear whether the coup organizers sought out U.S. approval.[56] What is clear is that the U.S. embassy was aware that a plot was in the making. One officer who participated in the coup claims that the organizers waited for and received a "green light" from the embassy three days before the coup was launched.[57] In an extremely well-researched study of the coup, Stanley suggests that while the MJM may not have sought the embassy's approval, they were nonetheless concerned about the Carter administration's reaction to a coup. Stanley argues that this may explain why some of the junior officers supported Gutiérrez, who was perceived to be well-connected to the embassy. Guerra y Guerra's presence on the junta, on the other hand, might have jeopardized U.S. support.[58]

Regardless of whether or not they waited for a "green light" from the Carter administration prior to staging the coup, the coup organizers did not have to wait long for the administration's public endorsement of the coup, which came the following day on October 16. Administration officials must have been pleased with the apparent ease with which the *golpistas* were able to oust Romero and the minimal resistance shown by units loyal to the president. Unlike in 1972, the security forces and air force did not come to the president's rescue.

The Limits of Reform

On the afternoon of 15 October 1979, President Romero and a group of senior aides and military officers boarded two Guatemalan planes headed for exile. A few hours earlier, Romero had been informed by the rebel officers gathered at the San Carlos barracks that the armed forces no longer supported his presidency. After confirming reports that all of the major army units were firmly under rebel officers' control, Romero accepted the officers' ultimatum.

That evening, Colonels Jaime Abdul Gutiérrez and Adolfo Arnoldo Majano read a proclamation over the radio explaining the officers' actions. Referring to the "anarchic situation" in the country resulting from the actions of "extremist elements" and the government's incapacity to respond decisively, the officers justified the coup as an attempt to reestablish constitutional order in the country. According to the proclamation, the armed forces would "direct the country's destiny" until which time the bases of a "real and dynamic democracy" could be established and free elections held.[59]

Although the proclamation seemed hardly different from those used to justify previous institutional coups, a second proclamation, issued within a few hours of the first, laid out a surprisingly comprehensive program of structural reforms.[60] In it, the officers condemned the Romero government for violating human rights, tolerating corruption, creating an economic and social "disaster," and discrediting the country and its armed forces. Blaming the country's problems on "antiquated economic, social and political structures," the proclamation outlined an emergency program, including the dissolution of ORDEN; an end to government corruption; the recognition of political and labor rights paving the way toward democratic elections; the adoption of measures to achieve a more equitable distribution of the national wealth (including an agrarian reform); and, finally, the reestablishment of diplomatic relations with Honduras and the strengthening of ties with other Central American countries.

For a brief moment, it seemed as though the junior officers who spearheaded the coup had created a unique opportunity to implement a far-reaching program of social, economic, and political reforms that might spare the country a bloody civil war. This seemed to be confirmed as the civilian members of the junta and cabinet were announced. On the junta, Guillermo Ungo, leader of the social democratic Movimiento Nacional Revolucionario (MNR), and Marco Antonio Andino, representing the more moderate elements of the private sector, joined Román Mayorga, the rector of the UCA. The cabinet was similarly pluralistic, including leaders from the Foro Popular—an alliance of opposition political parties, trade unions, and peasant organizations—and representatives of the private sector. Without a doubt, it was the most broadly representative government the country had ever experienced.

How was it, then, that within ten weeks of the coup the junior officers' movement had lost control to a group of conservative senior officers who were only superficially committed to the reform program laid out in the October 15 proclamation? We argue that in addition to a series of well-documented tactical errors, the junior officers' vision of reform was much more limited than most accounts of the coup would suggest. Except for a handful of junior officers, most were committed to preserving the armed forces' institutional integrity, internal hierarchy, and unity in the face of a serious internal security threat.

The election of Majano and Gutiérrez to serve on the junta was a key turning point in the fate of the junior officers' initiative. Gutiérrez was responsible for appointing García as minister of defense, a decision made without consulting the other members of the junta or junior officers. Although junior officers had demanded that officers implicated in human rights abuses and corruption be tried and punished, García ordered the release of senior officers detained during the coup. Although some fifty to sixty colonels were given early retirement, none were ever tried. Those colonels who survived the purge assumed key commands within the armed forces. Most of them were close allies of García and represented three key *tandas* (1956–58).[61] (See table 5.4.) Thus, while the composition of the new government reflected the influence of reformist officers, the control of the armed forces was firmly in the hands of conservative senior officers. This is not to suggest that the MJM no longer exerted influence within the military; however, short of insubordination, there was little junior officers could do to prevent García and his allies from subverting the reform program. Consequently, conservative officers used their control of key commands to progressively marginalize the MJM.

The marginalization of the MJM was a result of several factors. First of all, during the months following the coup, the security forces greatly intensified the level of violent repression against popular organizations. The almost daily protests and occupations of churches and government ministries in the wake of the coup must have unnerved more conservative elements in the military. Whereas civilian members of the government and reformist officers cautioned restraint and sought to open a dialogue with popular organizations, conservative officers unleashed a brutal assault on the popular movement. Although a thirty-day truce of sorts held during most of the month of November, the violence intensified throughout December.[62] The result of this spiraling repression was to drive a wedge between reformist officers and their civilian allies and between the government and popular organizations.

The growing tension between the civilian members of the government and their erstwhile allies in the military came to a head in late December. Civilians were frustrated in their efforts to push through reforms needed to build a base of support for the junta. And, as a result of their inability to exert control over the military, they found themselves in the untenable position of supporting a government that was slaughtering unarmed civilians. On 28 December the civilian members of the junta and cabinet presented

TABLE 5.4
Officers Holding Key Positions in First Junta—October 1979

Position	Name	*Tanda*
Junta member	Adolfo Majano	1958
Junta member	Jaime Abdul Gutiérrez	1957
Minister of Defense	José Guillermo García	1956
Subsecretary of Defense	Nicolás Carranza	1957
Chief of Staff	Francisco Castillo	1958
Director, National Guard	Carlos Vides Casanova	1957
Director, National Police	Carlos R. López Nuila	1959
Director, Treasury Police	Francisco Morán	ranks
Commander, Air Force	Juan Rafael Bustillo	1957

COPEFA (Consejo Permanente de la Fuerza Armada) with an ultimatum: either the military submit to the authority of the junta or the civilian members would resign. The demands included that COPEFA replace the minister of defense as the intermediary between the armed forces and the junta; that COPEFA recognize the junta's authority as commander in chief of the armed forces; that all decisions made by the Ministry of Defense regarding internal promotions and appointments be subject to the junta's approval; that a dialogue be initiated between the government and COPEFA and with popular organizations to clarify the goals of the October 15 proclamation and to avoid future confrontations; and, finally, that restrictions be placed on the ability of the security forces to intervene in labor disputes, subject to specific procedures established by a junta-appointed commission.[63]

The fact that civilians directed their ultimatum to COPEFA, rather than to the minister of defense, was significant. Created by reformist officers to guarantee the junta's compliance with the reform program outlined in the October 15 proclamation, COPEFA was to provide for increased participation of junior officers in the military's internal decisions. Nevertheless, it never functioned as originally intended, and by the time civilian members of the government appealed to COPEFA in late December, it had already been brought under the firm control of the Ministry of Defense (see below).

On 1 January 1980, COPEFA flatly rejected the demands. COPEFA stated that, though it recognized the authority of the junta, it could not acquiesce in establishing mechanisms that might "politicize" the military institution. Having seriously overestimated the weight of reformist officers within the military, civilian members of the government had no choice but to resign, leaving the government with only the two military members of the junta, Majano and Gutiérrez, and the minister of defense, García.

During the ten weeks following the coup, the government became increasingly isolated from organized sectors of civil society. The popular organizations were energized by the Sandinista triumph in Nicaragua and saw the coup as an opportunity to press their demands for profound structural reforms. However, for the government's reform program to have any chance of success, it needed to build a popular base of support, which entailed reaching some understanding with the popular organizations. Such an alliance with popular organizations was unlikely given the military's deep-rooted distrust of autonomous popular mobilization. As an institution based upon norms of vertical command and discipline, the concept of "popular participation" was foreign to most officers.

With the collapse of the first junta in early January, the government became even more isolated. The repression, which continued unabated, drove a permanent wedge between the regime and the popular organizations. In succeeding months, many leaders of the popular movements were forced underground, and not a few declared their allegiance to one of the several guerrilla movements that had emerged. Although García and Gutiérrez were able to convince the military's historical enemy, the PDC, to participate in a second junta, the regime's political base had shrunk considerably. Unlike the first junta, the second junta failed to patch together a broadly representative government.

As in October 1979, the military was again forced to look for civilian partners with whom to maintain its political dominance. The PDC was a logical alternative, given its reformist credentials and history of opposition to military dictatorship. In the pact of 9 January 1980, which followed and made public the incorporation of the PDC into the junta, the High Command (includes the minister and subsecretary of defense, chief and deputy chief of staff, commanders of the Air Force and key army brigades, and directors of the police and security forces) agreed to certain PDC demands: (1) to draw up a timetable for carrying out the socioeconomic reforms promised by the first junta, (2) to exclude representatives of the private sector from the cabinet, and (3) to support amendments to the constitution.[64] Nevertheless, in exchange for progress on the reforms, the PDC accepted the *status quo ante* regarding civil-military relations. The best it could do was elicit a vague promise by the High Command to respect human rights and to support a democratic transition.

Although conservative officers were willing to compromise on the socioeconomic reforms, they were unwilling to accept what they considered a civilian intrusion into the military's internal practices and procedures. By not insisting on new mechanisms to enhance the junta's authority over the armed forces, the PDC had helped ensure the military's continuing domination of the junta. Throughout 1980, PDC leaders in the government looked on as conservative officers consolidated their power at the expense of Majano and the MJM.

The first crisis erupted only two days after the second junta assumed control. A petition signed by some fifty officers circulated among the barracks demanding the resignations of Colonels García and Carranza (subsecretary of defense). Both were accused of blocking the reforms outlined in the October 1979 Proclama. A second petition, signed by 186 officers, circulated on 15 January, the same day that an assembly of officers at the San Carlos barracks voted to demand the resignations of García and Carranza. The High Command sent a group of high-ranking officers, including Gutiérrez, to meet with the rebellious officers. Gutiérrez managed to defuse the situation by convincing junior officers that their actions threatened the unity of the armed forces and promising that García would carry through with the reform program. The standoff ended with both García and Carranza remaining in their posts.[65]

The High Command further undercut the Majanistas' influence within the military by tolerating the activities of extreme rightist groups. In early May 1980, a coup attempt organized by retired Maj. Roberto D'Aubuisson and a group of military and civilian supporters provoked a severe crisis within the armed forces. To build support for the coup, D'Aubuisson circulated copies of a video in which he denounced Majano as being a member of one of the guerrilla organizations and called for his removal from the junta. Subsecretary of Defense Col. Nicolás Carranza, who considered the video "very objective," authorized D'Aubuisson to show the video at a number of military barracks. Carranza claimed that García approved of the visits.[66]

The goal of D'Aubuisson and his supporters was twofold: (1) derail the reform program, and (2) eliminate the Majanista officers' influence within the armed forces. Regarding the reform program, the third junta had pushed ahead with its agrarian reform initiative despite intense opposition from landed interests. On 6 March 1980, the junta issued the Basic Law of Agrarian Reform. Phase One provided for the expropriation of private land holdings of five hundred hectares and over, and for the formation of agricultural cooperatives on those lands. Phase Two targeted for expropriation farms between 150 and five hundred hectares. A third phase, known as "land to tiller," was announced on April 28. It allowed those farming all rented or sharecropped plots up to seven hectares the opportunity to purchase the land.[67] Neutralizing Majano and the MJM was a key element in sabotaging the reform. With Majano out of the way, support for the agrarian reform within the armed forces would evaporate. Conservative officers would be in effective control of the armed forces, thus removing a major obstacle to a more ambitious offensive against the armed Left and popular organizations.

On 7 May, officers loyal to Majano captured D'Aubuisson and a group of twenty-three officers and civilians at a farm in Santa Tecla. They found documents detailing D'Aubuisson's collaborators within the military and names of individuals who were to assume positions in the new government. Several of the active-duty officers detained with D'Aubuisson worked with ANSESAL, the intelligence agency where D'Aubuisson had served. The civilians included prominent members of the right-wing organization, Frente Amplio Nacional (FAN).[68]

Although acting within his legal authority as the most senior military representative on the junta, the fact that Majano acted alone against D'Aubuisson and had to rely on the First Brigade (San Carlos barracks) to carry out the arrest demonstrated how weak his position had become within the armed forces. He could not count on Gutiérrez and García's support, given that the coup attempt was aimed at Majano and the Christian Democrats, not against conservative officers.[69]

Not surprisingly, D'Aubuisson's arrest exacerbated internal divisions within the military. Despite Majano's insistence that those detained be prosecuted for endangering state security, a week after their arrest, the military prosecutor, obviously under instructions from García, ordered their unconditional release.[70] García claimed that those arrested could not be detained for more than seventy-two hours without formal charges.[71] To bolster García's position, the High Command organized a general assembly of officials to decide which of the two military representatives on the junta should be commander in chief of the armed forces. The vote was 313 to 187 in favor of Gutiérrez.[72] Two days later, on 14 May, Gutiérrez announced the indefinite suspension of Phase Two of the reform, and the immediate halt to further expropriations under Phase One.[73] The coup attempt was foiled, but D'Aubuisson and the FAN came very close to achieving all of their goals.

The suspension of Phase Two effectively tore the guts out of the agrarian reform. This phase would have affected much of the country's principal coffee *fincas,* seriously undermining the oligarchy's economic base. In contrast, coffee farms were hardly affected by Phase One, which primarily targeted for expropriation lands dedicated to cotton, sugar, and cattle grazing. Up to 60 percent of the land was laying fallow or unusable except for grazing.[74] Furthermore, the implementation of Phase One and the more limited Phase Three was accompanied by a significant increase in violence and repression. Some military commanders used the reform to further their counterinsurgency efforts in the countryside. Under a state of siege announced following the promulgation of the reform, the military and security forces occupied large estates targeted for expropriation. There were numerous reports of the security forces' involvement in executing leaders of newly formed agrarian reform cooperatives. By the end of 1981, forty agrarian reform workers had been murdered as well as ninety-two members of the UCS.[75]

Progress toward the other goal of D'Aubuisson and the FAN, Majano's marginalization and that of officers allied with the MJM, began even before the May crisis. Conservative officers used their control of key commands to undermine the MJM's influence within the armed forces. For example, from his position as minister of defense, Col. García complicated the efforts of junior officers to bring their collective influence to bear on the High Command and the government. The MJM had hoped to use COPEFA as an instrument to guarantee the junta's implementation of the reforms outlined in the October 15 proclamation. According to coup organizer Salazar Brenes, the commission, which was to have 4–5 members, was to function as a parallel body to the junta. However, when COPEFA was established in early November, it included two representatives from every military unit.[76] Moreover, because conservative officers viewed COPEFA as a threat, it never functioned as originally intended. Conservative officers felt threatened by COPEFA on two scores. First, it provided the MJM with a mechanism through which it could pressure the junta. Second, it enabled junior officers to exercise unprecedented influence within the military institution, thereby threatening traditional norms of hierarchy.

Less than six weeks after COPEFA's inauguration, the High Command moved to neutralize it. On 18 December, in a meeting with representatives of COPEFA, García and other members of the High Command demanded that COPEFA be restructured and that officers allied to the MJM be replaced with officers loyal to the High Command, the majority of whom had not even participated in the coup.[77] Thus, not only had the MJM lost control of an important instrument of pressure, but the newly restructured COPEFA became largely irrelevant.

Through its control over internal personnel decisions, the High Command was able to marginalize junior officers allied to the MJM. According to Stanley, several young officers who participated in the coup were assigned to troop commands in conflictive zones. Besides making it difficult for them to attend important COPEFA meetings, the intention was to undermine the MJM's organizational cohesiveness.[78] Other officers were sent abroad and some were put on "availability status." As early as November 1979, Mena Sandoval claims, Gutiérrez had planned to send him abroad on a scholarship.[79] Following the collapse of the first junta, Salazar Brenes, who had served as private secretary to the junta, was sent to the Salvadoran consulate in Washington, D.C.[80]

The final blow to the MJM came on 1 September 1980 when García issued a general order removing some fifteen Majano loyalists from their commands. The officers were to be reassigned to administrative posts, sent to study abroad, or assigned to obscure diplomatic missions. As Dunkerley writes, "if these appointments were accepted, complete control of the military apparatus would fall into the hands of the hard-liners."[81] The order, which had not been approved by Majano nor the civilian members of the junta, provoked a showdown between the Majanistas and Gutiérrez. In a press conference from the Zapote barracks—a Majano stronghold—on 4 September, Majano called the general order "unjust and illegal" and warned of "a serious military crisis." That same day a group of junior officers took over a radio station in the capital to publicize their grievances. Meanwhile, members of the High Command toured the barracks to shore up support in case of a military confrontation.[82]

The civilian members of the junta, led by Napoleon Duarte, offered a formula to defuse the crisis. The proposal called on Majano to accept the general order, but that all future orders would have to be approved by the entire junta.[83] After three or four days of great tension and uncertainty, both Gutiérrez and Majano accepted the proposal on 8 September. It appeared that, after measuring their support within the institution, neither side was willing to risk a bloody military confrontation that might threaten the armed forces' institutional unity. Junior officers who might otherwise have rejected the compromise had little choice but to accept it. At a minimum they could feel somewhat reassured by the High Command's reluctance to remove Majano from the junta.

The High Command's decision to leave Majano on the junta was probably a tactical one. With the September purge, Majano's influence within the armed forces was greatly diminished. The MJM had been effectively neutralized and any pockets of resistance could be dealt with easily. The civilian members of the junta were not about to risk their relationship with the military by supporting Majano. Duarte, especially, had sided with Gutiérrez on more than one occasion. Thus, the High Command could afford to bide its time before moving against Majano.

On 6 December, when Majano was in Panama meeting with Gen. Torrijos, a general assembly of officers voted 300 to 4 to remove him from the junta. This was confirmed on 13 December with the announcement of a "governmental reorganization." The "reorganization" offered something for everybody. Duarte and Gutiérrez became president and vice president of the junta, respectively, and Gutiérrez was made the sole commander in chief of the armed forces. García stayed on as minister of defense but, to placate the Carter administration, the ruthless Col. Carranza was removed as subsecretary of defense.[84]

As outlined above, the failure of the reformist officers to consolidate their control of the military was partly the result of their own tactical errors and the political acumen of conservative senior officers. However, also important in understanding the fate of the MJM was the limited "programmatic consensus" among reformist officers.[85] Reformist officers could agree on the following points: (1) that the armed forces' corporate survival depended upon the implementation of structural reforms, (2) that the Romero regime was incapable of implementing needed changes, and (3) that the military was the only institution capable of implementing a reform program. Nevertheless, despite the fact that reformist officers preferred reform over repression, there was never any consensus regarding the issue of political participation in the reform process nor as to the extent to which the military institution itself should be reformed.

Although most reformist officers viewed structural reforms as necessary to prevent a violent social revolution, they failed to understand the importance of popular participation in the reform process. There was never any agreement on how to incorporate popular organizations and the armed Left into the political process. Lacking such a consensus, and in light of the security forces' assault on popular organizations, individual efforts to establish a dialogue with the armed Left were doomed to failure.

The issue of the security forces was a matter of much discussion and disagreement among reformist officers, as well as within the armed forces as a whole. Some officers, realizing the need to establish a dialogue with popular organizations and the armed Left, argued in favor of dismantling the security forces. For them, the junta's decision to formally dissolve ORDEN was largely cosmetic and still left the security forces completely intact. Other reformist officers, however, believed that dismantling the security forces would provoke a countercoup, given the security forces' close relationship with important sectors of capital. Moreover, by dissolving the security forces, the military would lose a vital intelligence-gathering capability, essential in its struggle against the armed Left.[86]

Within the context of a growing insurgency, the bulk of reformist officers, including Majano, attached a high priority to preserving the armed forces' institutional unity. In this regard, they were not so different from conservative officers. Thus, in those instances when a military confrontation between the MJM and conservative officers seemed imminent, both sides eventually backed down, preferring to avoid a bloody showdown that might create an opportunity for the armed Left. In fact, only a handful of reformist officers were ever willing to countenance a direct confrontation with conservative officers.[87]

In addition to their concern over preserving institutional unity, most reformist officers were uncomfortable violating traditional norms of hierarchy. For example, those junior officers who supported Gutiérrez over Guerra y Guerra to serve on the junta did so partly out of respect for Gutiérrez's seniority vis-à-vis Guerra. Moreover, when Gutiérrez appointed García as minister of defense, few junior officers were willing to challenge his decision. Not surprisingly, given the military's traditional norms of hierarchy and vertical command structure, the creation of COPEFA provoked significant resistance on the part of senior officers. If COPEFA had been allowed to function as originally intended, it would have had a profound impact on the military institution, opening up a democratic "space" for junior officers through which to influence decision making by the High Command.

Thus, what was at stake for the military in the wake of the October coup was not so much the socioeconomic reforms, but rather the entire conception of the armed forces as an institution. Given the failure of reformist officers to articulate more clearly an "alternative" vision for the armed forces, and their lack of progress in disseminating such a vision among the officer corps, the bulk of officers did not understand the need for reforms and were easily manipulated by more senior conservative officers.[88] Few of the reformist officers in their own schooling had been exposed to alternative programs of structural change. Instead, they relied on civilian allies, including intellectuals at the Jesuit university, to help them formulate a program of structural reform. Not surprisingly, then, they never succeeded in forming the necessary cadre of officers committed to their reform program.

The lack of a programmatic consensus among reformist officers contrasted with the more solid consensus among senior conservative officers. Conservative officers disagreed somewhat as to the need for structural reforms. For example, whereas García was not at all inclined to support the reforms, Gutiérrez viewed them as an essential component in a successful counterinsurgency program. Nevertheless, conservative officers were united in their resolve to destroy the armed Left and to dismember the popular organizations. Their fervent anticommunism provided their counterinsurgency reform program with some ideological cohesion. Unlike reformist officers, they could count on a large cadre of officers schooled in the conservative national security doctrine who would support their consolidation of power at the expense of the MJM.

Even if the civil-military junta that emerged out of the October 1979 coup had lasted for a period of years with its original members in place, even if the popular organizations and the armed Left had made their peace with the new government and supported its reform program, the issue of the role of the armed forces would still have remained a bone of contention. Not even the most reform-minded officers were willing to contemplate, much less countenance, the prospect of civilian control over the military. Although reformist officers in the past had relied on civilian partners to help maintain the military's political dominance, they never seriously considered handing formal power over to a civilian president. This reflected not only a basic mistrust of civil politicians, but also a conviction that the armed forces made up the only institution capable of defending the state and preserving internal order. Thus, while reformist officers were willing to enter into an alliance with different political and social forces, their overriding commitment was to the defense of the state and the military institution's own core interests.

Reformist officers were also unwilling to give up the military's network of social control in the rural areas. In the second proclamation, there was only one reference to the historic role of the armed forces in the countryside: ORDEN was to be abolished, but not the *patrullas cantonales,* not the obligatory military service, and not civic action. The reformists could initiate land reform and nationalize the banks, they could enter into an alliance with the military's erstwhile political enemies, but they could not consider separating the military from its rural power base. In urban areas, autonomous political institutions could be allowed to evolve, albeit within a restricted political space. However, in the countryside there was no place for labor organizing, permanent party structures, demonstrations of grievances, or even cooperative ventures. There was only room for the *patrullas cantonales,* the local comandantes, the National Guard, and Acción Cívica Militar. All else was off limits, including democracy.

THE END OF REACTIONARY DESPOTISM?

Was the October 1979 coup a watershed event, a historic rupture, or was it just the latest in a series of coups aimed at averting a more serious crisis that might jeopardize the state's very existence? Baloyra argues that the coup brought an end to the system of authoritarian domination—reactionary despotism—that emerged in El Salvador after 1932. The "inability to maintain order led to the rupture of the historical nexus between the Armed Forces and the leaders of the reactionary coalition."[89] While the coup did not immediately lead to a "viable alternative coalition" or the pacification of the country, it was different from previous coups in a number of aspects. According to Baloyra, the October 1979 coup produced a series of reforms that succeeded in displacing the reactionary coalition and undermining the basis for continued oligarchic domination. Central among these was the agrarian reform, with all its shortcomings, and the nationalization of the banks and the export trade in coffee. The coup also led to an opening of the political sphere that came to include the PDC and its affiliated labor and peasant organizations. Finally, Baloyra argues, the coup opened the possibility for relatively free and fair elections in 1982 (see the next chapter).

Without a doubt, the military's system of political domination had entered into a profound crisis, the implications of which were uncertain. Never before had the armed forces been confronted with such a highly assertive and organized opposition. And not since 1932 had the armed forces faced an armed challenge of such proportions. Moreover, this time they were poorly equipped to confront the challenge. In July 1979, in an ominous-sounding confidential cable, the U.S. embassy in El Salvador questioned the military's capability for sustained combat: "If confronted with a Nicaragua-type situation the El Salvadoran military establishment could easily collapse in four to six weeks."[90]

In assessing whether the 1979 coup brought an end to reactionary despotism, Baloyra understates the central role of the armed forces in the system of political domination that emerged during the 1930s. According to Baloyra, the "core elements" of the reactionary coalition included: "the largest agricultural planters who monopolize control of sectoral associations, cattle ranchers, large merchants with linkages to agricultural interests, financiers and bankers whose main creditors or 'factors' are engaged in the export trade and in real estate speculation, former government officials and retired military officers who have embezzled public resources, and individuals committed to the repression of opposition elements either in an official or in a paramilitary capacity."[91] Moreover, Baloyra goes on to say that under reactionary despotism the government maintains "a division of labor which assigns the security function to the military and the economic 'mission' to the leadership of the coalition."[92] In other words, the military is not granted any independent theoretical status as an actor, but rather viewed as an instrument of the state.

Because he understates the central role of the military institution in the model of reactionary despotism that developed in El Salvador, Baloyra's discussion of the 1979 coup is limited primarily to its impact on the interests of the agro-financial and agro-industrial elites. We agree that the oligarchy's economic domination was severely challenged by the crisis that erupted in 1979. Besides agrarian reform and export nationalization, as we see in the next chapter, the oligarchy also had to accept the uncertainty of a process of liberalization that led to restricted electoral politics and the PDC's inclusion into the officially sanctioned political arena.

Nevertheless, Baloyra's analysis fails to consider fully the impact of the coup on the military's political domination, which is a key element in the particular form of reactionary despotism that evolved in El Salvador. Despite the seriousness of the crisis, the military was able to hold onto political power. In the year following the coup, conservative senior officers who had been denied advancement during the Romero regime succeeded in consolidating their power at the expense of young reformist officers. They resisted any attempts by civilian members of the junta and cabinet to subject the armed forces to greater civilian control. And, moreover, they succeeded in doing what no military regime before them had done: implementing an agrarian reform over the objections of conservative landowning interests.

The military's continued political domination came at a price. As the armed opposition to the regime threatened to develop into a full-blown civil war, the armed forces became increasingly dependent on external support from the United States. In return for U.S. assistance the armed forces would have to follow through with their commitment to reform, permit the election of a civilian-led government, and demonstrate greater sensitivity regarding human rights. However, despite these "costs" the military retained its ability to control key political decisions.

The implementation of reforms, particularly the export nationalization in December 1979 and the agrarian reform program in March 1980, carried an additional cost of complicating the military's uneasy alliance with the oligarchy. Conservative landholding interests, while in a much weaker position than in 1976, still had the capacity to destabilize the junta and jeopardize U.S. support. In fact, although opposition from the oligarchy was not sufficient to derail the reform program, it did succeed in blocking the all-important Phase Two of the agrarian reform. Furthermore, the activities of extreme right groups linked to conservative landholding interests contributed to the marginalization of Majano and the MJM.

Nevertheless, the "historic nexus" between the armed forces and the agro-export elite was not ruptured beyond repair. Even though the officers that consolidated their control over the military and government in the wake of the coup felt it necessary to enter into an alliance with previously excluded political forces and to implement an agrarian reform program, they did so in order to prevent the state's overthrow by a violent social revolution. As Rouquié puts it, they acted to defend the state from itself, since those administering the state were no longer capable of providing stable political direction and management.[93] In acting to defend the state, they were not attempting to overhaul it or to create a new social and economic order. They were acting to preserve a state that was dominated by the armed forces and committed to fostering a model of agro-export development that primarily benefitted the small coffee elite.

The October 1979 coup signaled the exhaustion of traditional forms of political control and the search for a more viable system of domination. The old power apparatus was severely shaken but the military managed to retain its power and thus postpone more profound changes. Reactionary despotism as Baloyra defines it may have come to an end when General Romero headed into exile on the afternoon of 15 October 1979. However, the Salvadoran armed forces were not yet willing to raise the white flag.

THE MILITARY AND DEMOCRATIZATION DURING THE 1980S

PARADOXICALLY, DURING the 1980s at the very time that a military-dominated junta was transferring formal power to a civilian president, the armed forces were successfully consolidating their presence in the state, expanding their network of control in the countryside, and maintaining their institutional autonomy. Though the military no longer governed directly, its political role expanded nonetheless, largely in response to demands of the war.

Although one might characterize the post-1979 period as one of transition from authoritarian rule, it in no way constituted a transition toward democracy. As Przeworski has argued, it is important to distinguish between *liberalization* and *democratization*. According to Przeworski, liberalization "is a process whereby the power apparatus allows some political organization and interplay of interests but maintains intact its own capacity to intervene."[1] The final outcome of such a process is what Przeworski refers to as "tutelary democracy: a regime which has competitive, formally democratic institutions, but in which the power apparatus . . . retains the capacity to intervene to correct undesirable states of affairs."[2] The crucial step in any transition from liberalization to democratization "is not necessarily the withdrawal of the army into the barracks or the opening of the elected parliament but the crossing of the threshold beyond which no one can intervene to reverse outcomes of the formal democratic process."[3]

During the 1980s, in response to internal and external pressures, the Salvadoran armed forces presided over a controlled political opening. Formally competitive elections were instituted as was some limited autonomous political organization. Nevertheless, at no time did the military forfeit its capacity to control outcomes that affected its core interests. In fact, a series of political pacts negotiated between the High Command and civilian political leaders reinforced the military's ability to intervene in political decisions. Moreover, the process of liberalization did not exhibit any linear progression. On the contrary, steadily declining voter turnout throughout the decade reflected the opposite trend. Whereas during the 1982 Constituent Assembly election over 1.5 million Salvadorans turned out to vote, during the 1989 presidential election turnout was down to just over one million. Finally, throughout the decade, periods of limited opening were abruptly interrupted with successive waves of repression in which those responsible went unpunished.

As Przeworski points out, liberalization is "inherently unstable." Limited openings can easily escape the control of authoritarian rulers. Pent-up dissent can erupt into unprecedented levels of popular mobilization, causing a regime to balk at further liberalization and leading to periods of retrenchment. In the Salvadoran case, the degree of uncertainty accompanying the political opening was exacerbated by the context of the civil war. Liberalization was one component of the regime's more global counterinsurgency program. Political spaces were opened and closed partly in response to the dynamics of the war. An intensification of the conflict usually triggered a deterioration in the human rights situation and greater limits on autonomous organization. Likewise, a lull in the fighting sometimes resulted in a period of limited political relaxation. Also adding to the uncertainty was the impact of external pressures, most notably U.S. policy toward El Salvador. Throughout the period, the Reagan and Bush administrations exerted variable pressure on the regime to keep the liberalization process on track. Thus, when the regime may have seen it in its short-term interests to step up the repression of the popular organizations, pressure from Washington may have produced the opposite response.

While we might characterize the period after 1979 as an uneven process of liberalization, there was no significant breakthrough toward a democratic transition until the peace accords were signed in January 1992. Unlike liberalization, democratization "is a process of subjecting all interests to competition, of institutionalizing uncertainty. It is thus this very devolution of power over outcomes which constitutes the decisive step toward democracy."[4] In the Salvadoran case, such a "devolution of power" required a political compromise among the country's principal political actors. As Karl argues, in addition to agreement on the basic "ground rules" of the new political regime, some consensus was also needed on a number of substantive issues, including past human rights abuses, land reform, the incorporation of the FMLN into the political process, and the future of the two contending armies.[5] However, elections during the 1980s were used by the regime as an alternative to negotiating these issues with the armed Left. Consequently, the exclusion of the FMLN from the electoral process blocked progress toward forging the political consensus necessary for a genuine process of democratization.

Thus, although one might expect a positive correlation between a transfer of power to civilian rule and a reduction of the military's political power, the opposite was true in the Salvadoran case. This chapter attempts to explain this apparent paradox by analyzing the impact of four conditioning variables: (1) the context of the civil war, (2) a series of political pacts between the military High Command and civilian political leaders, (3) internal factionalism within the officer corps, and (4) U.S. military assistance. It is our contention that these variables reinforced traditional obstacles to achieving civilian control over the military. For example, the intensification of the armed conflict bolstered the military's perception that it was the only national institution capable of defending the state. Moreover, whereas internal factionalism may have undermined the cohesiveness of the officer corps, a series of political pacts confirmed the military's expanded political role and U.S. military assistance only served to legitimate this trend.

IMPACT OF THE CIVIL WAR

In the wake of the October 1979 coup, very limited progress was made in reducing the military's colonization of the state. Given the intensification of the armed conflict, the High Command viewed the armed forces' control of key public institutions as essential to ensuring the state's survival. During the first three civilian-military juntas, civilians did replace military officers at the helm of the national water works (Administración Nacional de Acuaductos y Agua, or ANDA) and the state industrial development corporation (Instituto Salvadoreño de Fomento Industrial, or INSAFI), and occupied the bulk of cabinet portfolios, including the Ministry of Interior. However, this did not represent a radical departure from the past; traditionally, civilians had held most of the positions in the cabinet. Moreover, the civilian-military juntas were dominated by military members, and the most important autonomous institutions remained under the direction of military officers. Among others, these included ANTEL (Administración Nacional de Telecomunicaciones), CEPA (Comisión Ejecutiva Portuario Autónomo), ISSS (Instituto Salvadoreño de Seguro Social), CEL (Comisión Ejecutiva Hidroeléctrica del Río Lempa), Dirección General de Transporte Terrestre, Dirección General de Estadística y Censos, the Customs, Civil Aeronautics, and the Postal Service. Finally, officers served as minister of public health and subsecretaries of interior and agriculture.

It is important to remember that the appointment of officers to head up state institutions predated the conflict. The practice was part of a patronage system designed to "reward" officers removed from key leadership positions within the armed forces. In some instances this was a convenient way by which military presidents dealt with potential rivals or particularly controversial officers, at other times it was a way of rewarding loyal officers slated for retirement. Control of such entities as ANTEL and CEPA provided an important source of additional income for "deserving" officers, where bribes and kickbacks were the norm.[6]

During both the Magaña (1982–1984) and Duarte (1984–1989) governments, there was a more concerted effort to appoint civilians to replace military officers in important public positions, but again the results were mixed. Both presidents appointed civilians as ministers of interior and replaced those military officers serving as ambassadors. Duarte tried to bring the Instituto Salvadoreño de Transformación Agraria (ISTA) under civilian control, and he created the new Vice Ministry of Public Security to separate the security forces from military control (discussed below). What little progress was made, however, was reversed during the subsequent Cristiani government (1989–1994). Military officers once again assumed direction of the port authority, CEPA, as well as of ANDA (directed by civilians during most of the Duarte government), and a retired military officer was appointed minister of interior, a post that had been occupied by a civilian since 1979.

While on the one hand replacing military officers with civilians in some important positions, Duarte also followed the pre-1979 pattern of appointing military officers as presidential private secretaries. For example, one of his first administrative decisions was to appoint retired Major Salazar Brenes as private secretary.[7] A few years later he appointed Col. Benjamín Ramos to the same position.[8] Both officers had played important roles in the 1979 coup: Salazar was one of the coup organizers and Ramos was head of intelligence for the First Brigade, a Majano stronghold. While Duarte's decision to appoint the officers as his private secretaries obviously reflected his concern over relations with the High Command, it also served to undermine his timid efforts to demilitarize the Salvadoran state. This is not surprising given that the Duarte government's very existence depended on the support of the armed forces.

Militarization at the macro level also manifested itself in the array of prerogatives retained by the military throughout the 1980s. The armed forces maintained control of the security forces and intelligence agencies; the military court system continued to cover large areas of civil society, and the domain where military personnel could be tried in civil courts remained very narrow; the executive exercised little control of the military personnel decisions or the defense budget; legislative oversight was nonexistent since the High Command seldom provided the legislature with detailed information regarding the budget or other defense matters; and the military played a leading role in formulating defense policy and directing the war effort, again with little executive oversight.[9]

Many of the military's institutional prerogatives were enshrined in the 1983 Constitution, which, like previous ones, accorded the armed forces primary responsibility for (1) ensuring the national defense and internal law and order; (2) guaranteeing compliance with the constitution and other laws; and (3) defending the "democratic" system of government, including universal suffrage. Moreover, the provisions regarding executive and legislative oversight were weak at best. As one officer put it, civilian politicians "handed over the keys of the nursery to the military."[10]

MILITARIZING EVERYDAY LIFE

Beyond attending to responsibilities assigned by the constitution, the military also attempted to expand its functions through the nation's counterinsurgency program, which contained political, economic, social, and psychological elements as well as military ones. The goal of the counterinsurgency program, like previous civic-action programs, was to defend, and to enhance social control of the countryside. Without a doubt, the struggle for the "hearts and minds" of the civilian population was at least as important as the military battle.

Despite continued efforts to "militarize everyday life," by 1983 it became clear that the armed forces were losing the war on this front. In response to the FMLN's growing military capacity, U.S. and Salvadoran officials developed the National Campaign Plan, which "placed emphasis on civic action and developmental projects behind a security screen."[11] The idea of the plan was to restore local authorities and government services to selected conflictive zones where the army succeeded in eliminating guerrilla control. Typically, such operations included not only removing the guerrillas from the area but also the civilian population suspected of supporting them. After securing the areas, central government ministries were to move in to repair damaged infrastructure, implement the land reform program, and extend basic services. The Comisión Nacional para la Restauración de Areas (CONARA) was created in 1983 to coordinate the AID-funded initiative. Initially, the plan was to target conflictive zones in San Vicente and Usulután.[12]

The plan was not very successful for a number of reasons. First of all, the military was unable to hold targeted areas for sufficient time to implement development projects. As U.S. Military Group (MILGROUP) Commander Col. Joseph Stringham put it, the "El Salvadoran Armed Forces got way out in front of the developmental aspect of the plan, perhaps too far out in front. They outstripped their own capability as far as support systems were concerned."[13] In San Vicente, the guerrillas initially retreated from the area, but as soon as the military reduced its troop presence, guerrilla activity resumed "at about the same level as it was before the program began."[14] Moreover, the response by the displaced population to the plan was lukewarm at best. Potential participants in the repopulation program were generally suspicious of the army's intentions and particularly concerned with the plan's civil defense provisions. Finally, the military insisted on controlling the initiative, seriously eclipsing the civilian leadership's participation in the effort at both the local and national levels.[15]

Given the limited success of the National Campaign Plan, in 1986 the military launched another plan, Unidos para Reconstruir (UPR). The UPR consisted of three phases. First, the military was to eliminate the guerrillas and suspected civilian sympathizers from designated areas. Next came the consolidation phase, when the military was to establish permanent control in the zones. And third was the resettlement and reconstruction phase. As with the previous National Campaign Plan, the UPR was "based on the reformation of communities organized, structured, and controlled" by the armed forces.[16] In practice, this meant that potential participants were screened by the military to determine their political loyalties. Also, like the earlier plan, the armed forces, and not the civilian leadership, directed the initiative. A March 1986 agreement between President Duarte, Defense Minister Gen. Vides Casanova, and Army Chief of Staff Gen. Adolfo Blandón created a "National Joint Coordination Committee" for the UPR to be headed up by Blandón. The agreement also established "a chain of command from him to the fourteen Department Joint Coordination Committees, in which the local military commander is designated General Coordinator with control over local CONARA activities."[17] The military assumed direct control over CONARA, which was to coordinate the efforts of the various civilian ministries implementing UPR reconstruction projects. Moreover, the sites for projects were chosen by departmental military commanders and approved by Blandón.

Unlike the previous National Campaign Plan, the UPR was to be implemented in all fourteen departments, "so that each of the regional military commanders would get a piece of the pie."[18] As Bacevich et al. point out, the problem with such an approach was that by "spreading its development effort around to keep the officer corps happy, the government insured that nowhere would its effort be decisive."[19] Instead of saturating a particular area with civic-action projects, development initiatives were carried out in an uncoordinated, almost haphazard fashion.

The lack of success in forming civilian defense patrols hindered both the National Campaign Plan and the UPR. Besides relying on traditional mechanisms of control, such as the *patrullas cantonales* and local *comandantes,* the military—under U.S. guidance—set up a system of civil defense patrols throughout the country. By late 1987, it was estimated that there were 240 civil defense units; however, only one hundred had been "certified"—meaning they had received a minimum of training—and few were operating in conflictive zones. In Chalatenango there were seven detachments and in Morazán only one.[20] Moreover, only about half of the units were new, the rest consisting of the old *patrullas cantonales* and *escoltas militares.*[21]

Through its control of the UPR and CONARA, the military enabled local commanders to force the civilian population to join civil defense patrols. One of the criteria used to decide whether or not to fund local projects was the establishment of civil defense units in the area. Despite the use of economic assistance and food aid to facilitate the formation of civil defense patrols, the military's efforts did not fulfill the expectations of its U.S. sponsors. In general, the civilian population viewed them as little different from traditional paramilitary units: local instruments of intimidation and repression. More importantly, the costs of joining far outweighed the benefits. According to Bacevich et al., the "benefits" of being a member of the civil defense units were few:

> Training ammunition will be in short supply. He will receive neither uniform nor pay. If his unit is attacked, he will discover that the local ESAF commander has no plans to come to his rescue. If wounded, he will not be evacuated to a Salvadoran military hospital. If he is killed in the line of duty, the government will provide a $1,000 gratuity to his family and nothing more.[22]

On the other hand, as a member of a civil defense patrol, one was certain to be targeted by the guerrillas. Not surprisingly, faced with such choices, most peasants sought ways of avoiding service without drawing the wrath of local military authorities.

The military's support for the civil defense patrols—largely a U.S. initiative—was lukewarm at best. Schwarz suggests that the military was reluctant to share its assets "with the campesinos it despises."[23] In addition to their contempt for the peasantry, local commanders' reluctance to adequately equip the units stemmed from the fact that the poorly trained civil defense patrols were easy prey for the guerrillas. Providing the patrols with better equipment in larger quantities might have resulted in aiding rather than hindering the guerrillas. Moreover, MILGROUP's concept of civil defense was foreign to the Salvadoran armed forces. While both viewed civil defense as an instrument of social control, supplementing the regular army's efforts to secure the countryside, MILGROUP envisioned civil defense as a vehicle through which entire villages could protect themselves from guerrilla attacks. As we have seen, historically, the Salvadoran paramilitary network "served less as a vehicle for protection than as a source of extortion, repression, and intimidation."[24] Consequently, most Salvadoran officers found it difficult to swallow the idea of civil defense patrols as "a first line of defense" against the enemy.

The increasing militarization of everyday life did not go unchallenged. Significant areas of the country either fell under guerrilla control or remained "contested" throughout much of the war. Although the "space" available for autonomous social organization and mobilization was extremely limited by state repression, popular organizations aggressively challenged the military's domination at the local level. This was reflected after 1982 in the continued growth of peasant organizations and trade unions, and in the appearance of new organizations at the grassroots, such as women's movements, the Christian base community movement, and neighborhood associations.[25] Moreover, "everyday forms" of resistance, while less visible, were also extremely important, especially in rural areas.[26] Indeed, the failure of the civil defense patrols discussed above was at least in part the result of peasants resorting to a multitude of footdragging strategies to avoid serving in the patrols. Indeed, the FMLN's ability to challenge the military's system of social control depended on both the passive and active resistance of peasants. For example, when the military passed through rural communities in pursuit of the guerrillas, peasants often feigned ignorance or provided false information as to the guerrillas' whereabouts. These varied forms of resistance exerted constant pressure on the armed forces' network of control.

POLÍTICOS AND OLIGARCHS

Not only did the civil war facilitate an expanded political role for the military, but it also helped to shape the military's perception of itself and of

political society generally. Throughout this period, the officer corps continued to regard the armed forces as the only national institution able to defend the state and to guarantee public order. This view, combined with a
perception that civil society was weak and ineffective, was only reinforced by
the habit of civilian politicians to turn to the military for rescue in crisis situations. Such a situation occurred in April 1982 when the Constituent Assembly reached a political stalemate in selecting a civilian president. In
March 1982, after much fanfare, elections were held for a constituent assembly, which was to draft a new constitution and elect a transitional president who would serve until 1984. Although the Christian Democrats won a
plurality of the seats, two right-wing parties, the Partido de Conciliación Nacional (PCN) and the Alianza Republicana Nacionalista (ARENA), together
controlled a majority of seats. When it appeared likely that Roberto
D'Aubuisson would be named provisional president, the Christian Democrats chose to boycott the proceedings.

The elections were a key component in the Reagan administration's policy toward El Salvador. As Karl points out, the election of a civilian-led government could serve to improve the regime's international image, deflect
pressures for a negotiated settlement, and convince Congress that the administration was committed to promoting democracy. Furthermore, it was
hoped that elections would damage the FMLN's credibility—forcing it into
the uncomfortable position of boycotting the electoral process—and generate divisions within the guerrilla leadership.[27]

Given his unsavory past and embarrassing campaign rhetoric, D'Aubuisson was unacceptable to the Reagan administration. D'Aubuisson's assumption of the presidency would have jeopardized a major increase in military
and economic assistance by an already skeptical Congress. Ironically, administration officials had been convinced that the elections would result in
a Christian Democratic government. Instead, "the radical right wing had
been legitimized in power through elections, a somewhat embarrassing and
unexpected outcome."[28]

Although within the Salvadoran military D'Aubuisson had his backers,
Col. Gutiérrez and others were adamantly opposed to D'Aubuisson's selection. Like administration officials, they were concerned about endangering
future U.S. assistance. Moreover, officers like Gutiérrez and García had their
own political ambitions. Gutiérrez, who was the real power within the civil-
military junta, viewed the elections as part of a strategy by the Reagan administration to remove the military from power. As a way out of the stalemate, he favored a PDC proposal whereby a new provisional junta would be
formed, including one representative each from the PDC, the opposition,

and the armed forces.[29] García, on the other hand, favored the appointment of an independent as provisional president, which would allow him to exert effective political control from his position as minister of defense.[30] The Reagan administration also favored a compromise choice for president and dispatched special envoy Gen. Vernon Walters to San Salvador to prod political party leaders and the High Command into working toward such an outcome.

Borrowing a page from their Honduran counterparts, the High Command imposed its preferred candidate on the politicians.[31] Soon after the party leaders were informed of the High Command's decision, the Constituent Assembly duly elected Alvaro Magaña provisional president. The selection of Magaña was not accidental. Magaña had been president of the Banco Hipotecario for many years and had developed close ties to a number of officers. Over the years, officers could count on Magaña to receive loans on favorable terms, and many sought him out for general advice and counseling. A longtime "friend" of the military establishment, Magaña was a safe bet for the High Command. He was also the preferred candidate of the U.S. embassy, who saw him as a reasonable compromise choice that would be acceptable to most of the key players. Given the alternatives, the Christian Democrats were likely to sign on, as was the PCN, which could be counted on to support the military's candidate. ARENA, while it resented the Reagan administration's "meddling," could at least find comfort in D'Aubuisson's election as president of the constituent assembly. Moreover, Magaña had no popular mandate and, with a majority of the seats, the Right could control the legislative agenda.

Another situation that reinforced the military's general contempt for civilian politicians arose during the kidnapping of President Duarte's daughter in September 1985. The president's decision to accede to the FMLN demand that twenty-two political prisoners, including Comandante Nidia Díaz, be released was opposed by several high-ranking officers who believed such concessions only undermined the government's credibility and projected an image of weakness and vulnerability. Believing that his daughter was being held in Chalatenango, a guerrilla stronghold, Duarte ordered the suspension of all offensive operations in a forty-square-kilometer area of Chalatenango. Col. Sigfredo Ochoa, commander of the Fourth Brigade in Chalatenango, resented the order and circulated a document rejecting any concessions to the FMLN.[32] Although a number of senior officers shared Ochoa's dismay over the prisoner swap and the decision to suspend offensive operations in the midst of a war, Defense Minister Vides Casanova succeeded in convincing the officer corps to support the government's position. Vides, no doubt, was sympathetic to Duarte's predicament, given that a year earlier his brother had been kidnapped by the guerrillas and Duarte supported a prisoner exchange to secure Vides's brother's release.[33] Thus, an institutional crisis was averted, but the incident reinforced the military's notion that civilian politicians put personal and partisan interests before the national interest.

Besides helping to consolidate the military's position in the state and confirm its distrust of civilians, the civil war enabled the military to maintain its institutional autonomy vis-à-vis the state and society. During the course of the 1980s, the military became much less dependent upon the oligarchy and much more autonomous as an institution with its own set of interests. Always a somewhat stormy relationship, the distancing of the Salvadoran armed forces from the country's oligarchy became even more profound with the decision of the former to support an agrarian reform program. As Jeffrey Paige points out, as objectionable as land reform was to coffee elites, of most concern to them was the government's decision in December 1979 to nationalize the country's export trade in coffee. "Because most coffee holdings were not affected by the first phase of the agrarian reform . . . nationalizing the coffee trade had the largest effect on the fortunes of Salvadoran capital in general and the agro-export sector in particular."[34] To manage the government's new monopoly over the coffee trade, the junta established the *Instituto Nacional de Cafe* (INCAFE). Coffee growers and processors alike viewed INCAFE—and, hence, the military and the Christian Democrats—as responsible for the "collapse" of the coffee industry. Their main bone of contention was the price differential between the international price for coffee and the price that INCAFE paid to producers. During the 1980s, producers received between one-half to one-fourth of the international price. "The difference between the international and local price showed up as a government foreign-exchange surplus."[35]

Clearly, this represented a dramatic change from the past, when military governments pursued policies generally favorable to the interests of the agro-export sector. Over time, however, military officers increasingly came to view the oligarchy as disloyal and only concerned with its own profit. The military looked on angrily as wealthy oligarchs withdrew their capital from the country and sent their sons and daughters abroad when collapse seemed imminent. On the other hand, some sectors of the oligarchy came to view the military as a dangerous competitor in the economic realm, bristling at the military's unfair advantages. Prior to the civil war, individual officers typically received special benefits and perks and often used their positions for personal financial gain. During the 1980s, however, the massive influx of U.S. military assistance created opportunities for corruption on a grand scale. For example, during the course of the war, the Cooperativa de la Fuerza Armada grew "from a small shop to a shopping mall, complete with a supermarket and a three-story department store."[36] Many of the goods sold at the Cooperativa were brought into the country duty-free. Another example of such unfair competition was Promarisal, a fishing company run by the head of the navy, Col. Humberto Villalta. Unlike other fishing companies, Promarisal paid no municipal taxes or social security taxes for its employees.[37]

Beyond the illicit business dealings of individual officers, the military's social security fund (IPSFA—Instituto de Previsión Social de la Fuerza Armada) "allowed the military to become the single most powerful economic and social institution in El Salvador."[38] Receiving a portion of every conscript's salary, IPSFA's reserves grew from less than $2 million in 1980 to over $100 million by the end of the decade, making it the country's largest source of liquid capital. While all soldiers paid into the fund, only disabled conscripts or the families of the dead received payments. Officers and their families, on the other hand, could receive mortgage and car loans from IPSFA that were unavailable to conscripts. As IPSFA's reserves continued to grow, it began investing heavily in real estate. In 1989, it purchased a beach resort on the Costa del Sol and invested in a major housing development in one of San Salvador's suburbs.[39]

In addition to the military's increasing economic power, a series of kidnappings of wealthy business people greatly exacerbated the already strained relations between the armed forces and the oligarchy. In one highly publicized case in 1986, three officers from the *tandona* (the "big class" that graduated from the military academy in 1966) were implicated in a kidnapping ring and arrested by the National Police. Despite the efforts of the vice minister of public security, Col. Carlos Reynaldo López Nuila, to bring the officers to justice, their colleagues in the *tandona* successfully intervened on their behalf. One of the officers implicated, Col. Mauricio Staben, returned to active duty as commander of the elite Arce Battalion.[40] Besides the involvement of military officers in the kidnappings, equally infuriating to the business community was the military's unwillingness or inability to punish those responsible.

Thus, the convergence of interests between the military and its supporters within the oligarchy was severely tested during the 1980s. As the military progressively developed its own separate set of priorities, it became more concerned with protecting its core interests than with defending the oligarchy at all costs. As we see in chapter 7, during the peace negotiations between the FMLN and the Salvadoran government, officers would feel betrayed by those in the oligarchy that came to view the military as a bargaining chip to be used to gain concessions on socioeconomic issues.

PACTING WITH THE DEVIL

Another factor that contributed to the military's developing autonomy during the 1980s was a series of political pacts negotiated between the High Command and political leaders. On the one hand, the pacts helped to establish the ground rules of civil-military relations; on the other hand, they confirmed the political role of the military and assured its institutional autonomy vis-à-vis the civilian political leadership. Furthermore, the exclusive nature of these pacts contributed little to forging the consensus necessary for a genuine democratic transition.

The first such pact that affected civil-military relations in a significant way was the founding document of the second junta, drawn up in January 1980. As discussed in the previous chapter, the armed forces agreed to go forward with the socioeconomic reforms promised by the first junta in return for the status quo ante regarding civil-military relations. Given that it made no provisions for enhancing the junta's authority over the armed forces, the agreement all but guaranteed the military's domination of the junta. A subsequent agreement in mid-December 1980 reinforced the military's autonomy vis-à-vis civilian leaders in the government. The agreement provided for the restructuring of the junta, whereby Duarte was named president of the junta and Gutiérrez became the sole commander in chief of the armed forces. Previously, the entire junta, including its civilian members, was commander in chief of the armed forces. However, as the September 1980 purge of remaining Majanista officers demonstrated, Gutiérrez was already the de facto commander in chief. The December agreement, then, simply formalized this situation. In addition, García, Gutiérrez, and Vides Casanova were promoted to general, thereby enhancing their authority within the armed forces. And finally, several important D'Aubuisson allies were removed from command positions. Figuring prominently on the list was Subsecretary of Defense Col. Nicolás Carranza, whom D'Aubuisson planned to make minister of defense had his coup plot been successful. Of the other officers removed, some had been arrested with D'Aubuisson in May 1980.[41]

The Christian Democrats on the junta would never have been able to secure the removal of these officers had it not been for the pressure exerted by the Carter administration. On December 5, two days after the four American churchwomen were killed by members of the National Guard, the

Carter administration announced the suspension of all U.S. military assistance to El Salvador. The announcement of the junta's restructuring and the removal of the officers linked to D'Aubuisson on December 13 must have satisfied the conditions laid down by the Carter administration. A few days later, the administration announced that it was renewing economic assistance to the junta, and in mid-January $25 million in military assistance was released.

Another pact that confirmed the autonomy of the military came in the form of a secret agreement between President-elect Duarte and Minister of Defense Eugenio Vides Casanova, initiated on the eve of Duarte's inauguration in June 1984.[42] The agreement served to reassure both the High Command and the government-elect that their vital interests would be protected. It also helped to formalize a workable relationship between the Duarte government and the High Command, which both considered essential for the war effort.

In general terms, Duarte was concerned that the High Command allow his government to carry out its basic program. Several high-ranking officers were closely identified with the ARENA party and, during both the 1982 and 1984 elections, there had been incidents where brigade commanders campaigned openly in support of ARENA candidates. Vides Casanova, for his part, was concerned with defending the armed forces' institutional autonomy and, in particular, maintaining intact the team of officers he had assembled to direct the war effort.

While addressing the concerns of both civilian and military leaders, the document is at times contradictory. For example, regarding Duarte's desire to improve the regime's human rights record, the agreement committed the military to place a special emphasis on respecting human rights in all of its training programs, to eradicate the death squads, and to investigate the most egregious cases of human rights abuses. In addition, the agreement provided for the creation of a new Vice Ministry of Public Security. The idea, which had little or no support within the High Command, was to separate the security forces from the military command structure and bring them under more direct civilian control. Although the minister of defense was to exercise ultimate authority over the new vice ministry, the vice minister was to have wide latitude in restructuring the security forces. Included in this was a specific provision to establish a separate academy for officers in the security forces. Nevertheless, despite the apparent concern for improving the human rights situation and investigating past abuses, Duarte agreed not to prosecute military officers involved in past human rights abuses, promising, instead, to start with a clean slate—"borrón y cuenta nueva."

The agreement also recognized the right of the new government to seek a negotiated settlement to the conflict. However, this was to be carried out by "breaking the FMLN-FDR alliance" and attempting to "incorporate the FDR into the democratic process." Moreover, the document affirmed the military's duty to maintain a permanent offensive aimed at defeating the FMLN. To this end, the agreement called for the creation of a comprehensive counterinsurgency program with military, political, economic, and social components, and the establishment of "permanent units of combat and control of the population." Also, a new joint chiefs of staff was to be created—the Estado Mayor Conjunto (EMC)—incorporating the three branches of the armed forces. The new EMC was to be responsible for formulating a national military plan that included the policies of the new government and responded to the human and material needs resulting from the conflict.

On the issue of institutional autonomy, Duarte promised to defend the unity and integrity of the armed forces, accepting the current composition of the High Command and agreeing to work with Vides Casanova regarding the transfer of other officers. The agreement, which accorded the military a leading role in the war effort, also confirmed the defense minister's role of safeguarding "national interests, institutional interests, and government interests." Finally, Duarte accepted the High Command's insistence that any decisions affecting the military institution be implemented by the institution itself and not imposed by others. In exchange for Duarte's respecting the military's institutional autonomy, Vides Casanova agreed that the armed forces would not participate directly in the electoral process nor allow themselves to be manipulated by any political party.

Despite the contributions that such pacts can make in furthering a transition from authoritarian rule, their negative consequences are well known.[43] Given the small number of participants involved, pacts are inherently undemocratic. They also tend to freeze into place the existing power structure and limit the possibilities for more far-reaching change. Nevertheless most observers argue that, in terms of democratic consolidation, the benefits outweigh the costs. For example, O'Donnell and Schmitter contend that one of the lessons of recent democratic transitions is that opposition leaders must accept that the armed forces' "institutional existence, assets, and hierarchy cannot be eliminated or seriously threatened."[44] Likewise, Rouquié argues that "avoiding direct confrontation, dissipating any personal or corporate concerns among the officers most involved in the repression can in a curious way facilitate a gradual movement toward the rule of law and representative procedures."[45]

What these observers may fail to see, however, is that pacts can present major impediments to the establishment and consolidation of democratic rule. In El Salvador, pacts helped delineate more precisely the relationship between the civilian political leadership and the military's High Command. By reassuring both that their vital interests would not be threatened, the agreements minimized the potential for conflict. While this did, indeed, pave the way toward a more harmonious relationship between civilian leaders and the military, at the same time the pacts worked to reinforce the military's dominant position in the state, as well as its institutional autonomy.[46] Consequently, even though the armed forces tolerated a limited political opening, including the election of civilian leaders, they retained their right, and ability, to intervene in what they deemed undesirable situations. Their continuing political domination was a formidable obstacle to democratizing civil-military relations.

A MILITARY DIVIDED?

As has been discussed throughout this book, the military's political power was not without limits. Historically, internal factionalism within the officer corps restricted the armed forces' ability to implement policy initiatives that challenged the economic domination of the agro-export elite. In the wake of the 1979 coup, for example, the lack of programmatic consensus undermined the efforts of reformist officers to implement profound structural reforms. Disagreements over the extent and pace of reforms, and over the question of military reforms, did not simply disappear with the marginalization of *Majanista* officers. During the course of the 1980s, however, these issues were eclipsed by other concerns, namely the war effort and institutional politics.

Regarding the war effort, initial disagreements arose over whether to adopt the counterinsurgency strategy advocated by MILGROUP. Under the low-intensity warfare approach, the Salvadoran military was to adopt the same strategies as the guerrillas to defeat them. This included a shift toward smaller military units to provide greater mobility and enhanced response time; the use of selective repression as opposed to massive repression; efforts to improve relations with the civilian population; and an effort to keep the guerrillas constantly on the move and dispersed.[47] Given that this strategy sought to build up popular support for the regime over the long haul, it also required keeping the reform program on track.

Contrary to the long-term "low-intensity" strategy being promoted by MILGROUP, a number of officers preferred a "quick" resolution of the conflict. While eager to adopt the military elements of U.S. counterinsurgency doctrine, these officers were generally opposed to the reform program initiated by the civil-military juntas. For them, more important than building up popular support was annihilating the FMLN and its supporters in the shortest time possible. The "total war" approach was supported by some younger officers with significant combat experience who were frustrated by the restrictions imposed on the armed forces because of human rights considerations. With no end in sight to the conflict, the "total war" strategy was an appealing alternative. One well-known proponent of this strategy was Col. Sigfredo Ochoa, commander of the Second Detachment in Cabañas. He believed the military was being "held back" in conducting the war effort. His "success" in cleansing the Cabañas department of guerrillas in the early 1980s was held up as a model for the "total war" strategy. During one operation in 1981, Ochoa's troops were responsible for depopulating large areas of the department, killing suspected guerrilla sympathizers or forcing them to flee to San Salvador or Honduras.[48]

THE OCHOA UPRISING

Occasionally, disagreements over how to conduct the war evolved into very public confrontations. Other issues, including political differences and the personal power ambitions of individual officers, fueled these confrontations. One of the most serious occurred in January 1983. On 6 January, Col. Ochoa declared his troops in open rebellion and demanded the resignation of Defense Minister Gen. García. Ochoa's revolt was prompted by a 31 December 1982 general order stipulating his transfer to the post of military attaché in the Salvadoran embassy in Uruguay. In an interview the following day, Ochoa declared: "Cabañas Department has come under military control, under my control."[49] He accused García of being a corrupt "behind-the-scenes dictator" and of making arbitrary, politically motivated decisions. Ochoa also pointed to his success in eradicating the guerrilla threat in Cabañas and suggested that there were "better elements within the armed forces, who could take over the defense sphere."

Gen. García, who was due to complete his thirty years of service in February, refused to step down and insisted that Ochoa obey the general order. He portrayed Ochoa's revolt as an Arena-backed coup attempt that had been brewing for several months. Not surprisingly, Ochoa's well-known relationship with D'Aubuisson and other Arena leaders was partly behind García's decision to send Ochoa into diplomatic exile. Also important, however, is that García viewed officers like Ochoa as a threat to his own authority. Despite their opposition to the junta's reform measures, Ochoa and other young commanders were praised by MILGROUP officials for their willingness to adopt U.S. counterinsurgency tactics. Promoting the battlefield exploits by these young commanders contrasted with MILGROUP's lukewarm endorsement of García.

Col. Adolfo Blandón, commander of the First Brigade, paid Ochoa a visit on 7 January, offering to serve as a mediator. After emerging from the meeting, Blandón referred to Ochoa as a "great commander" and promised to search for a "just solution" to the crisis. Two days later, García sent a high-level negotiating team to Cabañas, headed by National Guard Director Gen. Vides Casanova. That same day, the High Command issued a communiqué denouncing the revolt; however, Col. Blandón and Col. Juan Rafael Bustillo, commander of the air force, refused to sign the document. According to Blandón, on 10 January, during a meeting of commanding officers, he and Bustillo called on García to resign, a position supported by the majority of officers.[50] A high-level meeting with Ochoa produced an agreement whereby the colonel would spend a year of study at the Inter-American Defense College in Washington, D.C. In return, García agreed to offer up his resignation by mid-April. When it appeared that García would attempt to stay on past the agreed-upon deadline, Col. Bustillo publicly threatened to disavow García's authority beyond 15 April. On 18 April, President Magaña accepted García's resignation and appointed Gen. Vides Casanova to replace him as minister of defense.

Disagreement over military strategy provides only a partial explanation for the Ochoa revolt. Clearly, MILGROUP officials viewed García as an obstacle to implementing needed changes in the military's war effort. And García's replacement, Gen. Vides Casanova, would prove much more willing to work with MILGROUP in implementing the "low intensity" approach. However, also important were the personal power ambitions of individual officers. Blandón and Bustillo viewed Ochoa's rebellion as an opportunity to enhance their own positions within the armed forces. Blandón, in fact, was made chief of staff not long after García's removal. Bustillo also stood to gain from García's replacement. Vides Casanova, the High Command's choice to succeed García, came from the same *tanda* as Bustillo. Given the traditional solidarity among members of the same *tanda,* Bustillo's position as commander of the air force probably was more secure with Vides Casanova as defense minister.

Finally, although it is unclear to what extent Arena leaders were behind Ochoa's uprising, officers opposed to the reforms gained the upper hand in the wake of the incident. Soon after his appointment, Vides returned to active duty several important D'Aubuisson allies. Several of these officers had been removed from command positions in late 1980 to placate the Carter administration. For example, in June 1983, the infamous Col. Carranza was placed in charge of the Treasury Police. Lt. Col. Mario Denis Morán, former head of intelligence for the National Guard, was made commander of the garrison in Zacatecoluca. In January 1981, Morán's bodyguard participated in the assassinations of José Rodolfo Viera, president of ISTA, and AIFLD (American Institute for Free Labor Development) advisors Mark Pearlman and Michael Hammer. According to the March 1993 United Nations Truth Commission report, Morán concealed information vital to the investigation of the incident.[51] Lt. Col. Jorge Adalberto Cruz, who participated in D'Aubuisson's failed coup attempt in April 1980, was given command of the Fourth Detachment in Morazán.[52] Both Morán and Cruz were from the same *tanda* (1963) as D'Aubuisson and used their positions and resources to actively support D'Aubuisson's candidacy during the March 1984 elections.

Tensions Over Human Rights

The return of officers opposed to the reform program was in part a reflection of the Reagan administration's policy. At least until late 1983, some administration officials expressed less concern than their predecessors about further reforms or about human rights abuses. This was especially true among MILGROUP officials who praised the battlefield exploits of officers like Ochoa who were opposed to reform initiatives. By late 1983, however, the Reagan administration could no longer ignore the increasing death squad activity and human rights abuses in El Salvador. As Arson points out, during 1983 the FMLN made significant gains on the battlefield, demonstrating an ability to mobilize large units to engage the army in pitched battles.[53] A September attack on the Third Brigade in San Miguel, in which the guerrillas employed unprecedented firepower, symbolized the FMLN's increasing confidence to take on the army in its own backyard. A string of embarrassing military defeats and growing U.S. concerns over the ineffectiveness of field and staff commanders prompted a major reshuffling in the armed forces in late November 1983. Col. Adolfo Blandón, commander of the First Brigade, replaced Col. Reyes Mena as chief of staff. In addition, three rapid deployment battalion commanders, and the military commanders of seven departments were replaced. Several officers with significant battlefield experience took over key commands within the army. For example, Col. Domingo Monterrosa, the much touted commander of the U.S.-trained Atlacatl Battalion, was made commander of the all-important Third Brigade in San Miguel.[54] Nevertheless, despite the publicly stated goal of achieving greater coordination and communication within the army, *tanda* affiliation seemed to have been at least as important as battlefield experience in determining the changes, with the 1963 *tanda* benefitting most from the changes.[55]

To reverse the tide on the battlefield, the Reagan administration planned to request a substantial increase in military assistance for FY 1984 (see table 6.1); however, the prospects of Congress approving such a dramatic increase were dim. Concerns over continuing human rights abuses and the government's failure to investigate past abuses, including the murders of the four American churchwomen, prompted Congress to place a cap of $64.8 million on future military aid and to tie 30 percent of the aid to a trial and verdict in the churchwomen's case.[56] Also adding to the administration's problems was the upsurge in death squad activity during the fall of 1983. Whereas a year earlier, Ambassador Deane Hinton had been reproached for delivering a harsh attack on death squad violence, his successor, Thomas Pickering, was backed up by administration officials when he delivered a scathing attack on "extremists on the right."[57] In fact, in November the embassy in El Salvador leaked names of officers believed to be linked to the death squads.[58] The leaks to reporters were followed by Vice President Bush's highly publicized visit to El Salvador in December 1983, during which he met with the High Command and demanded that officers implicated in human rights abuses be exiled or expelled from the military.

Following Bush's visit, the High Command took a number of steps to placate the Reagan administration. On 15 December, the High Command issued an unusual communiqué signed by the armed forces general staff

TABLE 6.1
Direct U.S. Military Assistance to El Salvador (in $ millions)

Year	IMET Training	Loans	Financing	Total
1980	0.2	5.7	—	5.9
1981	0.5	10.0	25.0	35.5
1982	2.0	16.5	63.5	82.0
1983	1.3	46.5	33.5	81.3
1984	1.3	18.5	176.8	196.6
1985	1.5	10.0	124.8	136.3
1986	1.4	—	120.4	121.8
1987	1.5	—	110.0	111.5
1988	1.5	—	80.0	81.5
1989	1.4	—	79.9	81.3
1990	1.4	—	79.6	81.0

Sources: Agency for International Development, *U.S. Overseas Loans, Grants and Assistance from International Organizations, 1980–90;* U.S. Library of Congress, Congressional Research Service, *El Salvador Under Cristiani: U.S. Foreign Assistance Decisions* (Washington, D.C.: 20 July 1993).

and commanders of the military and public security forces, in which they publicly affirmed their "firm decision to oppose the death squads and terrorist groups by all means in our power and in every possible way until they are totally eradicated."[59] A few days later, Capt. Eduardo Ernesto Alfonso Ávila was arrested in connection with the murders of Pearlman and Hammer, and in early January two officers suspected of death squad activities— Maj. Ricardo Pozo, chief of intelligence for the Treasury Police, and Lt. Col. Arístides Alfonso Marqués, chief of intelligence for the National Police— were sent abroad and another, Lt. Francisco Raul Amaya Rosa, was dismissed from the army. Finally, the security chief of the Constituent Assembly and longtime collaborator of D'Aubuisson was relieved of his duties.[60]

The Reagan administration's growing concern over the human rights situation in the country affected the balance of power within the Salvadoran armed forces. As Stanley argues, more moderate officers now could insist on improvement in human rights as important to the military's institutional interests.[61] Without significant progress, increased levels of U.S. assistance would be jeopardized, ultimately benefitting the FMLN. Duarte's election in March 1984 strengthened the hand of more moderate officers. While few could boast of exemplary human rights records, officers like Defense Minister Gen. Vides Casanova and Vice Minister of Public Security Col. López Nuila at least understood the political urgency of reining in the death squads.

Although Duarte hoped that his strong personal relationship with Vides Casanova and López Nuila would enable him to improve the human rights situation in the country, he encountered significant resistance within the armed forces. In fact, his pact with Vides Casanova, in which he agreed not to prosecute officers involved in past abuses, sent the wrong message to the officer corps. Instead of asserting civilian authority over the armed forces, the pact reinforced the military institution's autonomy from civil power and its position above the law. In short, the agreement failed to set a precedent for punishing those officers guilty of human rights abuses.

A key component in Duarte's efforts to improve the human rights situation was the creation of the Vice Ministry for Public Security. As discussed above, the pact between Duarte and Vides provided for the establishment of the new vice ministry under López Nuila's leadership. López Nuila, the former director of the National Police, believed that for the security forces to do a more efficient job of public security, they had to receive more specialized training in policing. As it stood, the security forces functioned less like police forces and more like poorly equipped units of the army. During his tenure, López Nuila did succeed in establishing the Academy for Public Security, which was to provide agents with opportunities to participate in specialized officer training courses, and in arresting over one thousand military and police for common crimes. However, because of resistance from the High Command, López Nuila failed to accomplish his main goal, which was to make the security forces more autonomous from the military command structure.[62]

Most high-ranking officers viewed control of the security forces as a fundamental core interest. Traditionally, military officers headed up the different security forces and the army relied heavily on them for their intelligence-gathering capabilities. As discussed in chapter 5, even reformist officers balked at dismantling the "eyes and ears" of the armed forces. Particularly worrisome to senior officers was the possibility that the security forces might be turned against the military if given too much autonomy. López Nuila's efforts to investigate the involvement of officers in kidnapping rings only served to reinforce these fears.

In April 1986, López Nuila announced that he had broken up one of several kidnapping rings in which three members of the *tandona* were implicated—Colonels Roberto Mauricio Staben and Joaquín Ernesto Zacapa, and Lt. Carlos Zacapa. At the time, Staben was commander of the elite Arce Battalion and Joaquín Zacapa was executive of the Cavalry Regiment. Other members of the *tandona,* who had risen to key positions within the armed forces, viewed the arrests as an attack on the *tandona* as a whole.[63] In an attempt to undermine his credibility, influential officers from the *tandona* accused López Nuila of attempting to separate the security forces from the military and called for his removal as vice minister of public security. The intense campaign against López Nuila succeeded in shielding the *tandona* members from prosecution. In fact, Col. Staben returned to active duty as commander of the Arce Battalion, while the Zacapa brothers fled the country.[64]

THE TANDONA'S ASSAULT ON POWER

Without the minister of defense's full support, López Nuila's efforts were fruitless. Vides Casanova, in fact, turned out to be a wholly unreliable ally to Duarte. When Duarte fell ill in May 1988, Vides Casanova moved to consolidate his power by eliminating potential rivals within the High Command. Instead of filling key positions with officials from the *tandas* next in line (1963 and 1964), Vides drew from the *tandona,* with whom he had developed a special relationship since the *tandona*'s days at the military academy. Unlike more senior officers, members of the *tandona* were combat veterans, many of whom had commanded special elite battalions that bore the brunt of the fighting during the 1980s. Not surprisingly, the *tandona*'s "warrior class" viewed U.S. pressures regarding human rights abuses as an obstacle to the war effort. In July and November 1988, Vides appointed *tandona* members to head up the National Guard, Treasury Police, National Police, the First, Third, and Fifth Brigades, and the Cavalry Regiment *(tandona* members remained in command of the Fourth and Sixth Brigades), and to key positions within the Estado Mayor. And in November 1988, Vides appointed Col. René Emilio Ponce chief of staff to replace retiring Gen. Adolfo Blandón, and Col. Gilberto Rubio as deputy chief of staff, both prominent members of the *tandona*.[65] The upshot was that Vides skipped over two *tandas* to move up his unconditional supporters from the *tandona*.

Vides Casanova's attempts to consolidate his power within the armed forces at the expense of traditional norms of hierarchy did not go unchallenged. Blandón recommended that Col. Miguel Méndez, former commander of the Third Brigade, replace him as chief of staff. Blandón was supported by a group of officers mostly from the 1964 *tanda*.[66] In a lengthy memorandum dated 15 September 1988, Colonels Roberto Rodríguez Murcia (commander of the Comando de Apoyo Logístico), Carlos Alfred Rivas (commander of the Centro de Entrenamiento Militar), Benjamín Ramos (commander of the Second Brigade), and Miguel Vasconcelos (commander of the Artillery Brigade), warned Vides Casanova about the "institutional crisis" within the armed forces. According to the colonels, the crisis had been provoked by the General Order dated 30 June 1988, which resulted in the replacement of several commanders of "great trajectory and professionalism" with less senior officers of "less capacity." The officers also warned about the efforts by the *tandona* to pressure the High Command "so that all of its compañeros come to occupy key positions within the institution." Such activities only served to sow divisions within the military and politicize the officer corps, thereby undermining the armed forces' institutional unity and threatening its ability to defeat the insurgency.[67]

The memorandum is surprisingly candid in its discussion of the internal disunity and low level of morale within the armed forces. It refers to the "bad examples" set by less senior officers who disobey the orders of their superiors and the criminal activities of some officers (including auto theft, kidnapping, and corruption) that only serve to undermine the institution's credibility. Moreover, it points to the intention of some officers to use their positions within the armed forces or at the head of state institutions to impose conditions on the victors of the upcoming (March 1989) elections. The officers end the memorandum with a recommendation that Vides Casanova establish a commission to study the problems outlined in the document and report back to him in thirty days.

The impact of the memorandum, according to one of its authors, was to persuade Vides Casanova to rethink his planned appointment of Ponce as chief of staff. Despite the opposition, Vides went ahead and made the appointment in November. It was from his position as chief of staff that Ponce orchestrated the *tandona*'s final assault on power. While Ponce himself would have to wait until 1990 to conquer the ultimate prize, minister of defense, by June 1989 the *tandona* was effectively in complete control of the armed forces (see table 6.2).

Although historically, one *tanda* usually dominated the High Command, never before had any one *tanda*'s domination been so overwhelming. For example, between 1979 and 1984 key commands within the armed forces were distributed among four or five *tandas* (see table 6.2). This pattern, however, was ruptured with the *tandona*'s rise to power in 1989. Except for the positions of minister of defense and commander of the air force, the *tandona* occupied all of the key positions within the High Command. In the case of minister of defense, incoming President Alfredo Cristiani's appointment, Gen. Rafael Humberto Larios, was a compromise choice. Both Ponce's and Bustillo's supporters had lobbied intensely for their candidates. Although Cristiani apparently favored Ponce, the appointment of a colonel instead of a ranking general as minister of defense would have broken traditional norms of hierarchy and created a serious rift within the armed forces. As Cristiani vacillated publicly over choosing Vides Casanova's successor, the air force made known its opposition to Ponce, grounding aircraft at the Ilopango air base for two days in early May. "A few days later, during Soldier's Day celebrations, Air Force jets buzzed the reviewing stand of the outgoing Defense Minister, Gen. Vides Casanova, drowning out his speech and embarrassing officers and diplomats alike."[68] In any case, Larios served for just over a year and was virtually powerless given the *tandona*'s almost total control of key commands.

During 1989 and 1990, resentment over the *tandona*'s growing monopoly on power grew within the armed forces. The growing rift within the officer corps resulted from a number of factors. First of all, officers belonging to those *tandas* (1967–69) immediately following the *tandona* were denied opportunities to assume key commands and in some cases were sent abroad. One of the more notorious cases was that of Col. Román Alfonso Barrera, considered one of the leaders of the 1967 *tanda* and a likely candidate to succeed Ponce. Barrera, who participated in the 1979 coup against Romero, had made his way up the ranks during the 1980s. In December 1989 he was appointed to the key position of chief of operations for the Estado Mayor. Less than two years later he was sent into diplomatic exile, becoming the military attaché for the Salvadoran embassy in Colombia. According to senior officers and a former MILGROUP commander familiar with his career,

TABLE 6.2
Officers Holding Key Positions

	First Junta—October 1979	
Position	Name	*Tanda*
Junta Member	Adolfo Majano	1958
Junta Member	Jaime Abdul Gutiérrez	1957
Minister of Defense	Jose Guillermo García	1956
Subsecretary of Defense	Nicolás Carranza	1957
Chief of Staff	Francisco Castillo	1958
Director, National Guard	Carlos Vides Casanova	1957
Director, National Police	Carlos R. López Nuila	1959
Director, Treasury Police	Francisco Morán	ranks
Commander, Air Force	Juan Rafael Bustillo	1957

	Magaña Government—May 1982	
Position	Name	*Tanda*
Minister of Defense	Jose Guillermo García	1956
Subsecretary of Defense	Francisco Castillo	1958
Chief of Staff	Rafael Flores Lima	1958
Director, National Guard	Carlos Vides Casanova	1957
Director, National Police	Carlos R. López Nuila	1959
Director, Treasury Police	Francisco Morán	ranks
Commander, 1st Brigade	Adolfo Blandón	1960
Commander, 3rd Brigade	Jaime Ernesto Flores	ranks
Commander, Air Force	Juan Rafael Bustillo	1957

	Duarte Government—June 1984	
Position	Name	*Tanda*
Minister of Defense	Carlos Vides Casanova	1957
Vice Minister of Defense	Rafael Flores Lima	1958
Vice Min. of Public Security	Carlos R. López Nuila	1959
Chief of Staff	Adolfo Blandón	1960
Director, National Guard	Arístides Napoleon Montes	ranks
Director, National Police	Rodolfo Revelo	1958
Director, Treasury Police	Reinaldo Golcher	1961
Commander, 1st Brigade	Jaime Ernesto Flores	ranks
Commander, 3rd Brigade	Domingo Monterrosa	1963
Commander, Air Force	Juan Rafael Bustillo	1957

	Cristiani Government—June 1989	
Position	Name	*Tanda*
Minister of Defense	Rafael Humberto Larios	1961
Vice Minister of Defense	Juan Orlando Zepeda	1966
Vice Min. of Public Security	Inocente Orlando Montano	1966
Chief of Staff	René Emilio Ponce	1966
Deputy Chief of Staff	Gilberto Rubio	1966
Director, National Guard	Juan Carlos Carrillo	1966
Director, National Police	Carlos Gúzman Aguilar	1966
Director, Treasury Police	Napoleon Hernández	1966
Commander, 1st Brigade	Francisco Elena Fuentes	1966
Commander, 3rd Brigade	Mauricio Ernesto Vargas	1966
Commander, Air Force	Juan Rafael Bustillo	1957

Source: Diario Oficial, 1979–89.

Barrera was sent abroad because members of the *tandona* viewed him as a potential rival. Other officers, like Col. Roberto Pineda Guerra (1967 *tanda*), who had relatively clean human rights records, were given commands where they were sure to "dirty their hands." In Pineda Guerra's case this included stints as commander of the Fourth Brigade in Chalatenango and as director of the infamous Treasury Police.

Also fueling the resentment of these officers were the pervasive acts of corruption perpetrated by members of the *tandona* and the High Command's unwillingness to punish those officers involved. Officers interviewed during the course of the research for this book, while freely admitting to the existence of corruption within the armed forces, uniformly agreed that under the *tandona* corruption reached unprecedented levels. Although in response to U.S. pressure some members of the *tandona* were sent into diplomatic exile because of their involvement in corruption or human rights abuses, many stayed on until well after the January 1992 peace accords were signed. The *tandona's* inaction only reinforced the perception that it was willing to sacrifice the armed forces' institutional credibility in exchange for protecting its own members.

Disagreement over the issue of negotiations also contributed to the growing rift within the armed forces. Prior to 1989, a negotiated solution to the conflict was a remote possibility. Although negotiations were attempted during both the Magaña and Duarte presidencies, neither side in the conflict was willing to make the kind of concessions necessary to move the process forward. Also extremely important in undermining a negotiating strategy was the Reagan administration's commitment to a military solution. For example, while Duarte won the 1984 presidential elections campaigning on a platform of peace and economic reconstruction, a dramatic increase in U.S. military assistance following the election led to a major escalation of the war (see table 6.1). Likewise, during the period following the October 1985 peace talks at La Palma between the Salvadoran government and the FMLN, the Reagan administration actively supported the High Command's hard-line position, which set strict parameters on Duarte's freedom to negotiate.[69]

Without pressure from the Reagan administration, the High Command could afford to pay lip service to negotiations without softening its position regarding concessions to the FMLN. Nevertheless, the costs of avoiding a negotiated solution began to accumulate for both sides. By 1989, there were growing pressures, both domestic and international, in support of a negotiated settlement. Within the country, war weariness and continued economic decline had a major impact on public opinion. In June 1989 the UCA released a poll showing that the overwhelming majority of Salvadorans (76 percent) favored negotiations with the FMLN.[70] Moreover, the more moderate faction led by Alfredo Cristiani gained ascendency within the ARENA party. This group, which included a number of coffee miller-exporters affiliated to the Asociación de Beneficiadores y Exportadores de Café (ABECAFE) and agro-industrialists, voiced support for a negotiated settlement and limited democracy.[71] At a regional level, the Central American Peace Process under Oscar Arias's leadership provided momentum in the direction of negotiations. And finally, the incoming Bush administration seemed more favorably inclined toward a negotiated strategy in both El Salvador and Nicaragua.

Despite the growing pressure in support of negotiations, the High Command remained divided on the issue. Whereas some *tandona* members, like Col. Mauricio Ernesto Vargas and, to a lesser extent, Col. René Emilio Ponce, appeared inclined to make concessions to the FMLN, hardliners, like Colonels Zepeda and Elena Fuentes, were adamantly opposed to any changes in the structure of the armed forces. As Gibb and Smyth point out, there were considerable institutional interests at stake.[72] During the 1980s, the armed forces had grown dramatically (see table 6.3), including a significant increase in the size of the officer corps.[73] Any negotiated settlement that called for a significant reduction of the armed forces would result also in a major contraction of the officer corps. The institution also stood to lose economically from a negotiated end to the conflict. As discussed in greater detail below, during the civil war the defense budget mushroomed both in absolute and relative terms, as did levels of U.S. military assistance. A negotiated settlement was certain to increase domestic pressures to cut the budget and to lead to an immediate reduction in U.S. assistance. Finally, officers feared that, as a condition for a peace accord, the armed forces would have to accept a purge of the officer corps.

TABLE 6.3
Estimated Troop Strength of the Salvadoran Military

Year	Army	Navy	Air Force	Total	Security Forces
1980	7,000	100	150	7,250	5,000
1983	22,000	300	2,350	24,650	9,500
1986	38,650	1,290	2,700	42,640	11,600
1988	39,000	1,000	2,000	42,000	12,600
1989	40,000	1,300	2,200	43,500	12,600
1990	40,000	2,200	2,400	44,600	13,400

Source: International Institute for Strategic Studies, *The Military Balance, 1978–1994* (London: 1994).

One last factor that exacerbated tensions within the armed forces was the High Command's behavior during the FMLN's November 1989 offensive. Even after receiving advanced warning, the High Command was completely unprepared to respond to the magnitude of the offensive. The commander of the air force, Gen. Bustillo, and several other senior officers were not even in the country when the offensive was launched.[74] It was only after several days of intensive bombing of the northern and eastern barrios on the periphery of San Salvador that the military succeeded in forcing the FMLN to retreat from the capital.[75] Even then, the military largely passed up the opportunity to pursue the retreating rebel forces. Further damaging the High Command's credibility was the decision during the heat of the offensive to murder the six Jesuit priests. During the early hours of 16 November, soldiers from the U.S.-trained Atlacatl Battalion entered the Jesuits' residence on the campus of the Universidad Centroamericana (UCA), killing the six priests, their housekeeper, and her daughter. According to subsequent investigations of the incident, including the United Nations Truth Commission report, senior members of the *tandona* were present at the meeting on 15 November, when the decision was made to kill the priests.[76] As one officer put it, "with that fatal decision we had lost the war."[77]

The murder of the Jesuits provoked widespread outrage and further undermined the already damaged credibility of the armed forces. It also jeopardized future U.S. assistance to the Salvadoran armed forces, and thus their ability to defeat the FMLN. In October 1990, the Congress voted to withhold 50 percent of the $85 million in military assistance requested for FY 1991 and condition its release on progress in the Jesuit murder investigation and in the peace talks.[78] The November offensive served, then, to reinforce officers' resentment toward the *tandona*.

Going into the peace negotiations, the armed forces were far from united. Internal factionalism resulting from generational cleavages, disagreements over military strategy and the issue of negotiations, and the personal power ambitions of individual officers seriously undermined the cohesiveness of the officer corps. With the *tandona*'s rise to power, the accumulation of tensions reached a boiling point. Faced with growing domestic and international pressures, the *tandona* was left with few options but to accept a negotiated settlement.

THE PRICE OF U.S. ASSISTANCE

Adding to the armed forces' vulnerability to outside pressures was its dependence on U.S. military assistance. U.S. military assistance and training expanded dramatically after 1980 and was a major factor in the massive buildup and expansion of the Salvadoran armed forces (see tables 6.1 and 6.3), modernization of their arsenal, and dramatic improvement in their war-fighting capabilities. Military assistance also increased as a percentage of total aid to El Salvador (see table 6.4). For example, whereas direct military assistance accounted for 9.2 percent of total aid in 1980, it reached 48.9 percent in 1984, before declining to 21.8 percent in 1989. The massive increase in military assistance between 1983 and 1984 was in large part a response to the deteriorating situation on the battlefield and the recommendations of the January 1984 Kissinger Commission report.[79] Similarly, Economic Support Fund (ESF) aid, much of which was security related, increased from 14.1 percent of total aid in 1980 to 42.8 percent in 1983, finally reaching 52.1 percent in 1989. Although the massive increase in U.S. aid during the 1980s was adequate to prevent a guerrilla victory, it was not sufficient to assure total military victory. It also meant that, in the wake of the war, efforts to reduce the size of the military and its drain on the national budget would be difficult.

By the end of the 1980s the Salvadoran military was a much more sophisticated, complex institution than had been the case prior to 1979. The officer corps forged during the war years included officers with extensive battlefield experience and superior training. Nonetheless, modernization did not lead inevitably to "democratic professionalism." According to J. Samuel Fitch, democratic professionalism "accepts not only the political subordination of the armed forces to the democratically determined will of the nation, but also their professional subordination to constitutionally designated state authorities."[80] Although it is unclear what degree of importance U.S. officials attached to this goal, it is clear that progress was negligible. This was reflected in the military's continuing involvement in human rights abuses and in the pervasiveness of corruption within the institution.

Regarding the armed forces' human rights record during the 1980s,

TABLE 6.4
U.S. Military Assistance as a Percentage of Total U.S. Aid to El Salvador

	1980	1981	1982	1983	1984	1985	1986	1987	1988	1989
Development Aid	66.9	23.2	15.9	18.0	9.8	15.4	19.2	24.0	17.9	16.1
ESF Aid	14.1	28.7	38.0	42.8	28.4	49.9	40.5	50.3	48.4	52.1
Food Aid	9.7	25.5	19.0	14.3	12.9	9.1	12.4	5.8	13.5	9.9
Military Aid	9.2	22.7	27.1	24.9	48.9	25.6	27.8	19.9	20.2	21.8

Source: U.S. Foreign Affairs and National Defense Division, El Salvador, 1979–1989: A Briefing Book on US Aid and the Situation in El Salvador (Washington, D.C.: 28 April 1989).

much has been written.[81] For our purposes, what is important is examining the impact of U.S. assistance and training on changing the military's actual behavior. Although it is difficult to get exact figures on human rights abuses during the period of the conflict, most independent human rights organizations agree that after 1983 there was a dramatic reduction in abuses carried out by the army and security forces and by military-linked death squads. For example, whereas during the early 1980s targeted killings by the armed forces and death squads numbered in the thousands, in 1987 they were down to 96, only to increase to 152 the following year.[82] Moreover, the reduction in human rights abuses parallels the increase in direct U.S. military assistance, which jumped from $5.9 million in 1980 to $82 million in 1982, reaching a peak of $196.6 million in 1984. Military assistance would remain above $100 million through 1987 (table 6.1).

The relationship between U.S. military training and assistance and the Salvadoran armed forces' performance on human rights has been the subject of much debate. Claims by MILGROUP officials that U.S. training programs for Salvadoran officers made them more sensitive to human rights issues were echoed in the Kissinger Commission report, which argued on behalf of increased funds for training Salvadoran officers. Yet as Schwarz points out, this line of reasoning ignored the fact that "between 1965 and 1977 the United States had trained the majority of the Salvadoran officer corps and that it was precisely these officers who carried out the worst bloodletting in Central American history."[83] Moreover, the elite counterinsurgency battalions (BIRIs—Batallónes de Infantería de Reacción Inmediata), that were the pride of U.S. trainers, were some of the more brutal units of the Salvadoran military. For example, the Atlacatl Battalion was responsible for some of the worst massacres that took place during the war, including "massacring 700 peasants in El Mozote in 1981, killing dozens of villagers from Tenancingo and Copapayo in 1983, and slaughtering 68 in the hamlet of Los Llanitos and 50 at the Gualsinga River in 1984."[84] Finally, members of the Atlacatl Battalion were the ones who carried out the killing of the six Jesuit priests and their helpers in November 1989.[85]

A somewhat more plausible explanation is that the Reagan administration used military assistance as a blunt instrument to force a change in the Salvadoran military's human rights performance. Such a policy was necessitated by congressional restrictions on U.S. military aid to El Salvador. In December 1981, Congress passed a certification law that required the president to end military assistance unless he could report to Congress "that the Government of El Salvador is making a concerted and significant effort to comply with internationally recognized human rights" and "is achieving substantial control over all elements of its own armed forces, so as to bring to an end the indiscriminate torture and murder of Salvadoran citizens by these forces."[86] As Arson writes, although by "delegating to the president the authority to make the certification, Congress in essence guaranteed that it would be made," the certification law did force the administration to pay more attention to human rights: "It kept a low flame burning."[87] Thus, despite the fact that the administration succeeded in repeatedly certifying a good faith effort by the Salvadoran government, it did feel obligated to occasionally send U.S. officials to San Salvador on highly publicized visits during which they admonished the Salvadoran High Command about continuing abuses by individual officers and pressed the government to prosecute those responsible. While all of this made for good political theater, there were few concrete results. In some cases, immediately following these visits, officers responsible were arrested, later to be released and often returned to active duty (see below).

A related explanation is that the reduction in abuses by the Salvadoran military was more a reflection of political expediency than any genuine attitudinal change on the part of officers. In other words, given the certification law, the Salvadoran High Command had to do something about its principal public relations problem. Indeed, while the number of abuses declined significantly after 1983, the repression continued unabated, albeit at lower levels. The shift away from large-scale massacres toward more selective repression also reflected a shift in military strategy. As discussed above, Vides Casanova, who replaced García as minister of defense in April 1983, was much more receptive to MILGROUP's counterinsurgency approach, which stressed the need to win over "the hearts and minds" of the rural population. Huge massacres of unarmed civilians undermined such an approach. Finally, one must consider the supply dynamic. The early phase of intense repression effectively drove opposition leaders and activists underground, into the ranks of the FMLN, or into exile, and forced entire rural communities to flee to urban centers or across the border into Honduras. In short, the pool of potential targets for repression was dramatically reduced by 1983.

The High Command's unwillingness to punish those responsible for human rights abuses is further proof that U.S. assistance and training failed to produce a significant attitudinal change on the part of the Salvadoran officer corps. The case of the Las Hojas massacre is illustrative.[88] On 22 February 1983, members of the Batallón Jaguar from the Sixth Detachment in Sonsonate rounded up and murdered sixteen campesinos, several of whom were members of the Las Hojas cooperative. According to the official version, the campesinos were killed in a clash with the guerrillas. An investigation ordered by the minister of defense at the time, Gen. García, cleared of any wrongdoing the officer in charge of the operation, Cap. Carlos Alfonso Figueroa Morales, and his superiors, Maj. Oscar León Linares and Col. Elmer González Araujo. This was despite the fact that several eyewitnesses claimed that there had been no clash and that they had seen members of the Batallón Jaguar and the civil defense patrol dragging the victims from their homes shortly before being murdered.

After failure by the attorney general's office to indict those responsible, the U.S. embassy pressured successfully to reopen the case in July 1986. In January 1987, Cap. Figueroa Morales signed an affidavit detailing his involvement in the massacre along with Col. González Araujo, commander of the Sixth Detachment, and Maj. León Linares, commander of the Batallón Jaguar.[89] According to Figueroa Morales, on 21 February 1993 Col. González ordered him and León Linares to "eliminate a suspected guerrilla cell" but to make it appear like a clash. In spite of expressing his objection to what he considered an illegal order, Cap. Figueroa carried out the order the following morning. Upon completing the operation, Figueroa briefed Col. González, who responded, "Brutal, así era la babosada (Great, that's the way it should have been done)." Figueroa also stated that Col. Alvarado, in charge of investigating the incident, told him what he should say in his sworn declaration.

Despite the new evidence and pressure by the U.S. embassy, in March 1987 a lower court ruled that the charges against the officers be dropped. In August 1987, the appeals court overturned the lower court's decision, ruling that the case go to trial. Nevertheless, in July 1988, the Supreme Court ruled that since the October 1987 Amnesty Law applied to the Las Hojas case, the officers could not be prosecuted for their involvement in the massacre.

The officers' participation in the incident did not seem to seriously affect their career advancement. For example, Col. González, who also had been implicated in a major corruption scandal (see below), was transferred to the Ministry of Defense in November 1983, where he remained on active duty for several years. Maj. León Linares moved on to a number of key commands, including commander of the Atlacatl Battalion (June 1989–May 1990), commander of the Fourth Detachment (June 1990–December 1991), and commander of the Fourth Brigade (January 1992–April 1993).[90] Finally, Cap. Figueroa was transferred to *maestranza,* where he remained on active duty for several years.

The San Sebastian massacre in September 1988 was another case that U.S. officials considered a test of the Salvadoran military's resolve to punish officers responsible for human rights abuses.[91] On 20 September 1988, elements of the Fifth Brigade's Batallón Jiboa murdered ten suspected guerrilla collaborators in the community of San Sebastian, Department of San Vicente. As news filtered out about the tragedy, the High Command strongly denied reports that a massacre had taken place, claiming that the victims had died during a clash with the guerrillas. This was despite forensic reports that revealed that the peasants were shot at short range.

Not until Vice President Quayle's high-profile visit to San Salvador in February 1989 did the High Command begin to back away from its original denials.[92] During his visit with members of the High Command, Quayle warned that continued U.S. assistance was contingent upon improvements in the military's human rights performance. He also gave the High Command a list of three officers whom the U.S. embassy claimed were responsible for the San Sebastian massacre, demanding that they be brought to justice. Soon after Quayle's visit, the commander of the Fifth Brigade, Col. José Emilio Chávez Cáceres, who was on the list, was temporarily suspended. Arrest warrants were issued for nine persons, including three officers, two of whom were on Quayle's list. Nevertheless, as in the Las Hojas case, little progress was made in bringing those responsible to justice. Despite significant pressure from U.S. officials, Col. Chávez Cáceres, a member of the *tandona*, reassumed command of the Fifth Brigade, and charges against two of the three officers were dropped. Only Maj. Mauricio de Jesús Beltrán Granados, intelligence chief for the Fifth Brigade, and an enlisted man remained in custody awaiting trial.

For the handful of officers who favored punishing those responsible for human rights abuses, the obstacles were formidable. A unique opportunity presented itself in February 1989. Shortly after Quayle's visit to El Salvador, Defense Minister Vides Casanova asked Col. Benjamín Ramos, commander of the Second Brigade in Santa Ana, to head up a commission to investigate the worst cases of human rights abuses committed during the war.[93] Although Ramos was suspicious of Vides's motives for appointing him—at one point Vides told Ramos that "you can get us out of this situation"—he was provided with adequate support to conduct the investigations. Vides supplied him with an office and a team of lawyers and assistants, and access to original reports from earlier investigations. According to Ramos, the commission interviewed family members of the victims, eyewitnesses, soldiers, and commanding officers implicated in the abuses. After two months of investigation, Ramos presented the commission's findings, detailing the involvement of several senior officers in human rights abuses. Upon reviewing the report, Vides told Ramos that "we can't give this to the gringos." While

Ramos is unsure as to what Vides finally turned over to the U.S. embassy, it must have been sufficient to satisfy U.S. officials, who knew that Ramos was directing the commission but never contacted him during any stage of the investigation.[94]

United States' assistance and training also had little impact on stemming the widespread corruption within the officer corps. By way of example, one can look to the Salvadoran air force, where corruption was especially pervasive. As one former high-ranking officer in the Salvadoran air force put it: "Everything the Left said about the air force under Gen. Bustillo—the contraband, the car thefts, the drug running—all of it was true."[95] An August 1989 U.S. General Accounting Office (USGAO) report documented how during 1986–88 the air force transferred U.S. Military Assistance Program (MAP)–funded fuels to third parties without U.S. government consent.[96] These transfers included: (1) 61,107 gallons of MAP-funded fuels sold to the crews and pilots of the Contra supply operation, (2) an unknown quantity sold to private and commercial aircraft, and (3) 942,509 gallons sold to U.S. government aircraft. The air force received at least $1.6 million for these transfers. While the report claimed that the payments received were used for "the construction of facilities at Ilopango [air base] and other operational requirements," a subsequent USGAO report issued in September 1990 concluded that between June 1987 and September 1989, "Salvadoran officials spent over $1.1 million of fuel sales proceeds to purchase items, including an automobile, camera equipment, and a $300,000 building that MILGROUP officials believed may have been overvalued."[97]

Even more disturbing to U.S. officials was the Nordac case in 1983, in which two senior Salvadoran officers accepted almost $300,000 in bribes to intercede on behalf of a U.S.-based defense contractor.[98] The officers, Colonels Jorge Rivera and Elmer González Araujo, headed the armed forces' Purchasing Commission. In the summer of 1983, Nordac Manufacturing Corp. received a $4.8 million contract financed with U.S. aid money to provide the Salvadoran military eighteen million rounds of ammunition. However, instead of supplying American-made ammunition, as stipulated by federal law, Nordac purchased the ammunition from a Yugoslavian supplier, repackaging it to make it appear U.S.-made. Nordac also paid nearly $300,000 in bribes to Rivera and González to "grease the way for the ammunition fraud."[99] Furthermore, it turned out that much of the ammunition was defective. Soon after the first deliveries, troops in the field complained that the new bullets caused their M-16 automatic rifles to jam. Federal investigators later traced the ammunition to Nordac and its Yugoslavian supplier. What was particularly disquieting about the incident was that, as a result of their corrupt activities, senior Salvadoran officers had endangered the lives of troops in the field.

Despite the fact that Nordac's owners pleaded guilty in 1986 to paying bribes to González and Rivera, the Salvadoran High Command took no action against them. In fact, Col. Rivera stayed on as chief of finance at the Ministry of Defense and González, while leaving his position on the Purchasing Commission, assumed another post within the Ministry of Defense. Although during a visit to Washington in August 1986 Defense Minister Vides Casanova told U.S. officials that the case had been turned over to a civilian prosecutor for investigation, no arrests were ever made.[100] In fact, about the same time, Ministry of Defense spokesman Col. Mauricio Hernández referred to the charges against the officers as a "dirty maneuver in the United States."[101]

The reluctance of officers to punish those involved in human rights abuses and corruption was partly the result of the *tanda* system which, despite bitter complaints by U.S. officials, remained essentially intact throughout the 1980s. Under the *tanda* system

> each graduating class, or *tanda*, from the military academy moves up the ranks together, regardless of ability. Members of the same *tanda* establish deep bonds of loyalty and reciprocity toward each other—often serving as godfathers to one another's children—and help shield fellow members from prosecution or punishment. . . . officers are not held accountable for their actions, no matter how egregious they may be; human rights abuses therefore go unpunished, military incompetence is tolerated, and corruption runs rampant.[102]

Loyalty to one's *tanda* often took priority over loyalty to the institution. Not surprisingly, throughout the 1980s there were numerous examples of officers protecting their fellow *tanda* members implicated in human rights abuses or other crimes despite the potential damage to the credibility of the institution as a whole.

Decisions regarding promotions and key appointments also were based on *tanda* loyalties and ties of *compadrazgo* rather than on merit. Minister of Defense Vides Casanova's appointment of then-Colonel René Emilio Ponce as chief of staff is a case in point. Instead of filling key positions with more senior officers, Vides appointed members of the *tandona*, with whom he had developed a special relationship during the *tandona*'s days at the military academy.

The lack of progress in professionalizing the armed forces also was reflected in the absence of a clear chain of command within the military. Authority continued to be greatly decentralized among the brigade commanders, who acted as warlords in the departments under their control. An example of this flawed command structure was the difficulty in implementing a national basic training program, to be located at the facilities of CEMFA (Centro de Entrenamiento de la Fuerza Armada) in La Unión. Despite the fact that the minister of defense issued a general order to the effect, the plan was resisted by departmental brigade commanders.[103] By relinquishing their recruits to the national basic training center, brigade commanders would have lost access to an important source of corruption: funds allocated for recruits' salaries, food, and uniforms.[104]

In short, U.S. military assistance made little headway in professionalizing the Salvadoran armed forces, let alone fostering democratic professionalism. United States military aid may have contributed to a more efficient war-fighting machine, but it failed to overcome the chief obstacles to a more professional armed forces. As long as the *tanda* system remained intact, and officers involved in human rights abuses and corruption scandals went unpunished, no amount of U.S. assistance was enough to professionalize the Salvadoran officer corps.

Conclusion

The process of militarization that began even before the military's assumption of power in 1931 did not come to a halt after the 1979 coup. As this chapter demonstrates, throughout the 1980s the armed forces sought to expand its colonization of the state and of everyday life despite the formal transfer of power to civilian leaders. As armed opposition to the regime developed into a full-blown civil war, the military succeeded in preserving its control of key state institutions and its wide-ranging constitutional prerogatives, and expanding its paramilitary network in the countryside. A series of political pacts between the High Command and civilian leaders, as well as U.S. assistance and training, only served to reinforce this trend.

Nevertheless, although the military retained its ability to control key political decisions throughout the decade, its political power was not without limits. First of all, the military's network of control in the countryside was challenged by the FMLN and by other less visible forms of resistance. Moreover, as the war intensified the military became increasingly dependent on

U.S. assistance. The extreme level of dependency, combined with internal divisions within the officer corps, made the Salvadoran military exceedingly vulnerable to U.S. pressures. The price of U.S. assistance included the implementation of social and economic reforms, elections for civilian-led governments, improvements in the area of human rights, and, ultimately, a negotiated settlement to armed conflict.

Despite U.S. pressure, the Salvadoran military exhibited an extraordinary degree of institutional autonomy. For example, while the High Command occasionally sent officers into diplomatic exile to placate U.S. officials, at least until 1990, not a single Salvadoran officer was prosecuted for human rights violations. Moreover, whereas U.S. advisors complained that the *tanda* system was "the chief barrier to a competent officer corps,"[105] one's graduating class, not merit, remained the principal criterion for advancement within the armed forces. The military's enduring capacity to resist both external and domestic pressures would pose a formidable obstacle to demilitarization in the aftermath of the peace accords.

THE ARMED FORCES AFTER THE
PEACE ACCORDS

O N 16 JANUARY 1992, in the Chapultepec Castle in Mexico City, representatives of the government of El Salvador and the FMLN signed a
historic peace agreement, culminating almost two years of intensive negotiations mediated by the United Nations. The accords represented an important step toward a genuine process of democratization and national reconciliation. More specifically, they provided a unique opportunity for
subordinating the armed forces to civilian control, thereby dramatically re-
versing the military's traditional role in politics.

During the negotiations leading to the accords, the issue of the armed
forces was a major sticking point. Whereas the High Command insisted that
the structure of the armed forces was not subject to negotiation, the FMLN
demanded a major overhaul of the armed forces, including a sweeping
purge of the officer corps, the dismantling of the security forces, and the integration of the two armies. Between June and September 1990, the talks
bogged down over the issue of reforms to the military. The FMLN's position
hardened, especially regarding the issue of human rights abuses by military
officers. Whereas before the FMLN had demanded that officers involved in
the four most infamous cases of human rights violations be punished, now
the list was expanded to include almost all human rights abuses since 1980.[1]
Also, toward the end of the year the FMLN began talking about the dissolution of the two armies as opposed to their merger.

Despite the apparent deadlock, the U.S. Congress's decision in October
1990 to withhold 50 percent of $85 million in military assistance for FY
1991 may have contributed to the High Command's softening its position.
In late 1990 there were indications that the High Command was willing to
make concessions, and in January 1991 it agreed to several UN-sponsored

reforms, including an overall troop reduction, transfer of the police to the Ministry of Interior, and dismantling the civil defense patrols. However, it continued to oppose any sweeping purge of the officer corps or discussion about merging the two armies.

By February the High Command began to backtrack from its earlier concessions. It seems that the Bush administration's decision in mid-January to release the remaining $42.5 million in military assistance was interpreted as a vote of confidence by the High Command.[2] Although in April 1991 the two sides reached agreement on a package of constitutional reforms, including reforms limiting the scope and authority of the armed forces, negotiations over restructuring the armed forces remained deadlocked.

The impasse was broken in September during high-level negotiations in New York, in which President Cristiani and the FMLN General Command participated. The FMLN dropped its demand to merge the two armies, settling instead for the incorporation of FMLN combatants into a new civilian police force that would replace the security forces. The "New York Agreement" also provided for the creation of an ad hoc commission charged with "cleansing" the armed forces. The agreement provided a comprehensive framework that facilitated the rapid completion of negotiations on subsequent issues, culminating in a preliminary accord signed on 31 December 1991.

Although the accords were comprehensive in scope—covering electoral, judicial, and socioeconomic reforms in addition to military reforms—at first glance it appeared that the big loser was the Salvadoran military.[3] Under the terms of the accords and the constitutional reforms agreed to in April 1991, the role and doctrine of the armed forces was completely redefined.[4] The military's primary responsibility was to be national defense. Its role in public security was to be limited to situations of national emergencies and then only under strict executive control and after notification of the legislature. The armed forces doctrine was redefined to stress "the preeminence of human dignity and democratic values, respect for human rights," and subordination to the constitutional authorities.[5]

Besides ending the military's role in public security, the accords called for the dissolution of the security forces and the creation of a new civilian police force under executive control. Further, the military-controlled intelligence agency was to be dissolved and a new one set up under direct civilian control. The armed forces' educational system was to be revamped, incorporating into its training programs the new constitutional mission and doctrine. And a new academic council for the military academy, made up of civilians and military, would be charged with overseeing curriculum, admissions procedures, and faculty appointments.

The accords also called for "cleansing" the officer corps, based upon the recommendations of a special Ad Hoc Commission made up of three prominent Salvadorans and charged with evaluating the entire officer corps. The commission was to base its recommendations on officers' past records on human rights, professional competence, and ability to adapt to a democratic society.

Finally, the accords provided for the reduction and restructuring of the armed forces. The size of the armed forces was to be reduced to approximately thirty-one thousand over a two-year period; the specialized combat battalions (BIRIs), civil defense patrols, and *servicio territorial* were to be disbanded; and a new military service law and system of reserves was to be implemented.

Implementing the Peace Accords

Implementation of the reforms affecting the armed forces proved to be an uneven process at best. As Stepan has pointed out, reducing the military's prerogatives usually produces an increase in the level of conflict between the civilian government and the armed forces. For example, in Argentina, the Alfonsín government's decision to prosecute high-ranking officers implicated in past human rights abuses resulted in an intensification of conflict. Similarly, in Chile, the creation of a national commission to investigate past human rights abuses generated tension between the Alywin government and the armed forces under Pinochet. What is interesting in the Salvadoran case is that the initiative for reforms related to the military did not originate with the civilian government; rather, the reforms were a product of a process of negotiations whose objective was to bring an end to the armed conflict. Consequently, implementation of these reforms generated conflict, not between the military and the civilian government of Alfredo Cristiani, but between domestic opposition forces and international actors on the one hand, and the armed forces and the civilian government on the other hand.

Initial problems arose concerning the military's failure to dismantle the security forces. According to the established timetable, the National Guard and Treasury Police were to be dissolved by March 2, 1992, and their agents dismissed or incorporated into the army. Although the government announced the dissolution of the National Guard and Treasury Police as scheduled on March 2, in fact, they were simply renamed (the National Border Guard and Military Police, respectively) and incorporated, structurally intact, into the army. Moreover, the two security forces remained in their original barracks.

Not surprisingly, "the FMLN accused the army of slight-of-hand and announced that it would postpone the demobilization of the first group of combatants."[6] The High Command's position was that the accords only called for "the suppression of the security forces in their public security functions," not their organizational dissolution.[7] The military's interpretation notwithstanding, the UN Observer Mission in El Salvador (ONUSAL) considered the actions a violation of the accords and, with the help of UN special envoy Marrick Goulding, mediated talks that produced an agreement whereby the security forces would be definitively dissolved by June 28. On 24 June, the Legislative Assembly repealed the laws creating the two security forces.

The High Command's unwillingness to comply with the accords regarding the dissolution of the security forces was a result of several factors. First of all, the High Command looked at the security forces as a bargaining chip to force FMLN compliance with the accords. In the 12 June agreement providing for the definitive dissolution of the security forces, the FMLN agreed to concentrate all of its forces by 25 June and complete the first phase of demobilization on 30 June. Secondly, the High Command's resistance reflected its unwillingness to give up its extensive network of social control in the countryside, of which the security forces were an integral part. And finally, opposition from within the security forces themselves was significant. Both the National Guard and Treasury Police had a long history and strong corporate identity that distinguished them from the army. Unlike the army, which relied on conscripts, the security forces traditionally relied on volunteers who made a career out of their service. Consequently, it was not surprising that lower-level career officers in the security forces would put up some resistance as would agents unwilling to be treated like conscripts upon their incorporation into the army.

Although the National Guard and Treasury Police were finally dismantled, many of their former members continued to serve in public security roles. In fact, after the signing of the accords, the National Police reinforced its numbers by incorporating over one thousand ex-agents of the security forces (932 from the Treasury Police and 116 from the National Guard) and entire units from one of the demobilized BIRIs.[8] In addition, the new Special Brigade for Military Security, which is housed in the former barracks of the National Guard, consisted largely of former guardsmen and Treasury Police agents.[9] The Special Brigade's functions were limited to military policing and border security; however, as part of the "dissuasive" deployment of regular army along the country's highways in July 1993 (see below), troops from the Special Brigade were assigned to patrol the main highway between San Salvador and the airport.

The accords also provided for the gradual phasing out of the National Police and its replacement by a new National Civilian Police (PNC) during a two-year transition period. However, delays in the deployment of the PNC complicated efforts to dismantle the National Police as scheduled. The delays resulted from several factors. First and foremost was the High Command's unwillingness to provide a suitable location for the new National Public Security Academy (ANSP), which opened four months late. The academy was to train agents for the new police force. The most appropriate location for the ANSP was the site of the former Public Security Academy, which had trained officers for the security forces. However, instead of turning over the installations to the ANSP, the High Command decided in December 1991 to relocate the military academy there. Given that the military academy's enrollment was to return to pre-war levels (about one hundred per year), its need for a 114-acre facility was questionable. Another possible site for the ANSP, the base of the soon-to-be demobilized Atlacatl Battalion, was also retained by the armed forces.[10]

Initially, the ANSP was located at an old technical school for the National Police in Santa Tecla (CETIPOL). Although the installations did not belong to the Ministry of Defense, the military stripped it clean prior to handing it over. Since it was clearly too small to accommodate contingents of three hundred trainees, the government agreed to refurbish facilities of the former Bracamonte Battalion in Comalapa. Conditions were so poor that the government estimated some $4.5 million would be needed to complete improvements to the facilities.[11]

The delay in deploying the PNC was also related to resource constraints. The estimated start-up and operating costs for the PNC's first two years were $127.7 million. The government pledged to provide $62.2 million, with the remainder presumably coming from outside sources. However, international commitments only covered about 7 percent of projected expenses for 1993–1994.[12] The military contributed to the PNC's early resource problems by refusing to hand over equipment previously delivered to Salvadoran security forces under the U.S. administration's police aid program. For example, according to a December 1992 GAO report, "of 1,000 9mm Beretta pistols purchased by the US, only 124 were in the hands of the National Police. The balance were being used by Army personnel or stored in a military warehouse."[13]

The delay in dismantling the National Police had serious human rights implications. ONUSAL human rights reports issued after the peace accords were signed indicated that the National Police continued to engage in systematic human rights abuses, including arbitrary detentions, torture, and executions. Although no longer part of the armed forces' command structure, active-duty military officers continued to direct the National Police, albeit under the Ministry of Interior's supervision. Given the composition and training of its agents and commanding officers, the National Police remained a "militarized" security force still engaged in public security functions.

Implementation of the accords became bogged down in October 1992 as a result of the High Command's resistance to the Ad Hoc Commission's recommendations. Because of the severity of human rights abuses during the conflict and the government's inability or unwillingness to punish those responsible, the accords had provided for the establishment of two commissions to address the issue of impunity.

The Ad Hoc Commission was to be installed on 16 May and given three months to conduct its evaluations and make its recommendations known to the UN secretary general and to President Cristiani. The commission was authorized to use information from any source it considered credible. Although it was required to interview officers before recommending administrative action against them, no review or appeals process was provided for under the accords. Moreover, the commission was not required to justify its decisions.[14]

The commission began work on 19 May.[15] In addition to evaluating information provided by both Salvadoran and international human rights organizations, the commission traveled to the United States to meet with officials of the State Department and Defense, and with congressional sources and human rights organizations. Given the enormity of the task—in effect, the commission was given three months to evaluate approximately 2,300 officers—the commission only interviewed some 230 officials, including all of the active-duty generals, colonels, and lieutenant colonels, and a handful of lower-ranking officers implicated in abuses. The commission asked for and was granted an extension until 23 September to present its recommendations. According to a new timetable, President Cristiani was to make the necessary administrative decisions by 23 October and to implement these by 22 November.

On 23 September, the commission presented its recommendations to UN Secretary General Boutros Boutros-Ghali and President Cristiani in New York. The commission's report, the contents of which were kept confidential, called for the removal of 102 officers, including the minister and vice minister of defense, most of the generals, and many of the colonels.[16] Fierce resistance on the part of the High Command prompted Cristiani to announce in late October that he was postponing action on the commission's recommendations until after the FMLN had demobilized completely.[17] Mediation efforts by UN envoys Marrick Goulding and Alvaro de Soto resulted in an agreement whereby the commission's recommendations were to be "incorporated into the year-end 'general orders' of the armed forces promotions and retirements to be announced on 30 November and December 31," scheduled to take effect by 6 January 1993.[18] Nevertheless, on January 7, 1993, Boutros Boutros-Ghali informed the UN Security Council that President Cristiani had failed to comply with the commission's recommendations regarding fifteen officers, including the minister and vice minister of defense.[19] Cristiani subsequently announced that he would defer action on eight of the officers until the end of his presidential term.[20]

The logjam was broken in March 1993 with the release of the long-awaited United Nations Truth Commission report.[21] Just days before the report became public, Minister of Defense Gen. René Emilio Ponce offered up his resignation, followed soon after by Vice Minister of Defense Gen. Juan Orlando Zepeda, who announced that he was retiring from the armed forces.[22] Unlike the earlier Ad Hoc Commission's report, never made public, the Truth Commission's findings unmasked for all to see the sheer brutality with which the Salvadoran armed forces conducted themselves during the course of the civil war. It described, in great detail, the involvement of over forty military officers in some of the most heinous human rights abuses committed during the conflict, including Ponce and Zepeda's role in planning the murders of the six Jesuit priests in November 1989. The report recommended that those officers named in the report that were still on active duty be dismissed from the armed forces and that those no longer on active duty be barred from public or political office for ten years.[23]

Pressure by the United Nations and the Clinton administration, which conditioned $11 million in military assistance on full compliance with the Ad Hoc Commission's recommendations, combined with the fallout from the Truth Commission's report, prompted President Cristiani to inform the UN secretary general in late March of his decision to remove the remaining officers by the end of June 1993. Although the minister and vice minister of defense, along with the rest of the High Command, stepped down on 30 June, the officers remained on "availability status" and were not slated for retirement until the end of 1993.[24] Moreover, several of these officers received special cash bonuses and other financial perks as an incentive to step down. On the other hand, those "good" officers who survived the purge faced less pay and benefits, and a smaller force and budget. One senior officer who was not purged but instead sent into early retirement by the *tandona* reflected on his predicament: "El único jodido aquí fui yo! Yo no recibí nada más que mi pensión" (The only fool around here was me! I didn't receive anything except for my pension).[25] The special incentives may have helped to break the logjam but they clearly went against the spirit if not the letter of the Ad Hoc Commission's recommendations.

Resistance within the military to the Ad Hoc Commission's recommendations was to be expected. As Zagorski has argued, "the more fundamental the interest, the greater likelihood of the high command's involvement in, or tolerance of, potentially risky or costly means of resistance."[26] Of most concern to the High Command was preserving the military's autonomy in the face of attempts to enhance civilian oversight. Ceding control over internal discipline, promotions, and assignments to civilians threatened to undermine a core interest of the military. Had the Ad Hoc Commission's report affected only members of the *tandona,* there would have been much less resistance. The general sentiment within the officer corps was that the *tandona* had overstayed its welcome, and it was time for a new generation of officers to assume the leadership of the armed forces. Nevertheless, the purge went well beyond the *tandona,* affecting officers from several other *tandas* who had been denied opportunities for exercising leadership. Furthermore, the *tandona* used the general orders at the end of 1993 to conduct its own purge, removing officers it considered as potential rivals, regardless of whether or not they were on the commission's list. By enlarging the scope of the purge, the *tandona* was able to convert it into a direct attack on the military institution.

The work of the Ad Hoc Commission confirmed officers' worst fears concerning civilian "meddling." Several officers interviewed, including junior officers, complained that those called before the commission were never given a chance to defend themselves. They also saw the commission as politically driven, bent on destroying the military's credibility. In short, the purge process reinforced officers' traditional resistance to civilian oversight.

In a recent study of military autonomy during democratic transitions in South America, Pion-Berlin distinguishes between institutional and political autonomy.[27] To illustrate he outlines twelve defense-related issue areas and locates them along a "professional-political continuum." For example, whereas human rights, internal security, and intelligence gathering are considered issues of largely political content, junior-level personnel decisions, force levels, military doctrine and education, and military reform are primarily professional matters. Falling in a "gray area" somewhere in between are arms production/procurement, military budget, defense organization, and senior-level personnel decisions. After surveying the evidence from recent South American transitions, Pion-Berlin argues that the armed forces are more likely to resist—and to have more success resisting—threats to their institutional autonomy rather than to their political autonomy. Nevertheless, he did find that exceptions do occur largely because of a "perceptual gap" between military and civilians regarding these issue areas.

Pion-Berlin's analytical framework may shed some light on the issue of autonomy in the Salvadoran case. The accords were quite novel in that they addressed issues across the "professional-political continuum." Nevertheless, the High Command's resistance to various reforms did not make sense according to Pion-Berlin's categorization of the different issue areas. As is demonstrated in the discussion that follows, the High Command was just as likely to resist threats to "core" professional issues as to "peripheral" political matters. It may be that Pion-Berlin's analytical construct is not entirely appropriate to the Salvadoran case, given the unique history of the armed forces. Historically, internal security and intelligence gathering were essential components in the armed forces' network of social control and could hardly be considered a "peripheral" interest of the Salvadoran military. Likewise, given its involvement in massive human rights abuses during the armed conflict, it was highly unlikely that the military would view it as an issue for civilians to decide. On the contrary, the work of the Ad Hoc and Truth Commissions had important institutional implications, especially as it affected internal personnel decisions. Consequently, while it may be possible to group the twelve issue areas into core and secondary interests, it may not be feasible to make such a clear distinction between institutional and political dimensions of military autonomy.

Other aspects of the reforms affecting the military encountered somewhat less resistance on the part of the High Command. As mentioned above, those reforms constituting a challenge to the military's core interests elicited the fiercest opposition. To most civilian politicians the creation of a new academic council for the military academy did not represent a direct challenge to the professional autonomy of the armed forces. However, top officers apparently considered control of the military academy to be a core interest. One high-ranking officer stated in an interview that, of all the conditions stipulated in the peace accords, the most unpalatable was that of creating an academic council for the military academy, which he viewed as "blatant meddling" by civilians in military affairs. Arguing that civilian participation in the council was "politically interested" and might make cadets more open to "leftist ideas," he insisted that "military officers don't serve on the academic councils of civilian universities."[28]

Despite getting off to a late start[29] and the initial resistance of several high-ranking officers, the academic council gradually gained wider acceptance within the military. Civilian and military members interviewed by the authors expressed satisfaction with the council's early progress.[30] Joaquín

Samayoa, vice rector of the Jesuit University and one of the civilian members of the council, was impressed by the harmonious working relationship with military members of the council. According to him, because the council aroused the interest of other Latin American militaries and governments, the High Command came to view the council as a way of improving the armed forces' image both at home and abroad.[31]

The High Command's growing acceptance of the council also reflected the "nonthreatening" composition of the council. Except for Samayoa, who is identified with the political Left, the other civilian members of the council were not viewed as hostile to the military's interests. Dr. David Escobar Galindo was a member of the government's negotiating team during the peace negotiations with the FMLN. Dr. José Luís Castelar is the son of a military officer and María Angélica Díaz served as minister of education during the Romero government and previously taught in the military academy. Nevertheless, despite the fact that some officers came to hold a positive view of the council, they continued to oppose the extension of civilian oversight to subsequent training courses.[32]

Reforms aimed at significantly reducing the military's control of the civilian population particularly in rural areas also encountered some resistance. Most Latin American militaries consider this a core interest only "when instability is seen as a serious threat to the state or the military itself."[33] As we have argued, however, the Salvadoran armed forces' role in establishing and administering the system of social control in the countryside has a long history behind it and was considered of vital interest as a preventive measure even when instability did not loom large on the horizon. The paramilitary network of control predated the 1932 uprising and was linked to the development and expansion of the agro-export model. The 1932 uprising gave a new sense of urgency to the tasks of social control. Control of the rural population also became increasingly important as the official military parties could mobilize this population for electoral purposes. Consequently, even though the peace accords brought an end to the armed conflict, these historical considerations in addition to the military's profound distrust of the FMLN complicated efforts to extricate the armed forces from their role in controlling the civilian population.

In addition to dismantling the security forces, the demobilization of the civil defense patrols, the dismantling of the *servicio territorial,* and the implementation of a new system of reserves were crucial to ending the military's control over the civilian population. The disarming and disbanding of the civil defense patrols was completed as scheduled by 30 June 1992; however, there were fears that members of the units would continue to serve as part of the armed forces' extensive paramilitary network, gathering intelligence and intimidating the civilian population. In a poor neighborhood of San Salvador, residents complained to one of the authors that ex-members of the civil defense patrol continued to force them to pay "protection money" even though the patrols supposedly had been dismantled. Residents were not at all convinced that members of the patrols would give up their traditional functions. Likewise, the Truth Commission report expressed concern over the demobilization and disarmament of the civil defense units, "in particular over the fact that hundreds of ex-members of the civil defense remain armed in the countryside."[34]

The *servicio territorial* was to be replaced by a new system of reserves by 31 May 1992. However, the new law for military service and reserves was not approved until 30 July. Also, the dismantling of the *servicio territorial* was pushed back until the end of November. Under the new system of military reserves all those completing their military service are required to serve as active reservists for the next seven years.[35] To administer the new system, the law provides for the establishment of fourteen departmental recruiting and reserve centers and thirty subsidiary offices located throughout the country. During 1993, the army opened fourteen departmental centers but only three subsidiary offices, citing a lack of resources.[36]

The intelligence apparatus of the armed forces, the National Intelligence Directorate (DNI), had worked in tandem with the security forces during the armed conflict. Under the terms of the accords, the government was to name a director for the new State Intelligence Organ (Órgano de Inteligencia de Estado—OIE) by 17 March 1992, who would oversee the dissolution of the DNI scheduled for 15 June. The OIE would be responsible for evaluating former DNI personnel interested in working in the new intelligence agency. In fact, the government did not appoint a director for the OIE until 12 June, even though it announced the dissolution of the DNI only three days later. Moreover, there was significant opposition to Cristiani's choice, Mauricio Sandoval, who had served as director of the Secretariado Nacional de Comunicaciones (SENCO). Under Sandoval's leadership, SENCO was responsible for several controversial publicity campaigns in support of the ARENA government. The FMLN and other opposition groups feared that the new intelligence agency would be driven by partisan political interests.[37]

Regarding the DNI's personnel, some were incorporated into the intelligence section of the Estado Mayor (C-2), but the bulk were absorbed by the OIE. What is unclear is whether or not the OIE conducted an exhaustive evaluation before admitting former DNI personnel and, if so, what were the criteria used. In its reports on the implementation of the accords, ONUSAL did not elaborate on these points. Finally, it appears that none of the files held by the DNI were handed over to the new intelligence agency. The military's refusal to turn over these files raised doubts about its sincerity in removing itself from intelligence functions.

Disbanding the five specialized combat battalions (BIRIs) also proved to be problematic. The accords called for the demobilization to begin in July 1992 and finish in December 1992. In October, after having demobilized the first two BIRIs (the "Ramón Belloso" and the Bracamonte), the High Command announced that it would not disband the Atlacatl as scheduled (by 19 October), arguing that the military would not allow itself to be weakened as long as the FMLN refused to fully demobilize its forces.[38] Under a revised timetable, the FMLN was to demobilize all of its forces by October 31. However, the failure of the two sides to resolve satisfactorily the land issue led to the FMLN's refusal to fully demobilize by the end of October.

A November agreement mediated by the UN provided for a new calendar whereby the Atlacatl was disbanded on December 8 and the last BIRI on February 6, 1993. Although the demobilization was considered a success by ONUSAL officials, as mentioned above, ex-members of the BIRIs and in one case entire units from the "Belloso" Battalion joined the ranks of the National Police.[39] Finally, in some cases units were integrated intact into the army instead of in an individual manner as called for by the accords.

Unlike the National Guard and Treasury Police, or even the *servicio territorial*, the BIRIs were a product of the armed conflict. While their existence may have been considered a core interest of the military during the war, this was no longer the case once the FMLN's demobilization was complete. Historically, during periods of relative stability the security forces and the *servicio territorial* were sufficient to maintain control over the rural population. Hence, the importance of the BIRIs had diminished significantly.

Although the High Command was willing to countenance some restructuring including the demobilization of some units, a drastic reduction of the army's overall troop strength was entirely out of the question. In fact, the reduction carried out under the terms of the peace accords was not nearly as dramatic as it appeared on the surface. At the time the accords were signed, the High Command claimed a total of 63,175 troops, including regular army and security forces. The military agreed to a 50.2 percent reduction, or to just over thirty-one thousand troops by January 1994. Given that the security forces, totaling some fifteen thousand, were to be separated from the armed forces under the accords, this left forty-eight thousand troops according to the High Command's figures. Nevertheless, most analysts agree that the armed forces (not including the security forces) numbered at most forty to forty-two thousand (and possibly less) in early 1992 (see table 7.1). Also important is that a significant number of conscripts were scheduled to complete their military service during the course of 1992 and then be incorporated into the military's reserve system. The fact that the military completed its reduction by March 1993, almost a year ahead of schedule, suggests that the number of soldiers demobilized was much less than claimed by the High Command. This seems to be confirmed by the scope of the technical programs for *desmovilizados* initiated in early 1993, which were only designed to service some eight thousand soldiers and ex-members of the security forces.[40]

Although the implementation of the accords concerning the armed forces was not without problems, significant progress was made in circumscribing the military's institutional prerogatives. The Ad Hoc and Truth Commissions' reports marked the first time in Latin American history that a military had submitted to an external review of its officer corps. While it may have been a bitter pill to swallow, it represented an important step forward in enhancing civilian control of the military.

LIMITATIONS OF THE ACCORDS

On paper, the accords offered an impressive blueprint for transforming civil-military relations. Nevertheless, they failed to address adequately several important dimensions of the military's political power. These include: (1) the military's position within the state; (2) the military's network of social control in rural areas; and (3) the military's institutional and political autonomy.

The accords did not mention the military's administration of key state institutions. Military officers (both active-duty and retired) traditionally directed an array of state institutions, including the National Telecommunications Administration (ANTEL), the National Administration of Water and Aqueducts (ANDA), the Port Authority (CEPA), the General Directorate of

Table 7.1
Estimated Troop Strength of the Salvadoran Armed Forces

Year	Army	Navy	Air Force	Total	Security Forces
1991	40,000	1,200	2,400	43,600	12,000
1992	40,000	1,300	2,400	43,700	6,000
1993	28,000	500	2,000	30,500	—
1994	28,000	700	2,000	30,500	—

Source: International Institute for Strategic Studies, *The Military Balance, 1978–1994* (London: 1994).

Land and Transport, the General Directorate of Statistics and Census, Customs, Civil Aeronautics, and the Postal Service.

During the armed conflict, the military could justify its control of key public institutions as essential to ensuring the state's survival. However, even in the wake of the accords, the military showed little willingness to hand over control to civilians. On the contrary, the Cristiani government continued the policy of appointing officers to head up state institutions. For example, soon after stepping down as minister of defense, Gen. Ponce was named to the board of directors of ANTEL.

It is important to remember that the military's control of these entities predates the conflict. The appointment of officers to head up state institutions was part of a patronage system designed to "reward" officers removed from key leadership positions within the armed forces. In some instances this was a convenient way by which military presidents dealt with potential rivals, at other times it was a way of rewarding loyal officers slated for retirement. Control of such entities as ANTEL and CEPA provided an important source of additional income for "deserving" officers, where bribes and kickbacks were the norm.[41] ANTEL was an especially prized commodity, given its role in wiretapping telephone conversations of political opposition figures.[42]

Although the accords provided for the dismantling of the security forces and the civil defense patrols, and the replacement of the *servicio territorial* with a new system of reserves, they did not go far enough in this endeavor. For example, the new military service law allowed the army to establish recruiting centers throughout the country and to maintain a large reserve system as it had in the past, thereby guaranteeing it a significant presence in the countryside, including those areas that were previously under the FMLN's control. Also, the accords failed to mention, let alone regulate, the armed forces' civic action activities.

As discussed in earlier chapters, the armed forces initiated a civic action program (ACM) in 1963. The scope and activities of ACM increased over time, particularly during the 1980s as part of the military's counterinsurgency program. In the wake of the peace accords, the High Command sought to preserve the military's traditional role in national development, stepping up its civic action activities. In addition to activities geared toward infrastructure repair, public health, and literacy, the ACM entered new areas like conservation and reforestation. According to the military's own figures, whereas during the period June 1991 through May 1992 the ACM carried out 258 activities benefitting more than one hundred thousand persons, during the following year it conducted 341 activities benefitting almost four hundred thousand inhabitants.[43]

In the aftermath of the peace accords the armed forces also came to play a role in the implementation of the Plan for National Reconstruction (PRN). Local military commanders continued to participate in *cabildos abiertos* (open town meetings) where municipal reconstruction projects were discussed, and local garrisons routinely participated in the public works projects sponsored by the PRN. According to the vice minister of defense, Col. Roberto Tejada Murcia, involvement in national reconstruction was a legitimate role for the military. Tejada stated in an interview that the purpose of ACM and related activities was to "contribute to the national objectives, support the government and the country's well-being."[44] This included a campaign in support of the PRN and the armed forces "integration" in the PRN through the Secretariat of National Reconstruction (SRN).[45] The military would carry out "parallel projects," such as the construction of schools and health clinics, in areas "beyond the government's reach."

The High Command's desire to preserve a role for the military in national development was a response in part to its lack of mission and fear of becoming irrelevant. Given the costs of reconstructing the country after twelve years of war, the military faced an uncertain future. Not surprisingly, the High Command eagerly sought out new tasks for the army, and particularly ones that might repair its damaged credibility. Interviews with senior officers revealed a strong emphasis on maintaining the military's involvement in national development. However, this view contradicted the armed forces' newly redefined mission under the terms of the peace accords. The accords made a clear distinction between the concepts of defense and security, stating that while national defense is the responsibility of the armed forces, security is a broader concept that, in addition to defense, includes "economic, political and social aspects which go beyond the sphere of competence of the armed forces and are the responsibility of other sectors of society and the State."[46]

The U.S. administration appeared to support the Salvadoran armed forces' involvement in national development as a legitimate role in the wake of the peace accords. According to a report on the implementation of the national reconstruction plan, "civic action activities were a part of the package presented to U.S. officials in discussion on the U.S.$40 million in U.S. military aid in FY1992."[47] Although in 1993 the United States denied a request for trucks to be used in reconstruction activities, the U.S. Army Corps of Engineers continued to collaborate with the Salvadoran army in the construction of schools and health centers. In April 1993, Gen. George Joulwan, commander of the U.S. Southern Command (USSOUTHCOM), explained to the Senate Armed Services Committee SOUTHCOM's plans to conduct joint engineering and training exercises with the Salvadoran armed forces. The Fuertes Caminos operation was to last from August through December 1993, starting back up again in May 1994. During the first phase, some four hundred U.S. troops were to participate. The plan was to build twelve schools, seven wells, and two community centers in sites worked out in consultation with the SRN.[48] According to Joulwan, the purpose of the operation "will be involvement by the ESAF and public works personnel in a joint and combined exercise to rebuild after the neglect brought about by a decade of war. The intended outcome of this effort is to strengthen democratic institutions in El Salvador" and to "reinforce the appropriate role of the military in a democratic political system."[49]

The U.S. administration's support for a developmental role for the Salvadoran armed forces appeared to go against congressional restrictions on U.S. military assistance to El Salvador, which required that such assistance be used "only in strict accordance with the newly defined mission of the Salvadoran Armed Forces as embodied within the Salvadoran Peace Accords."[50] Whether or not the Salvadoran military's continued participation in national development was a quid pro quo on its acceptance of the peace accords, as suggested by some analysts, is unclear.[51] Just as likely is that U.S. officials viewed civic action and reconstruction as logical activities for an army of thirty thousand no longer at war. Such a view ignored the history of civic action in El Salvador, an activity that has been anything but politically neutral.

Intelligence gathering is another traditional component of the armed forces' system of social control. Although the accords provided for the dissolution of the DNI and the establishment of a new intelligence organism under civilian purview, they did not remove the military entirely from the business of intelligence. For example, the Estado Mayor's intelligence wing (C-2) was not affected by the accords. On the contrary, it absorbed some personnel from the former DNI and in fact may have grown as a result. Furthermore, while most armed forces justify the development of an intelligence-gathering capacity based on the need to assess external security threats, in the Salvadoran context, intelligence activities have been almost exclusively focused on threats to internal security. This latter view of intelligence gathering persisted even after the accords. In an interview with one of the authors, the defense minister, Col. Corado, explained that the C-2's activities went beyond detecting external threats.[52] This was confirmed in the UN secretary general's report to the Security Council on 29 October 1993, in which he expressed preoccupation over "the fact that the military intelligence services continue to involve themselves in questions related to internal security."[53]

The accords also ignored the Escuela Nacional de Inteligencia (ENI).

Established in 1987 as part of a U.S. initiative, the ENI was designed to centralize the training of those involved in intelligence gathering. According to one of its former directors, it was modeled after similar intelligence schools in South Korea and the Philippines.[54] Instead of bringing the ENI under direct civilian control as in the case of the new intelligence agency (OIE), the ENI remained under the Ministry of Defense. According to an officer currently advising at the ENI, the school plans to train both civilians and military personnel for the OIE and for military intelligence.[55] In other words, the armed forces' control of the ENI ensured them a continuing role in intelligence and seriously jeopardized civilian administration of the OIE.

Although the accords went a long way in reducing the military's institutional prerogatives, they did not adequately address the issue of autonomy. The military's continued ability to maintain a high degree of decision-making autonomy presented a significant obstacle to establishing civilian supremacy. Senior officers' resistance to attempts at reducing the military's autonomy is rooted in a particular concept of national security that goes beyond defense. As formulated during the 1960s, the "national security doctrine" broadened the concept to focus on internal as well as external security threats and include national development as an essential component of national security. Such an expanded view of national security resulted in the armed forces assuming new responsibilities in addition to its traditional roles. As Rouquié states, the national security doctrine, "by enlarging the spectrum of threats and locating them within the nation itself, gave a corporate basis for the army's intervention in politics."[56]

In the Salvadoran context, this concept of national security was based on two assumptions: (1) that national security was the exclusive responsibility of the armed forces, and (2) that civilians had no legitimate role to play in formulating national security policy or in decisions affecting the military. These assumptions were rooted in a deep-seated contempt for civilian politicians and the perception that the military was the only institution capable of guaranteeing order and stability.

As the military consolidated its political power, it began to develop a separate set of political and institutional interests that did not always coincide with those of the coffee oligarchy. In other words, members of the military were not simply the "watchdogs of the oligarchy." During the course of the 1980s, the military became much less dependent upon the oligarchy and much more autonomous as an institution with its own set of interests. During the peace negotiations, officers felt betrayed by the oligarchy, sensing that the armed forces had been singled out as a scapegoat after having defended the system from "communist aggression." As the negotiations proceeded, that sector of the oligarchy convinced of the need for a negotiated settlement came to view the military as a bargaining chip that could be used, if not sacrificed, in exchange for concessions on socioeconomic issues. Thus the marriage of convenience was severely tested during the peace negotiations. By the time the peace accords were signed, the military was much more concerned with protecting its core interests than with defending the oligarchy at all costs.

Prior to the implementation of the peace accords, the complete lack of legislative oversight of the defense budget and internal promotions enabled the armed forces to maintain a high degree of autonomy. The peace accords alluded to the need to enhance legislative oversight; however, they did not provide any specifics regarding how this might be accomplished. Not surprisingly, little progress was made in this direction after the signing of the accords.

As before, the military continued to be the only state institution not held accountable for its expenditures. Legislators, even those serving on the defense committee, did not have access to the details of the military budget. They were provided with a general outline of the budget, including the categories of expenditures. Without a detailed breakdown of these expenditures, serious discussion and debate were impossible. In fact, prior to 1992, the minister of defense was not even required to appear before the legislature to discuss the budget. This changed in October 1992, when legislators succeeded in "forcing" Defense Minister Gen. Ponce to present the 1993 budget to the legislature. Nevertheless, it proved to be a pyrrhic victory, given that legislators lacked the information to ask anything but perfunctory questions.[57]

Also not addressed by the peace accords was the issue of internal promotions. This enabled the military to continue its practice of setting the boundaries for the promotion process. An example was the total lack of legislative input when the promotion law was reformed in April 1993. Likewise, the executive was constrained as in the past in influencing promotion decisions. This was evident in the summer of 1993 when a new High Command took over. President Cristiani did not have a free hand in making the appointments; rather, he was constrained by factional politics within the military (see below). Thus, while Cristiani had some influence over key appointments, his range of choices was sharply circumscribed by the incumbent High Command.[58]

The accords provided for the possibility of appointing a civilian as minister of defense, without making it obligatory. This was a serious omission given that appointing a civilian as defense minister is a key element in ensuring civilian supremacy. In the wake of the accords, senior officers showed little willingness to accept a civilian defense minister. Deputy Chief of Staff

Gen. Mauricio Vargas considered such a possibility "difficult," on the grounds that civilians lack the expertise and "political education" needed for that post.[59] He added that any civilian defense minister "would have to be respectful of the military institution." Another senior officer, Col. José Humberto Corado (later appointed minister of defense), argued that the public itself would oppose such a move since "a civilian would project an image of lack of solidarity" with the military institution, thereby "weakening the armed forces."[60]

Finally, although the accords called for the establishment of an academic council for the military academy, they did not provide for civilian oversight of subsequent military education and training. Given that most senior officers accepted the academic council only reluctantly, there was little likelihood that they would willingly invite civilian oversight of subsequent training courses. The chief of staff, Col. Jaime Gúzman, pointed out in an interview that civilians already participate in military education, a good part of the instructors being civilians. Moreover, in the case of the Universidad Militar, civilian instructors also serve on the university's academic council.[61] However, whereas in the case of the academic council for the military academy members were to be selected "on the basis of criteria of political pluralism," this is not the case for civilian instructors in other areas of military education. They are selected based on their political conservatism and support for the armed forces. Not surprisingly, these handpicked civilian instructors are not an effective instrument for civilian oversight.

In short, although the accords laid the groundwork for a significant reduction of the military's prerogatives, they did not go far enough in ensuring civilian supremacy over the armed forces. The military's realm of political action was greatly circumscribed, but it retained much of its autonomy intact.

MIXED SIGNALS

On the eve of the March 1994 elections, significant progress had been made in implementing the peace accords affecting the armed forces. However, as demonstrated above, by failing to address important aspects of the military's traditional domination of the political sphere, the accords had not succeeded in firmly establishing the armed forces' subordination to civilian authorities. During the year leading up to the elections, prospects for democratizing civil-military relations were mixed.

There were some encouraging developments. First of all, the new High Command led by Minister of Defense Col. José Humberto Corado Figueroa demonstrated a greater willingness to engage civilians in a dialogue concerning the future role of the armed forces. For example, in July 1993 the Universidad Salvadoreña (USAL) sponsored a seminar on civil-military relations. Approximately fifty officers and as many civilians attended, including the commander of CODEM (Comando de Doctrina y Educación Militar). The panel included two U.S. experts on the Salvadoran military, a sociology professor from the USAL, and a retired colonel. Despite the hostile reaction by some of the officers to the U.S. scholars' critical assessment of the state of civil-military relations, the following week they were invited to give the same presentation to a group of officers at the Special Brigade for Military Security.

On 7 October 1993, the minister of defense was the keynote speaker at a conference on civil-military relations organized by the Centro de Investigaciones Tecnológicas (CENITEC), a civilian-run research institute in San Salvador. Over 100 officers and some 250 civilians, including leaders from the FMLN, attended the morning session where, in addition to Corado, a representative of ONUSAL, the former defense minister of Guatemala, Gen. Héctor Gramajo, and one of the authors addressed the audience. During the afternoon session, all of the principal presidential candidates, except for Armando Calderón Sol, discussed the future role of the armed forces. Especially interesting was Rubén Zamora's presentation, in which he called on the officers present to bury the ax and to join him and other political leaders in forging new civil-military relations based on consensus and mutual respect. The event was historic in that it represented the first time that civilian politicians addressed a previously taboo subject.

Another important development was the creation of the School of High Strategic Studies in 1993. Administered by CODEM, in September 1993 the school launched a six-month course on strategic studies including eight military officers (all lieutenant colonels) and twenty-three civilians drawn from government ministries, private sector organizations, political parties (including the FMLN), and universities. The U.S. Military Group (MILGROUP) played a key role in getting the project off the ground, assigning a U.S. advisor to work full-time with CODEM. From MILGROUP's perspective, given the lack of civilian expertise on military matters, the course would fill an important gap. Nevertheless, because of the haphazard manner in which the course was organized and the lack of sufficient resources, U.S. officials had no illusions about its potential impact. At a minimum, though, they viewed it as a unique opportunity for civilians and military to engage in dialogue on issues of national interest.

Also encouraging were the severe resource constraints facing the military. Although the High Command was successful in protecting the defense budget from drastic cuts in the wake of the peace accords, U.S. military assistance was reduced dramatically (see tables 7.2 and 7.3).[62] In 1990, U.S. assistance stood at $81 million, but was down to $12.4 million for 1993.[63] As a result of the strain on resources, maintaining political influence in the countryside became much more problematic for the military. Prior to 1979, the military was able to exercise control over the rural population with relatively minimal resources; however, in the late 1970s this system of social control began to fall apart. Moreover, in the wake of the peace accords, the opening up of political space resulted in the emergence of new social and political forces determined to challenge the military's traditional domination of the countryside.[64]

Not so encouraging was the process by which the new defense minister was selected. President Cristiani did not have a free hand in the matter. Besides the fact that the military was unwilling to accept a civilian, Cristiani had to be sensitive to military hierarchy and internal military politics. Al-

Table 7.2

Budgetary Outlays for Regular Army and Security Forces (in thousand colones)

Year	Regular Army	Security Forces
1990	974,872 (81.1%)	227,181 (18.9%)
1991	888,615 (78.2%)	247,005 (21.8%)
1992	926,172 (80.0%)	231,101 (20.0%)
1993	866,483 (77.2%)	255,960 (22.8%)
1994	866,400 (69.4%)	381,600 (30.6%)
1995	866,400 (44.8%)	1,068,000 (55.2%)

Source: Ministerio de Planificación y Coordinación del Desarrollo Económica y Social, *Indicadores Económica y Sociales;* Dirección General de Estadísticas y Censos, *Anuario Estadístico;* and *Diario Oficial* for years in question.

Table 7.3

Direct U.S. Military Assistance to El Salvador (in $ millions)

Year	IMET Training	Loans	Financing	Total
1990	1.4	–	79.6	81.0
1991	1.0	–	65.9	66.9
1992	1.38	–	21.25	22.63
1993	0.3	–	11.0	11.3
1994	0.4	–	–	0.4

Sources: Agency for International Development, *US Overseas Loans, Grants and Assistance from International Organizations,* 1980–1995.

though the commander of the air force, Col. Héctor Lobo, had some support within ARENA, he was unacceptable to the *tandona* and to the U.S. embassy. The *tandona* viewed him as an archenemy and the embassy was concerned with the air force's past involvement in drug running. Although the U.S. embassy had little leverage given the suspension of military assistance, the *tandona*'s range of choices was limited as a result of the purge. Corado, while somewhat critical of the *tandona* for having overstayed its welcome, was loyal enough to have been appointed chief of operations of the Estado Mayor and then commander of CODEM. He also had served as chief of the Estado Mayor Presidencial (9/90–10/91), thus he was not an unknown quantity from Cristiani's perspective. What is clear, though, is that Corado owed his position to the *tandona* and was unlikely to completely sever the relationship.

During his swearing in as defense minister in June 1993, Col. Corado tried to distance himself somewhat from the outgoing *tandona*. Whereas Ponce delivered an embittered speech in which he lambasted the Ad Hoc and Truth Commissions (referring to them as "prejudicial, unjust and partial"), Corado avoided criticizing the peace accords or the FMLN directly, instead focusing on the need to "consolidate the peace process."[65] Nevertheless, during the CENITEC conference in October 1993, Corado stated that harmonious civil-military relations depended on military professionalism and political stability and he warned against governments with "radical programs." According to Corado, the armed forces desired "responsible governments that serve the national interests."[66]

Although the new High Command appeared to have accepted reluctantly the military's reduced institutional prerogatives, there was still significant resistance to civilian authorities exercising effective oversight of the military institution. As mentioned above, while some officers had a positive view of the academic council for the military academy, they were opposed to civilian oversight of subsequent training courses. Moreover, most officers were unwilling to accept greater civilian oversight of the defense budget even under peacetime conditions, and few were willing to tolerate a civilian defense minister. Finally, it was not at all clear that officers would accept a politically marginal role for the military.

An editorial in the July 1993 edition of *Revista Militar,* published by the Estado Mayor, reflected how little attitudes had changed within the armed forces regarding some of these issues. The editorial accused the FMLN of being behind the increase in crime in a transparent attempt to destabilize the government. It also accused the FMLN of trying to discredit and marginalize the armed forces, raising doubts about their utility in maintaining internal security. The FMLN had brought the military to "a new form of war and a new battlefield" and the question now facing the armed forces was: "what should be the armed forces' battle plan in this new class of war?"[67]

For some retired officers the answer was to join the political fray. For example, in July 1993 the PCN announced its decision to nominate General (retired) Juan Rafael Bustillo, former commander of the air force, as its presidential candidate for the March 1994 elections. Bustillo had been singled out in the Truth Commission report for his involvement in planning the murder of the six Jesuits. The PCN also nominated General (retired) Adolfo Blandón, former chief of staff, as its first legislative candidate for San Salvador. Although the PCN had served as an electoral vehicle for the armed forces during the 1960s and seventies, it tried to adopt a more civilian look during the eighties. Bustillo's candidacy represented a transparent attempt by retired officers to once again use the party as an electoral vehicle and to use their influence within the armed forces to influence the electoral outcome.[68]

Even after its reduction to some thirty thousand troops, the Salvadoran military was still large by Central American standards (see table 7.4). The troop to population ratio for El Salvador in 1994 was 5.2:1000 inhabitants, while for Honduras and Nicaragua it was 3.4:1000 and 3.2:1000 respectively. In Guatemala, where the military was involved in an armed conflict, the ratio was only 3.2:1000 inhabitants. In terms of military spending, El Salvador compared favorably with other Central American nations on military expenditures as a percentage of GNP and of central government expenditures (see table 7.5). However, El Salvador's military spending per capita surpassed Guatemala and was double that of Honduras and Nicaragua. The relative size of the Salvadoran armed forces and of the defense budget was especially troubling given that the country no longer faced an external threat—the border dispute with Honduras was definitively settled by the World Court—nor an internal civil war.

As discussed above, in the wake of the peace accords the High Command sought out new tasks for the army. These included traditional activities, such as civic action, collaboration with government ministries on national reconstruction projects, and "supporting" the police in its public security functions. Especially worrisome was President Cristiani's decision in July 1993 to call out the army to patrol the nation's highways and other high-crime areas where the new National Civilian Police (PNC) had not yet been deployed. A few months later, Cristiani asked the military to "protect" the coffee harvest. Although the FMLN opposed Cristiani's decision to deploy the army, it found itself in a difficult position politically. In a March

1993 poll, crime was considered the number two concern by citizens, and in a September 1993 poll, 66.5 percent expressed support for the army's deployment.[69] Despite the apparent public support for the measure, it set a dangerous precedent. Instead of assigning sufficient resources to the PNC, the government turned to the army to perform what were in fact public security functions, thereby legitimizing the army's involvement in public security.[70]

Another discouraging sign was the lack of initiatives from civil society aimed at transforming civil-military relations. For example, the School of High Strategic Studies was a Ministry of Defense initiative, not the product of a dialogue with organized sectors of civil society. Consequently, some institutions, like the Jesuit University, did not send representatives to partici-

TABLE 7.4
Estimated Troop Strength of Central American Militaries, 1994

Country	Army	Navy	Air Force	Total	Security Forces	Troops per1000 people
El Salvador	28,000	500	2,000	30,500	—	5.2
Guatemala	42,000	1,500	700	44,200	12,300	3.2
Honduras	16,000	1,000	1,800	18,800	5,500	3.2
Nicaragua	10,000	800	1,200	12,000	—	3.4

Source: International Institute for Strategic Studies, *The Military Balance, 1978–1994* (London: 1994); U.S. Arms Control and Disarmament Agency, *World Military Expenditures and Arms Transfers, 1995* (Washington, D.C.: April 1996).
Note: For El Salvador and Nicaragua, data on security forces are not included as they are no longer under the direct control of the armed forces.

TABLE 7.5
Central American Military Expenditures, 1994

Country	Military Expenditures per capita (in U.S. dollars)	Military Expenditures as Percentage of GNP.	Military Expenditures as Percentage of Central Govt Expenditures
El Salvador	18	1.2	9.1
Guatemala	16	1.4	15.2
Honduras	9	1.6	8.3
Nicaragua	8	2.6	5.7

Source: U.S. Arms Control and Disarmament Agency, *World Military Expenditures and Arms Transfers, 1995* (Washington, D.C.: April 1996).

pate in the course. Moreover, few research institutes or universities expressed a willingness to devote resources to research on civil-military relations.

THE MARCH 1994 ELECTIONS

The March 1994 elections were a great disappointment for many Salvadorans and most international observers. Billed "the elections of the century," the elections were supposed to be the culminating event of the peace
process, bringing an end to the bloody twelve-year civil war that had left the
country deeply divided. Nevertheless, the elections were not very different
from the flawed elections of the 1980s, marred by low voter turnout and
widespread irregularities. Despite the peace accords and significant international pressure, the electoral system had changed little.

Two important provisions of the peace accords that were to have been
implemented prior to the elections had not been fully implemented. In the
first place, the new civilian police force (PNC) was deployed only in about
half the country, primarily in the eastern and northern departments. Elsewhere, including most of San Salvador, the old National Police were in
charge of public security functions. Although no longer under the armed
forces' command structure, the National Police force was assigned to the
Ministry of Interior, headed by a retired colonel. Moreover, the director of
the National Police was an active-duty officer.

The failure to fully deploy the PNC and dismantle entirely the old security forces contributed to a climate of fear and intimidation during the
electoral process. In fact, in its ninth report on human rights in the country, ONUSAL found an increase in human rights abuses and other illegal
acts by National Police agents during the months of June through September 1993. This included a return to the use of torture, the excessive use of
force, arbitrary detentions, and executions.[71]

The intensification of death squad activities, including the assassination
and attempted assassination of several FMLN leaders, also contributed to
the climate of fear, especially evident in the countryside. During the week
preceding the election, one of the authors had the opportunity to travel to
former conflictive zones. Campesinos, when asked which parties had the
most support in their communities, referred to the FMLN as *el otro partido*
(the other party), reluctant to utter the initials aloud. In one community in
Usulután, Nueva Granada, residents pointed out that members of the former security forces still lived in the community and doubted that they had
"changed their attitudes."[72] There was also great concern about how the government might react if *el otro partido* won the elections. In a poor barrio on

the outskirts of San Salvador residents also talked about the climate of intimidation. Although they had not been personally threatened, for some the government's campaign propaganda, with its veiled threats of a return to violence if the FMLN triumphed, reinforced their sense of fear. One resident commented, "If I was stopped on the street by a journalist and asked what I think, what I think is that I had not better say anything."[73]

Another key provision of the accords, the land transfer program, also had not been fully implemented prior to the elections. The program intended to aid the reinsertion of ex-combatants into civilian life and to resolve long-standing land disputes in former conflictive zones. For electoral reasons, it was extremely important to the FMLN that the plan be implemented in an expeditious manner, since the FMLN needed to deliver material benefits to ex-combatants and its civilian followers in the countryside. Otherwise, ex-combatants and campesinos who had received nothing after two years of waiting might be discouraged from voting.

Delays in implementing the land transfer program resulted from a number of factors.[74] First of all, disagreement arose over the list of lands to be transferred. The government charged that many of the parcels included on the FMLN's list did not meet the criteria laid out in the accords. ONUSAL mediation produced agreement on a final list in October 1992, including some 4,600 parcels and approximately 250,000 *manzanas* of land. Second, the Land Bank's[75] insistence that only individuals could purchase properties, and that they provide an exact list of buyers, slowed down the process. Third, the adoption of market principles in carrying out the plan meant that landowners who had abandoned their land because of the conflict would benefit handsomely from postwar market prices. Peasants receiving the land, however, would be saddled with burdensome debts. Finally, the FMLN had problems convincing some potential beneficiaries to relocate to other regions of the country where land was available.

Besides the failure to implement these key provisions of the peace accords, as mentioned earlier, the electoral system itself was not fundamentally altered in the wake of the accords. Changes in the electoral law agreed upon during the peace negotiations guaranteed the opposition greater representation on the Tribunal Supremo Electoral (TSE) than in the past and reduced the opportunities for fraud on election day. However, the registration process was not altered significantly nor was the organization of election day voting. Despite offers of assistance from ONUSAL and other international organizations and governments, and constructive alternatives presented by opposition parties, the TSE insisted on conducting business as usual.

The TSE made very little effort to streamline the cumbersome registration process in preparation for the March 1994 elections. In July 1993, ONUSAL estimated that approximately 786,000 Salvadorans (or about 29 percent of eligible voters) did not have a voting card. However, it was only after intense pressure from domestic opposition forces and external actors, including ONUSAL, U.S. embassy officials, and the U.S. Congress, that some progress was made. A National Registration Plan, approved in late July, included mobile registration units and provided collaboration with national and international NGOs. In addition to its constant pressure on the TSE to do its job, ONUSAL provided crucial logistical support throughout the registration period. During September–November, the rate of applications increased dramatically. Nevertheless, 74,000 were rejected for lack of documentation, and some 350,000 Salvadorans who were registered never received their cards.[76] According to the TSE's own figures, just over 400,000 new voters received voting cards in the nine months leading up the elections.[77]

On election day itself, voting was disorderly to say the least. In some voting centers, voting tables were not ordered alphabetically, and in many centers voters were unable to locate their names on the electoral rolls. In one voting center in San Salvador, the Feria Internacional, 120,000 voters were assigned to vote there. Upon arriving, prospective voters first had to locate their names on the seemingly endless voting lists, before proceeding to the corresponding voting table. The system was particularly biased against illiterate voters, given that electoral officials made little effort to guide voters through the process. In fact, it was estimated that between 5 and 6 percent of voters were turned away, and that the rate was higher in some areas, particularly in ex-conflictive zones. This figure does not include those who were discouraged by the long lines outside voting centers or who never arrived because of the lack of public transport.[78] Not surprisingly, turnout for the first round was estimated at only 55 percent of registered voters and 45 percent during the second-round voting in April.[79] Although the overall turnout was higher than the 1991 election, it was lower than the elections in 1982 and 1984, despite the fact that the potential electorate had grown considerably.

Also disturbing was the deployment of combat troops in ex-conflictive zones on election day. For example, during the general election on 20 March, heavily armed troop contingents were highly visible along the highway to Chalatenango. This was also the case in areas of San Miguel and Morazán.[80] During the second round of voting on 24 April, it was reported that in Morazán "dozens of truckloads of troops were seen with heavy caliber machine guns, grenade launchers, and mortars."[81] While it is impossible to tell what impact the military's presence had on individual voters, it may have served to reinforce the climate of fear in areas most affected by the war. Also, it may have underscored Arena's dominant campaign theme, that a vote for the FMLN was a vote for a return to violence and destruction.

Needless to say, the Arena party won big in the elections. Its presidential candidate, Armando Calderón Sol, won 49.0 percent of the vote, compared to 24.9 percent for Rubén Zamora of the FMLN-led Coalition, and 16.4 percent for Fidel Chávez Mena of the PDC (Partido Demócrata Cristiano). In the second-round voting on April 24, Calderón Sol won easily with 68.3 percent to Zamora's 31.7 percent. In the legislative elections, Arena won thirty-nine seats, the FMLN twenty-one, and the PDC eighteen. The remaining seats were divided as follows: Partido de Conciliación Nacional (PCN)—4, Convergencia Democrática (CD)—1, and the Movimiento de Unidad (MU)—1. Finally, at the municipal level, Arena swept 212 of the 262 mayoralties.[82]

AFTER THE ELECTIONS

In the aftermath of the elections, there were some encouraging developments affecting civil-military relations. First was the demobilization of the National Police in December 1994. Back in October 1993, the Cristiani government had agreed to complete the demobilization of the National Police by October 1994. However, in January 1994, Cristiani announced that he had suspended the demobilization in order to combat the crime wave affecting San Salvador. Opposition leaders feared that the government would use the context of increasing levels of crime to justify incorporating the bulk of National Police agents into the PNC.[83] A May agreement mediated by ONUSAL led to yet another delay, postponing the final demobilization until March 1995.[84]

Any possibility of further delaying the National Police's demobilization was shattered after a bloody bank heist on 22 July 1994. Fifteen heavily armed men, some of whom were dressed in National Police uniforms, assaulted an armored vehicle outside the Banco de Comercio in San Salvador. A videotape of the heist implicated Lt. José Rafael Coreas Orellana, head of the National Police's Department of Investigations. Soon after, Vice Minister of Public Security Hugo Barrera announced that, in light of the recent events, the government was considering completing the National Police's demobilization by December 1994. Moreover, in early July, President Calderón Sol, faced with growing evidence linking the National Police's criminal investigation unit to organized crime, ordered the dismissal of six hundred of the eight hundred members of the unit and announced that the National Police would be placed under the authority of the vice minister of public security, also responsible for the PNC. Finally, on 31 December 1994, Calderón Sol officially dissolved the National Police, the last of the security forces.

Another positive development was the ouster of the PNC operations director, Major Oscar Peña Durán, in May 1994. Peña, formerly head of the U.S.-funded antinarcotics unit (UEA), had been appointed PNC operations director in July 1993. Peña's appointment was initially opposed by both the FMLN and ONUSAL, given that the position of operations director was to be reserved for a civilian. During his tenure, Peña "virtually eliminated UN involvement with the PNC and placed a number of his men in command positions, although they had not gone through the new public security academy and were supposed to be limited to anti-narcotics work."[85] In fact, at the end of 1993, 430 members of the UEA and 140 members of the National Police Special Investigative unit (SIU) were transferred wholesale into the PNC without receiving proper evaluations or training. The agents "were merely required to attend a one-week course at the Academy on PNC doctrine; even then, no roll was taken, and no examinations were given."[86]

After Peña's ouster, the new director of the PNC, Rodrigo Ávila, invited ONUSAL to work closely with the police. In June and July 1994 ONUSAL organized training courses for PNC officers and in September–October provided refresher courses for senior officers. Both Ávila and Vice Minister of Public Security Hugo Barrera publicly expressed their commitment to work with ONUSAL to address its concerns regarding the civilian police.[87] Finally, Calderón Sol demonstrated greater commitment than his predecessor in providing much-needed resources to the PNC. For example, whereas in FY 1994 the government earmarked 381.6 million colónes for public security, the 1995 budget included over 1 billion colónes for public security, an increase of 180 percent. Even more significant was that for the first time, public security received a larger share of the budget than defense (9.1 percent vs. 7.4 percent).[88]

Despite these positive developments, civilian control over criminal investigation remained problematic. According to Popkin's study of judicial reform in El Salvador after the peace accords, throughout 1994 there were "continuing efforts to bring former military or National Police officers into command positions."[89] A 28 July report by the Joint Group for the Investigation of Politically Motivated Illegal Armed Groups underlined similar concerns.[90] The Joint Group was formed in December 1993 to investigate the activities of death squads as recommended by the Truth Commission Report. After describing the activities of the death squads during the period of the armed conflict, the Joint Group report explains how, after the peace accords, death squads branched out into organized crime, including auto theft, kidnapping, extortion, drug trafficking, and contraband. Given the PNC's apparent inability to fully investigate the criminal activities of such groups, the Joint Group recommended the establishment of a special unit within the PNC's Division of Criminal Investigation, dedicated to combat both organized crime and politically motivated violence.

The report also pointed to other disturbing developments. One was the continued involvement of active duty officers and members of the National Police in politically motivated violence and other illicit activities. In fact, not long after the report became public, the vice minister of public security announced the arrest of Col. José Santiago Domínguez Zelaya, former subdirector of recruitment and reserves, for his involvement in auto theft and extortion. Barrera also revealed the capture of Cap. David Araujo Iglesias of the Engineering Battalion, accused of extortion. Three days later, on 12 August, Calderón Sol ordered the creation of special tribunals within the armed forces to investigate cases of corruption and criminal activity of their members. He also affirmed the government's conviction that the two officers accused of extortion should be tried in the civil courts.[91]

Moreover, the report found that some units of the military were still carrying out intelligence activities "in clear violation" of the constitution.[92] Warning against the possibility that such activities might be used for political ends, the Joint Group called on the new State Intelligence Organ (OIE) to fully assume its constitutional prerogatives and to thoroughly investigate the politically motivated violence of death squads and organized crime.

On the one hand, the climate of increasing criminal and political violence singled out by the Joint Group's report may have accelerated the dissolution of the National Police and spawned greater commitment on the part of the government in adequately funding the PNC. On the other hand, the growing violence also reinforced the government's resolve to preserve the armed forces' role in maintaining internal order. Adding to the growing violence throughout 1994 and 1995 was the increasingly militant posture of former members of the military and security forces.[93] Although the peace accords provided that demobilized soldiers and members of the security forces would receive one year severance pay and also suggested that they receive preferential treatment in the land transfer program, the language was somewhat ambiguous. The Cristiani government made the determination that only those former members of the armed forces with good records would receive benefits. Those excluded from receiving benefits included: (1) soldiers discharged for bad conduct, (2) members of the armed forces demobilized prior to the signing of the peace accords, and (3) members of the civil defense patrols. Moreover, programs designed to reintegrate former soldiers received inadequate government support and were unable to meet the demand. For example, a program of vocational training courses launched in early 1993 offered places for sixteen hundred ex-soldiers but still had a waiting list of over eight thousand.[94]

The most disturbing protests took place during January 1995, when groups of demobilized soldiers (estimated at between three and seven thousand) organized by the Asociación de Desmovilizados de la Fuerza Armada de El Salvador (ADEFAES) occupied the Legislative Assembly, the Ministry of Finance, the Armed Forces Social Security Institute (IPSFA), and a number of other governmental buildings. The demonstrators held hostage fifteen legislators and several hundred public employees for three days. The ADEFAES claimed that many of its members had not received benefits promised them under the peace accords and that others that should have been included in the benefits were not. The government succeeded in defusing the protest; however, it was able to do so only with ONUSAL's help. ONUSAL officials entered the legislative assembly, negotiated the release of the deputies, and escorted them out. In the aftermath of the incident, the government refused to address the organization's key demands. Consequently, the demonstrations continued throughout the spring of 1995.

The parallels with Nicaragua's demobilization process are striking. The inability of the Chamorro government to make good on its promises to ex-combatants after a peace treaty in 1990 contributed to a dramatic increase in urban and rural violence. Beginning in 1991, groups of ex-Contras (re-contras) took up arms to protest the government's failure to provide them with land and support services. Soon they were joined by ex-Sandinista soldiers (recompas) who also pressured the government for land. Although the Chamorro government was successful in negotiating disarmament agreements with most of these groups, after mid-1992 new groups of recontras began to appear. Unlike the earlier groups, this second wave of recontras was much less willing to negotiate with the government and stepped up attacks on military targets. By early 1994, the government had signed peace agreements with over forty armed groups. The problem, however, was that most of the ad hoc agreements provided for only short-term immediate compensation, "such as money, food, clothing and houses," and were not part of a more comprehensive plan for productive reinsertion of demobilized combatants.[95] Consequently, rural violence, especially banditry, continued throughout 1995 and 1996.

The Chamorro government's vacillation on the issue of property redistributed through the Sandinista agrarian reform also fueled the growing violence. In addition to the demands of recontras and recompas, former landowners, whose property was confiscated by the Sandinistas, returned to Nicaragua to reclaim their lands. This heightened the level of insecurity on the part of agrarian reform cooperatives and shanty town dwellers who had received titles to their lands under the Sandinista government. In the context of a deepening economic crisis,[96] the government's inability to meet the contesting demands of these groups exacerbated an already explosive situation.

Likewise, in El Salvador the government's failure to facilitate the land transfer program and adequately address the issue of demobilized soldiers and guerrillas contributed to an increase in political and criminal violence. Other factors included the lack of employment opportunities for ex-combatants and for poor Salvadorans in general; the widespread availability of guns in the aftermath of the war; and the influx of Salvadoran gang members deported from the United States.[97] With the dramatic rise in gang-related killings, El Salvador posted one of the highest homicide rates in the hemisphere for 1995. The crime wave was so bad in some parts of the country that some Salvadorans took matters into their own hands. In 1995, a new death squad, Sombra Negra, began targeting suspected gang members. In Usulután, an area that was especially affected by the war, shopkeepers and merchants staged a one-day strike in March 1996 to protest the government's inaction. In response, the Calderón Sol government introduced new legislation aimed at stemming the crime wave. The legislation provided the police with wide-ranging discretion to arrest suspected criminals and gang members, including those recently deported from the United States. Opposition leaders denounced the new legislation as a blow to human rights and for not addressing the social problems fueling the increase in criminal activity.[98] They also opposed the government's efforts to organize neighborhood watch committees (*juntas de vecinos*) throughout the country. Whereas the government viewed them as a way of enhancing citizen collaboration with the PNC, opposition leaders saw the *juntas de vecinos* as an attempt to resurrect the old paramilitary structures of repression.[99]

In the context of increasing violence, both criminal and politically motivated, the army continued to participate in "dissuasive" patrols along highways and in support of outgunned police units. The military also participated in putting down several demonstrations staged by trade unions and military veterans. As pointed out above, the military's fear of becoming irrelevant in the wake of the peace accords made it favorably disposed to taking on new—or in this case, old—responsibilities. The government argued that the army's deployment was a temporary measure taken under extraordinary circumstances. Moreover, unlike in the past, the army participated in these new public security functions in a subordinate fashion, with soldiers taking orders from PNC officers. The danger, of course, was that its role in public security would become permanent.

Conclusion

The peace accords created a historic opportunity to dramatically transform civil-military relations, thereby bringing an end to the Salvadoran military's prolonged political domination. The agreement provided for a comprehensive restructuring of the armed forces and their relationship to civilian authorities and mapped out a new, more limited role for the military. Nevertheless, the unique legacy of protracted military rule presented powerful obstacles to the full implementation of the reforms and complicated the possibilities for future progress.

Without a doubt, significant progress was made in circumscribing the military's institutional prerogatives. As a result of the accords, the military no longer had a prominent role in public security; the military academy was now subject to civilian oversight; and, for the first time, officers had to submit themselves to an external evaluation conducted by civilians. However, demilitarization requires more than just limiting the military's realm of action. Demilitarization at the state level consists not only of reducing the military's traditional prerogatives but also eliminating its ability to exercise tutelary power over the political process. At the level of everyday life, demilitarization implies the dismantling of the military's paramilitary network of social control. On both scores, the process of demilitarization initiated by the peace accords fell short.

If it is true that the peace accords did not go far enough in addressing the various dimensions of the military's political power, then questions remain as to what additional reforms may be necessary and as to the likelihood that the military will accept further changes. In the next chapter, we discuss the prospects for future reform efforts and lay out the broad outlines of a politically led strategy toward the military.

CONCLUSIONS
The Road Ahead

THIS STUDY argues that the extent and nature of militarization in El Salvador prior to 1992 produced powerful obstacles that limited the possibilities for demilitarization in the wake of the peace accords. Although the accords created a unique window of opportunity to fundamentally transform the military's political role, they failed to address several key aspects of the military's political power.

The process of militarization, at both the macro and micro levels, predated the 1931 coup, when the Salvadoran armed forces assumed direct control of the state. Already under the Araujo presidency, the military's creeping colonization of the state was reflected in Gen. Hernández Martínez's assumption of the vice presidency and his appointment as minister of war. Moreover, the armed forces' paramilitary presence in the countryside grew considerably during the 1920s. The 1932 uprising convinced the Hernández Martínez regime of the need for further militarization, as it set out to impose the discipline of the barracks on the entire country. Through a combination of control of state resources, the continued development of a paramilitary network in rural areas, and alliances with civilian groups and the United States, the regime succeeded in consolidating its power.

During the 1940s, a new generation of officers emerged to challenge Hernández Martínez's attempts at *continuismo*. Although the 1948 coup ushered in a number of changes in the way the military exercised its political domination, much remained the same. On the one hand, the Osorio government sought to promote industrialization, diversify agro-exports, and increase spending on social services and welfare. It also allowed greater political space for opposition parties to engage in electoral activities. On the other hand, the political opening during the 1950s did not translate into significant participation or representation by opposition groups and was limited to urban areas. Moreover, in the countryside, the military maintained its extensive paramilitary structure. At no time did either the Osorio or Lemus regimes consider reducing the presence of the *patrullas cantonales,* the *escoltas militares,* or the National Guard, all of which were indispensable to the military's effective control of rural areas and its electoral success. Thus, the period of the 1950s underscored the limits on the military's political power. Even though it came to view social reforms as essential to the preservation of the state, the military was incapable of implementing more profound reforms that might have threatened the agro-export elite's economic dominance.

The 1960s were years in which armies all over Central America were involved in a variety of activities designed to counter a perceived leftist threat emanating from revolutionary Cuba. The United States, through the Alliance for Progress and stepped-up military assistance, sought to promote social and economic reforms and guarantee military security. Thus the military regime in El Salvador found itself caught between the demands of the United States that it implement reforms, on the one hand, and the continued resistance of the coffee elite to implementing such changes as land reform, increased direct taxes, and free political expression, on the other. To complicate matters, reform-minded parties, like the Christian Democrats and Social Democrats, began to emerge and attract significant support, especially in urban areas. Finally, in the countryside, peasants, who experienced increasing hardships during the 1960s and seventies, became increasingly willing to take direct action against the regime.

The unsuccessful coup attempt in 1972 signaled the military's inability to mollify these conflicting interests through traditional means. Efforts during the 1960s and 1970s to strengthen and expand the armed forces' internal security system failed to stem the growing popular mobilization. Attempts at reform, such as Molina's tepid land reform program, were successfully blocked by conservative land-holding interests. Consequently, under the Romero regime the military stepped up its repression of opposition movements, fueling an escalating spiral of violence that precipitated the 1979 coup.

The coup in October 1979 signaled the exhaustion of more traditional forms of political control and the search for a more viable system of domination. In the wake of the crisis, the armed forces became increasingly dependent on U.S. assistance. As elsewhere in the region, the U.S. administration exacted a price for its support. The armed forces had to permit the election of a civilian-led government, show greater respect for human rights, and force through reforms over the objections of the oligarchy. Although the reforms strained the military's relationship with the agro-export elite, the historic nexus was not ruptured beyond repair. Moreover, despite the costs of U.S. support, the military managed to retain its power and postpone more profound changes.

The process of militarization did not come to a halt after the 1979 coup. Instead, during the 1980s, at a time when the military was transferring formal political power to civilian leaders, it succeeded in preserving its control of key state institutions and its wide-ranging constitutional prerogatives, and in expanding its paramilitary network in the countryside. Although the military retained its ability to control key political decisions, there were limits to its power. First, the growing guerrilla threat and less visible forms of resistance challenged the military's continued colonization of everyday life. Second, growing dependency on U.S. assistance, combined with internal factionalism, made the Salvadoran military increasingly vulnerable to U.S. pressures. Nevertheless, despite U.S. insistence on reforms of the armed forces, the Salvadoran military displayed an incredible capacity to resist both external and domestic pressures.

The implementation of peace accords affecting the armed forces proved to be an uneven process at best. Those reforms that constituted a challenge to the military's core interests elicited the fiercest opposition from the High Command. Especially controversial was the Ad Hoc Commission's recommendations, which called for the removal or transfer of over one hundred officers. In addition to the problematic aspects of the implementation phase, the accords failed to address adequately: (1) the military's position within the state, (2) the military's paramilitary network in rural areas, and (3) the military's institutional and political autonomy. In short, although the accords laid the groundwork for a significant reduction of the military's prerogatives, they did not go far enough in ensuring civilian supremacy over the armed forces. The military's realm of political action was greatly circumscribed, but it retained much of its autonomy intact.

Lessons from the Salvadoran Case

Without a doubt, the process of demilitarization unleashed by the peace accords is unprecedented in Latin America. Nevertheless, if the Salvadoran experience is to inform policy initiatives elsewhere in the region, a couple of points are worth making. First of all, compared to other militaries in Latin America, the Salvadoran military's capacity to resist reforms was seriously limited as a result of the armed conflict. The institution's credibility was damaged severely because of extensive human rights abuses committed by the army and security forces. Moreover, the Salvadoran military's increasing dependency on U.S. assistance during the 1980s left it highly vulnerable to external pressures in the wake of the accords.

Despite the Salvadoran military's limited capacity to resist changes, it took the full weight of UN and U.S. pressures to finally convince the High Command to swallow the bitter pill. And even then, the High Command was able to negotiate a number of face-saving compromises. For example, despite being singled out by the Ad Hoc and Truth Commissions, high-ranking members of the *tandona* were allowed to retire with honors, financial perks, and their pensions intact. Not only was the outgoing High Command able to impose its choice as minister of defense, but it also drew a line in the sand regarding any further reforms that went beyond the scope of the peace accords.

The Salvadoran case points to both the possibilities and limits of demilitarization. Elsewhere in Central America, with the end of the Cold War, international pressures to resolve internal conflicts and support for initiatives to enhance civilian control over the military facilitated progress toward demilitarization. In neighboring Guatemala, international mediation to end the thirty-five-year-old civil war created opportunities for significant military reforms. Even before the Guatemalan government and the guerrillas signed a final peace accord, important steps were taken to reform the military. Beginning in early 1996 the High Command began dismissing or transferring several officers accused of involvement in human rights abuses and criminal activities.[1] In September 1996, President Alvaro Arzú dismissed nine senior officers, including the deputy defense minister, as part of an investigation of a smuggling and theft ring operated by army and police officers. Given that in July the military *fuero*[2] was abolished, these officers now would have to answer to a civilian court. Finally, in December 1996 the two sides signed a definitive peace agreement. Similar to the Salvadoran accords, the Guatemalan agreement provided for the establishment of a new police force to take over public security functions, the creation of a new intelligence agency under presidential control, and the disbanding of the notorious civil defense patrols. The agreement also called for the military to reduce its force levels by 33 percent in 1997 and for a 33 percent reduction in the defense budget by 1999 (measured as a percentage of GDP).[3]

In Nicaragua, reforms to the Sandinista military also followed on the heels of a peace accord that brought an end to the decade-long Contra war. Like the Cristiani government in El Salvador, the Chamorro government was not very aggressive in asserting civilian control over the military. In fact, before assuming office in April 1990, President-elect Chamorro signed a transition agreement with the outgoing Sandinista leadership, in which she agreed to respect the "integrity and professionalism" of the armed forces and to allow Gen. Humberto Ortega to stay on as commander of the armed forces. Chamorro also accepted the Military Organization Law No. 75, passed two days before the elections, which provided the Sandinista military with a high level of institutional autonomy regarding internal promotions and personnel decisions, and control over its budget. In exchange for these concessions, Gen. Ortega agreed to immediate force reductions. Despite Chamorro's lack of assertiveness, there was significant internal pressure from the right wing of her electoral coalition, UNO, and from some of the *recontras*. Their principal demand was for Gen. Ortega's removal as army chief. There was also external pressure from Senator Jesse Helms and other Republican critics in Congress, who threatened to block U.S. assistance to the Chamorro government unless the military was brought under civilian control, and from United Nations and Organization of American States (OAS) observers monitoring the demobilization and reintegration of the ex-Contras.[4]

Although the Sandinista military resisted efforts to subject it to civilian control, it did agree to a dramatic reduction in force levels—from over ninety thousand in 1990 to twelve thousand by 1995—and grudgingly accepted sharp reductions in its budget. The troop reductions were much more dramatic than in El Salvador, especially given the very real military threat posed by armed groups of ex-Contras and demobilized soldiers. Moreover, in August 1994 the national assembly approved a new military code that enhanced civilian control over the armed forces. Unlike the previous law, which empowered the Military Council to select the army chief, the new military code gave the president the authority to select the chief of the armed forces for a fixed five-year term from a list proposed by the Military Council. The code also prohibited the use of military intelligence for political motivations and sharply circumscribed the jurisdiction of military courts. One shortcoming of the new law was its failure to ensure civilian oversight over the military's economic ventures. As in the Salvadoran case, the leading private sector association, the Consejo Supremo de la Empresa Privada, was vociferously opposed to the military's involvement in business activities.[5]

Particularly striking about the Nicaraguan case is that some of the impetus for restructuring the Sandinista military came from within the institution. This may have been partly a result of the different officer training. Unlike Salvadoran officers, whose training was steeped in Cold War ideology, most Sandinista military officers rose through the ranks based on their combat experience and lacked a more formal military education. Moreover, the relative youth of the Sandinista military—established as a regular standing army in 1979—may help explain its greater willingness to redefine its mission in the wake of the war. Recognizing the dramatic changes on the domestic, regional, and international scene, Gen. Ortega and his staff were quick to provide a blueprint mapping out a new role for the armed forces. As part of this new mission, the Sandinista military became involved in development projects, environmental protection, and combatting rural violence and crime.[6] To a large extent, the military was out ahead of civilians in creating a new model for civil-military relations.

Unlike the other cases, in neighboring Honduras, recent civil-military reforms were not the result of an internationally monitored peace accord. Moreover, in Honduras the civilian government played a lead role in asserting greater civilian control over the military. After assuming office in 1994, President Carlos Roberto Reina succeeded in removing several state institutions, including the national telecommunications agency, from direct military control. The Reina government also moved decisively to reduce the military budget and sponsor a constitutional reform replacing obligatory military service with a voluntary system. In September 1995, the National Congress approved a constitutional amendment to place Honduran security forces under civilian control. And finally, in September 1996, the armed forces were obliged to provide the legislature with details of its proposed 1997 budget.[7]

In addition to the assertiveness of the Reina government, there was considerable external pressure in support of the reforms. U.S. policy underwent a dramatic turnabout in the 1990s. With armed conflicts winding down in the region, Honduras was no longer a linchpin in United States policy toward Central America. The U.S. ambassador in Honduras, Cresencio Arcos, became an outspoken advocate in support of military reforms. Furthermore, key business associations, including the Consejo Hondureño de la Empresa Privada, joined the chorus of voices demanding greater civilian control over the military. As in El Salvador and Nicaragua, members of the private sector were angry at unfair competition from military-owned enterprises. Faced with such a broad antimilitary movement, the armed forces reluctantly accepted the reforms.[8]

What are some of the lessons that can be drawn from the demilitarization process in El Salvador and the rest of Central America? First of all, negotiated agreements ending long internal wars can create unique opportunities for transforming civil-military relations. The opportunities are especially great in cases where the accords are brokered and monitored by international actors. Even so, constant international pressure is required throughout the implementation phase and beyond. Second, domestic actors, including civilian leaders and organized groups in civil society, can make a major contribution to the process of demilitarization. Their efforts are particularly important in the absence of international pressure. Third, the possibility of military reforms is greater when some of the impetus for change comes from within the armed forces. Those militaries that are quick to comprehend new global and regional realities may be more likely to accept military reforms.

Without a doubt, significant military reform and restructuring occurred in Central America after 1990. Central American militaries witnessed significant reductions in their prerogatives and the threat of military coups subsided as civilian governments slowly gained confidence in their dealings with the military. However, as Richard Millet argues, while the traditional pattern of civil-military relations may have collapsed, no new one emerged in its place.[9] In fact, one of the most important lessons from the Salvadoran case is that formulating a new model of civil-military relations requires more than simply circumscribing the military's institutional prerogatives.

LOOKING AHEAD

Further progress in transforming civil-military relations in El Salvador is likely to be slow. As discussed in chapter 7, in the wake of the March 1994 elections there were mixed signals regarding the possibility of additional reforms. The changes achieved thus far, while unprecedented, did not originate from within the armed forces but were imposed from outside. Not surprisingly, while some officers came to accept reluctantly these reforms, they showed little willingness to countenance further changes. Instead, officers were likely to safeguard the institution's remaining autonomy from further "encroachments" by civilian authorities. The challenge, then, for civilian leaders was to craft a strategy of reform that minimized the level of conflict.

If further reforms are warranted given the limitations of the accords, how does one guarantee compliance on the part of the armed forces? Might not the military subvert the democratic system if it perceives its interests to be fundamentally threatened? On the issue of compliance, Adam Przeworski has written that compliance depends on the probability of winning within democratic institutions.[10] On the one hand, then, civilian leaders could approach the problem of compliance by asking how they might go about increasing the probability of the military "winning." A typical policy pursued by newly established civilian governments to avoid future coups is the hands-off approach. In more concrete terms, this approach implies policies that safeguard the military's autonomy and guarantee its needs are met. In this way, civilian leaders reduce the uncertainty of political outcomes affecting the armed forces. An example of this sort of approach can be seen in the Brazilian case, where the armed forces maintained a high degree of autonomy after the initial transition to civilian rule, including consistent increases in their budget.[11]

The problem with the "hands-off" approach, of course, is that it does nothing to enhance civilian control over the military. On the contrary, during the Sarney administration, the Brazilian armed forces demonstrated their autonomy from civilian authorities on a number of occasions. Most importantly, the Brazilian military succeeded in blocking a number of constitutional changes that would have reduced its institutional prerogatives.[12] An alternative strategy might be to convince the military that it has more to gain by accepting additional reforms than by resisting them. For example, prior to the March 1994 elections, Salvadoran officers were greatly concerned about the future of the defense budget, even if the Arena party held onto power. In interviews with one of the authors, senior officers commented that they would like legislators to visit military installations to gain a firsthand appreciation of the resource constraints facing the military. However, if the military wants to foster a constituency of defense hawks in the legislature, it would be to its advantage to disclose details of the budget. Only when the budget is made more transparent are legislators likely to become sympathetic to the military's needs.

Another key element in ensuring civilian supremacy is the appointment of a civilian as minister of defense. Here again, the military must be persuaded of the advantages of accepting a civilian defense minister. In conversations with the authors, officers often complained that the military only involved itself reluctantly in politics because of the inability of civilian politicians to put national interests before partisan political concerns. Most officers interviewed expressed a desire to disengage from politics and dedicate themselves to purely military affairs. If this is the case, then civilians should sell the idea of a civilian defense minister as a means of insulating the military from partisan politics and not simply as an instrument of control.

Similarly, in the area of military education, additional reforms might be viewed by some officers as beneficial. As discussed in chapter 7, under the peace accords, a new civilian-military academic council was established to oversee the military academy. Although the council was a major step forward in enhancing civilian oversight, one of the principal problems with military education and training programs is the lack of contact with civilian society. For example, in the military academy cadets are completely insulated from the outside world. Those who want to pursue credits toward a university degree while studying at the academy must do so at the military university. Because the Universidad Militar's course offerings are limited (only degrees in law and business administration are available), most cadets have to wait until some years later to pursue a university degree. A better idea would be to allow cadets to simultaneously pursue a university degree at a public or private university while studying at the academy. Such a program not only would allow cadets to have more choice and to finish their degrees sooner but also would facilitate greater integration with civilian society.

Interviews revealed that whereas senior officers generally opposed the idea on the grounds that they would lose control over cadets' education, junior officers were more supportive of the change. Unlike senior officers, junior officers were very concerned about uncertain career opportunities in the future. In the wake of the peace accords, the ranks of captain and major were bursting at the seams. This was a result of the armed conflict, when the military was training some two hundred new officers a year. With the end of the war, however, and the reduction and restructuring of the armed forces, there were less and less opportunities for junior officers to assume positions of command. Consequently, a significant number of junior officers were scheduled to be deactivated. In the meantime, an increasing number of officers took advantage of opportunities to enroll in degree programs at private universities as a hedge against an uncertain career in the military. These trends made junior officers and cadets more inclined to embrace additional changes in military education and training.

Without civilian leadership, however, it is unlikely that the military will be persuaded to accept any further reforms. During an informal seminar with a group of about thirty-five officers at a brigade in San Salvador in July 1993, one of the authors discussed the future role of the armed forces in El Salvador. Although several of the officers present expressed their willingness to accept the reduction of the military's prerogatives mandated by the peace accords, they were skeptical about whether civilians were prepared or willing to assume these new responsibilities. According to one of the officers, "civilians have given us these prerogatives over the years. It's not that we go looking to assume these responsibilities. The problem is that civilians don't want to take responsibility." This same sentiment was expressed during the CENITEC conference in October 1993. In response to one of the panelist's suggestion that a civilian be named minister of defense, an officer commented that to do so was equivalent to "putting an illiterate in charge of the Ministry of Education." If civilians are to exercise effective leadership, then, they must demonstrate a willingness to prepare themselves to assume those responsibilities previously within the military's domain.

Because of the likelihood that the military will resist direct challenges to what it considers basic, or core, interests, further demilitarization will entail more than simply reducing the military's prerogatives. As Stepan has pointed out, achieving more effective civilian control encompasses a multiplicity of tasks in which civil society, political society, and the state all have a role to play.[13]

First, in regard to civil society, universities and research institutions have important contributions to make. Ongoing, systematic study of the military is essential in developing new strategies to transform civil-military relations. By dedicating some of their resources to researching the military, universities and research institutes can help legislators to improve, and enhance, their oversight capabilities as well as help to educate the public on military affairs.

In El Salvador, for obvious reasons, academics have been unwilling to study the military in a systematic fashion. Not surprisingly, in the wake of the peace accords, there were few civilians with expertise in military affairs. Although such research may not have been feasible in the past, the changed political landscape after 1992 offered new opportunities for researching such a delicate topic. Raising public awareness and sharing their expertise with popular organizations and political parties are ways in which academics can contribute to the development of a *política militar*. Public organizations can also educate their membership about various dimensions of the military problem.

In the wake of the accords there were some encouraging signs at the level of civil society. As is argued throughout this book, the militarization of everyday life did not go unchallenged. Both direct and less visible forms of resistance were evident throughout the period of military rule. During the 1970s and 1980s, civil society did become more assertive despite the enormous obstacles. Although the space available for autonomous social organization and mobilization was extremely limited by state repression, popular organizations aggressively resisted the military's domination. After the peace accords, popular movements found new opportunities to organize and serve their constituencies, thus lending impetus to the efforts of civil society to mount an effective challenge to the military's traditional political dominance.

Also important at the level of civil society was the growing antimilitarist sentiment in the aftermath of the war. Even certain sectors of the oligarchy expressed concern regarding the liability of supporting a large, well-equipped military without a mission. Besides the continuing drain on the budget, business people also worried about the upsurge in kidnappings and other violent crimes as increasing numbers of former members of the army and security forces were demobilized. Moreover, as the Salvadoran economy became less and less dependent on labor-repressive agriculture, the oligarchy's need for a network of social control in the countryside diminished.[14]

Finally, private research institutes, like CENITEC and Centro DEMOS, were very active in educating the public about the peace accords and facilitating open, pluralistic debate about issues of national import prior to the March 1994 elections. For example, in January 1994 the Centro DEMOS sponsored a seven-month intensive course of studies on the Salvadoran *realidad nacional,* including representatives from the armed forces, government, opposition parties, the private sector, the trade union movement, universities and NGOs, and popular movements. Several sessions during the course focused on civil-military relations in El Salvador, including national security and defense, demilitarization and democracy, public security, and paramilitary groups.[15] Combined with the civilian presence on the military academy's academic council and civilian-military participation in the School for High Strategic Studies, these initiatives created unprecedented opportunities for exchanges between civilians and military, thereby facilitating a gradual opening of the armed forces to civil society. Over the long term, such incremental changes may produce unintended consequences that contribute to even greater civilian control.[16]

Second, it is in the interests of the political society to devise a clear strategy to enhance the legislature's oversight capacity. If the military is to be made accountable to elected officials, at the very least legislators will need access to the details of the military budget. Moreover, to be able to debate the military budget in an intelligent manner (when and if the budget details are disclosed), legislators need to develop expertise in military affairs. Whether this expertise comes as the result of establishing a permanent legislative committee for military affairs, as recommended by the Truth Commission, or by some other means, is less important than not having to rely solely on military officers for expertise.[17] By developing such expertise independently, political parties will be in a better position to contribute to the development of a *política militar.* After 1992, few of the parties made much progress in this regard; rather, most continued to hold a very short-term vision of civil-military relations, with little thought of how these might be transformed over the long run.

Besides reducing the military's prerogatives, the executive branch of government can provide essential leadership in formulating an alternative mission for the military and promoting democratic professionalism. One possibility might be to convoke a dialogue, open to all political and social forces, to take up and discuss the proper role of the military. In addition to bringing civilian attention to bear on the urgency of formulating a national *política militar,* such a dialogue also might persuade officers of the benefits of fostering democratic professionalism within the armed forces.

After 1992, the executive branch failed to exercise a leadership role in fostering debate on the future of civil-military relations or crafting an alternative *política militar.* Research institutes and the military itself launched several independent initiatives, but these were not part of a coherent effort coordinated by the civilian government. Although the government did send representatives to participate in these endeavors, its failure to take the lead only reinforced officers' doubts about the willingness of civilians to assume responsibility for military affairs.

One final task for political leaders is to convince the military of the costs involved in resisting additional changes. Przeworski argues that the likelihood of successful subversion and the costs associated with its failure depend on the willingness of other political forces to defend democratic institutions.[18] In other words, political leaders have to demonstrate a commitment to democratic institutions as "the only game in town," even when the outcomes of the democratic process are not always to their advantage. Convincing the military that all the major political forces will not resort to tactics that threaten to subvert the democratic system will not be easy. An essential element in shifting from the politics of confrontation to the politics of *concertación* (consensus building) is the creation of political and bureaucratic institutions that are capable of addressing citizens' needs. On the contrary, failure to achieve democratic governance is likely to provoke the military into assuming a more political role. Given that the peace accords did not address satisfactorily the structural roots of the conflict, further delay in implementing long-awaited socioeconomic reforms might prove costly. If the country's leaders are unable to lay the socioeconomic foundations of a democracy, they could soon find themselves faced with a crisis of governability and direct intervention by the armed forces.

An alternative view is that with the transition to competitive elections, politicians may have additional incentives for contesting the military's prerogatives. For example, in a recent study of civil-military relations in Brazil, Wendy Hunter argues that the "incentives unleashed by electoral competition soon led politicians to contest the military in Brazil's new democracy."[19] Given the clientelistic nature of Brazilian politics, politicians came to view the military budget as an unnecessary drain on resources that otherwise could be used for purposes of political patronage. Although the military's budget increased in nominal terms during the Sarney administration, since 1985 (with the exception of 1990) the military's budget as a percentage of the overall federal budget has declined steadily. According to Hunter, from "a rational choice perspective, Brazilian politicians followed instrumental calculations and contested the armed forces in order to improve their own electoral chances."[20]

Similarly, in El Salvador, we saw that in the wake of the peace accords and the transition to more competitive elections, politicians allowed the military's relative share of the budget to decline. At the same time, with crime becoming an important electoral issue, the PNC's budget increased dramatically to the point of overtaking the defense budget in 1995. Nevertheless, as Hunter herself admits, while politicians may have incentives in the new political context for reining in the defense budget, from an electoral standpoint they may have little motivation to pursue additional reforms that seek to reduce the military's political and institutional autonomy.[21] Only the constant pressure of organized groups of voters will convince politicians of the need for more systematic civilian control.

Ultimately, some of the impetus for change must come from within the military; if not, the Salvadoran armed forces risk becoming a total anachronism in the future. El Salvador no longer faces an external threat (the border dispute with Honduras was definitively settled by the World Court); the danger of a so-called communist menace in the region is gone; the new civilian police force is in charge of internal security; and the country has few resources to squander on a needless military machine. Coming to terms with this new era will be difficult at best for some officers, since it all points to a future armed force that will be politically marginal and obedient to its civilian masters.

NOTES

I. INTRODUCTION

1. Alfred Stepan, *Rethinking Military Politics: Brazil and the Southern Cone* (Princeton: Princeton University Press, 1988), xi–xii.

2. Guillermo O'Donnell and Philippe Schmitter, *Transitions from Authoritarian Rule: Tentative Conclusions* (Baltimore: Johns Hopkins University Press, 1986), 69.

3. Frances Hagopian, "'Democracy by Undemocratic Means?' Elites, Political Pacts, and Regime Transition in Brazil," *Comparative Political Studies* 23 (July 1990): 147–70.

4. For example, see Robert Putnum, "Toward Explaining Military Intervention in Latin American Politics," *World Politics* 20 (October 1967): 83–110.

5. See Guillermo O'Donnell, *Modernization and Bureaucratic Authoritarianism* (Berkeley: Institute for International Studies, 1973).

6. Samuel Huntington, *Political Order in Changing Societies* (New Haven: Yale University Press, 1968), 194.

7. Juan Linz and Alfred Stepan, *The Breakdown of Democratic Regimes* (Baltimore: Johns Hopkins University Press, 1978). See also Douglas Chalmers, "The Politicized State in Latin America," in James Malloy, ed., *Authoritarianism and Corporatism in Latin America* (Pittsburgh: University of Pittsburgh Press, 1977), 23–46.

8. Samuel Huntington, *The Soldier and the State: The Theory and Politics of Civil-Military Relations* (Cambridge: Harvard University Press, 1957).

9. For example, see Bengt Abrahamsson, *Military Professionalization and Political Power* (Beverley Hills: Sage Publications, 1972); S. E. Finer, *The Man on Horseback: The Role of the Military in Politics,* 2d ed. (Boulder: Westview Press, 1988); and Alfred Stepan, "The New Professionalism of Internal Warfare and Military Role Expansion," in Stepan, ed., *Authoritarian Brazil: Origins, Policies and Future* (New Haven: Yale University Press, 1973), 47–68.

10. For example, see Manuel Garretón, *The Chilean Political Process* (Boulder: Westview Press, 1989); and Alain Rouquié, *The Military and the State in Latin America* (Berkeley: University of California Press, 1987).

11. Stepan, "The New Professionalism," 52.

12. José Nun, "The Middle-Class Military Coup," in Claudio Veliz, ed., *The Politics of Conformity in Latin America* (London: Oxford University Press, 1967). Stepan, in his study of the Brazilian military, strongly refutes this view. See *The Military in Politics: Changing Patterns in Brazil* (Princeton: Princeton University Press, 1971), 30–56.

13. Huntington, *Political Order,* 222.

14. For example, see Miles Wolpin, "External Political Socialization as a Source of Conservative Military Behavior in the Third World," in Kenneth Fidel, ed., *Militarism in Developing Countries* (New Brunswick, N.J.: Transaction Books, 1975). Most statistical studies of the impact of U.S. military assistance find little or no correlation between levels of military aid and military coups. See J. Samuel Fitch, "The Political Consequences of US Military Aid to Latin America: Institutional and Individual Effects," *Armed Forces and Society* 5, no. 3 (1979): 360–86.

15. Finer distinguishes between short-term "disengagement" and long-term "neutrality." Finer, *The Man on Horseback,* 283–84.

16. Constantine Danopoulos, "Military Dictatorships in Retreat: Problems and Perspectives," in Danopoulos, ed., *The Decline of Military Regimes* (Boulder: Westview Press, 1988), 4.

17. Ibid.

18. Claude Welch, *No Farewell to Arms? Military Disengagement from Politics in Africa and Latin America* (Boulder: Westview Press, 1987). Chapter 2 provides a useful overview of the literature on military disengagement.

19. Finer, *The Man on Horseback,* 287 (emphasis in original).

20. Ibid.

21. For examples of this literature, see J. Samuel Fitch, "Military Professionalism, National Security and Democracy: Lessons Learned from the Latin American Experience," *Pacific Focus* 6 (1989): 99–147; Louis Goodman et al., *The Military and Democracy: The Future of Civil-Military Relations in Latin America* (Lexington, Mass.: Lexington Books, 1990); Dirk Kruijt and Edelberto Torres-Rivas, eds., *América Latina: militares y sociedad* (San José: FLACSO, 1991); and Paul Zagorski, *Democracy vs. National Security: Civil-Military Relations in Latin America* (Boulder: Lynne Reinner Publishers, 1992). An exception is Rouquié's *The Military and the State in Latin America.* His discussion of the prospects for demilitarization follows a lengthy analysis of the history of militarism in Latin America.

22. An exception is Richard Millet's study of the Nicaraguan National Guard. Richard Millet, *Guardians of the Dynasty* (Maryknoll, N.Y.: Orbis Books, 1977).

23. A notable exception is Gabriel Aguilera's work, *El fusil y el olivo: La cuestión militar en Centroamérica* (San Jose: DEI, 1989). Also, see Leticia Saloman, *Militarismo y reformismo en Honduras* (Tegucigalpa: Editorial Guaymuras, 1982) and Rafael Guidos Vejar, *El ascenso del militarismo en El Salvador* (San Salvador: UCA Editores, 1980).

24. See Robert Elam, "Appeal to Arms: The Army and Politics in El Salvador, 1931–1964," Ph.D. diss., University of New Mexico, 1968.

25. See Mariano Castro Morán, *Función política del ejército salvadoreño en el presente siglo* (San Salvador: UCA Editores, 1987).

26. For example, see Martin Needler, "El Salvador: The Military and Politics," *Armed Forces and Society* 17, no. 4 (summer 1991): 568–88. Notable exceptions are the works of José García and William Stanley. García's work focuses primarily on internal factionalism within the armed forces during the 1980s ("The Tanda System and Institutional Autonomy of the Military," 95–105 in J. Tulchin and G. Bland, eds., *Is There a Transition to Democracy in El Salvador?* [Boulder: Lynne Reinner Publishers, 1992]). Stanley's recent book explores the extreme levels of state-sponsored violence during the late 1970s and 1980s in El Salvador *(The Protection Racket State* [Philadelphia: Temple University Press, 1996]).

27. Joel Millman, "El Salvador's Army: A Force Unto Itself," *New York Times Magazine,* 10 December 1989. Also of interest is a collection of interviews with Salvadoran military officers, U.S. advisors, and other protagonists in the conflict. Max Manwaring and Court Prisk, eds., *El Salvador at War: An Oral History of Conflict from the 1979 Insurrection to the Present* (Washington, D.C.: National Defense University Press, 1988).

28. For example, see A. J. Bacevich et al., *American Military Policy in Small Wars: The Case of El Salvador* (Washington, D.C.: Pergamon-Bassey's International Defense Publications, 1988); Raul Benítez, *La teoría militar y la guerra civil en El Salvador* (San Salvador: UCA Editores, 1989); and Benjamin Schwarz, *American Counterinsurgency Doctrine and El Salvador* (Washington, D.C.: Rand Corporation, 1991).

29. Stepan, *Rethinking Military Politics,* 11.

30. Rouquié, *The Military and the State,* 11.

31. Stepan, *Rethinking Military Politics,* xii.

32. Ibid., 10. According to Poulantzas, the state "is the *site* and *center* of the exercise of power, but it possesses no power of its own." Nicos Poulantzas, *State, Power, Socialism* (London: New Left Books, 1978), 148.

33. Rouquié, *The Military and the State,* 284.

34. Ibid., 38.

35. Michael Lowy and Eder Sader, "The Militarization of the State in Latin America," *Latin American Perspectives* 12, no. 4 (fall 1985): 9. Our concept of militarization is distinct from Alfred Vagts's notion of militarism. Vagts defines militarism as "the unquestioning embrace of military values, ethos, principles, attitudes; as ranking military institutions and considerations above all others in the state; as finding the heroic predominantly in military service and action, including war—to the preparation of which the nation's main interest and resources must be dedicated, with the inevitability and goodness of war always presumed." Alfred Vagts, *A History of Militarism* (Greenwich: Meridian Books, Inc., 1959), 453.

36. Lowy and Sader, "The Militarization of the State in Latin America," 9.

37. Felipe Aguero, "The Military and Limits to Democratization," in Mainwaring, O'Donnell, and Valenzuela, eds., *Issues in Democratic Consolidation: The New South American Democracies in Comparative Perspective* (Notre Dame: University of Notre Dame Press, 1992), 166.

38. Jurgen Habermas, *The Theory of Communicative Action,* vols. 1 and 2 (Boston: Beacon Press, 1984, 1985).

39. Aguero, "The Military and Limits," 174.

40. Habermas, *The Theory of Communicative Action.*

41. According to J. Samuel Valenzuela, "reserved domains remove specific areas of governmental authority and substantive policy making from the purview of elected officials" (64). "Tutelary powers," on the other hand, "attempt to exercise broad oversight of the government and its policy decisions while claiming to represent vaguely formulated fundamental and enduring interests of the nation-state" (62–63). Valenzuela, "Democratic Consolidation in Post-Transitional Settings," in Mainwaring, O'Donnell, and Valenzuela, eds., *Issues in Democratic Consolidation: The New South American Democracies in Comparative Perspective* (Notre Dame: University of Notre Dame Press, 1992).

42. For a similar view, see Rouquié, *The Military and the State.*

43. Rouquié, *The Military and the State,* 285.

44. Stepan, *Rethinking Military Politics,* 128–45.

45. Stepan defines *política militar* as a "politically-led strategy toward the military." Stepan, *Rethinking Military Politics,* 138.

2. THE 1931 COUP AND THE CONSOLIDATION OF MILITARY RULE

1. Salvador Peña Trejo, with Quino Caso (Joaquín Castro Canizales), "Narración histórica de la insurrección militar del 2 de diciembre de 1931," *Diario Latino,* 2 June 1964 and subsequent issues. Castro Canizales was one of the original members of the *directorio militar* that replaced President Arturo Araujo, whereas Peña Trejo became minister of defense in 1944.

2. The motives behind Araujo's assassination were never clarified. For a detailed discussion of the Araujo government, see Rafael Guidos Vejar, *El ascenso del militarismo en El Salvador* (San Salvador: UCA Editores, 1980), 68–75.

3. Everett Alan Wilson, "The Crisis of National Integration in El Salvador, 1919–1935." Ph.D. diss., Stanford University, 1970, 49–55.

4. Ibid., 105–06.

5. Ana Patricia Alvarenga, "Reshaping the Ethics of Power: A History of Violence in Western Rural El Salvador, 1880–1932." Ph.D. diss., University of Wisconsin-Madison, 1994, 266–68. Local political violence between competing factions during the 1920s in the eastern department of Usulután is described in a taped interview with General Enrique Claramount Lucero; Claramount states that when he was the governor of the department he persuaded the political factions to field consensus candidates and thus there were "only one or two" people killed during the campaign. Taped interview with Enrique Claramount Lucero in possession of the authors, no date but probably early 1950s.

6. El Salvador, Ministerio de Guerra, Marina y Aviación, *Memoria de 1922* (San Salvador: Imprenta Nacional, 1923), 89. The Escuela Politécnica Militar was closed down as a result of the rebellion in 1922 and not reopened until 1927.

7. El Salvador, Ministerio de Guerra, Marina y Aviación, *Memoria de 1930* (San Salvador: Imprenta Nacional, 1931), 17–20. According to Alvarenga, the military had a permanent presence in each department by 1885 and a total strength of 3,200 by 1893 (368 officers and 2,832 soldiers); there was no significant increase in these numbers for the next thirty years. Alvarenga, "Reshaping the Ethics of Power," 155–56.

8. Alvarenga, "Reshaping the Ethics of Power," 13.

9. Ibid., chapter 4, especially 185–90.

10. Ibid., 156–59.

11. "Lista de comandantes de barrio y de cantón con sus respectivas escoltas del Departamento de Ahuachapán," Archivo Nacional, Ministerio de Gobernación, 1925 (unclassified).

12. Alvarenga, "Reshaping the Ethics of Power," 292–335. See also Wilson, "The Crisis of National Integration in El Salvador," especially 189–94, which discusses the rhetoric of Alberto Masferrer, the principal ideologue of reformist groups at the time.

13. Mariano Castro Morán, *Función política del ejército salvadoreño en el presente siglo* (San Salvador: UCA Editores, 1984), 49–53.

14. Wilson, "The Crisis of National Integration in El Salvador," 199–200, 206–08. Alvarenga, "Reshaping the Ethics of Power," 334–35.

15. Wilson, "The Crisis of National Integration in El Salvador," 214–18.

16. Carmelo F. E. Astilla, "The Martínez Era: Salvadoran-American Relations, 1931–1944," Ph.D. diss., Louisiana State University, 1976, 32–34.

17. Peña Trejo and Quino Caso, "Narración histórica de la insurrección militar." See Minister Curtis's account of the coup: U.S. Department of State, *Foreign Relations of the United States, 1931* (Washington, D.C.: Government Printing Office), vol. 2, 177–85.

18. Interview with Colonel Luis Lovo Castelar, San Salvador, 7 July 1995. Lovo Castelar was a junior lieutenant assigned to the military school when the coup against Araujo took place. Kenneth J. Grieb, in his "The United States and the Rise of General Maximiliano Hernández Martínez," *Journal of Latin American Studies* 3, no. 2 (1970), 151–72, quotes U.S. minister Curtis to the effect that the junior officers involved in the coup were "little more than half-witted" and "utterly irresponsible" and had absolutely no plan for government.

19. Castro Morán, *Función política del ejército salvadoreño*, 89. Castro Morán states that the junta was approached by civilians seeking to ingratiate themselves with the new government but that they were rejected with the argument that "civilians had led the country to failure" and that what was needed was a "strictly military government."

20. Grieb, "The United States and the Rise of General Maximiliano Hernández Martínez," 158–59.

21. The peasant/Indian rebellion of 1932 has been studied quite extensively. Among others, Thomas P. Anderson's *Matanza: El Salvador's Communist Revolt of 1932* (Lincoln: University of Nebraska Press, 1971) is probably the best-known book to date. Héctor Pérez Brignoli has written an excellent synthesis under the title "Indios, comunistas y campesinos: La rebelión de 1932 en El Salvador," *Cuadernos Agrarios* 5 (San José: Escuela de Historia, Universidad de Costa Rica, 1991). More recently, see Alvarenga's "Reshaping the Ethics of Power," and Erik Ching's "Una nueva apreciación de la insurrección del 32" in *Tendencias* 44 (Septiembre de 1995): 28–31 (San Salvador). The last three stress ethnicity as one of the driving forces behind the insurrection.

22. See Grieb, "The United States and the Rise of General Maximiliano Hernández Martínez," 163–65.

23. Ching, "Una nueva apreciación." According to Ching's research in the Comintern archives, the Communist Party was riven by dissension and seriously limited by lack of resources.

24. "Memoria de los Ministerios de Gobernación, Fomento, Trabajo, Beneficiencia y Sanidad para 1932." *Diario Oficial* 114, 45 (23 February 1933): 333–43.

25. "Memoria de Gobernación . . . para 1932," 335. In Castaneda's own words: "El ideal, para oponerse a los avances doctrinarios del funesto comunismo, no es otro que la elevación de todos o de la mayoría de los habitantes del país a la clase de 'pequeños propietarios.'"

26. "Memoria de Gobernación . . . para 1932," 337. Alvarenga states that in the western coffee-growing regions of the country the landlords handled the distribution of identity papers, giving them the power to decide who would or would not enjoy "basic rights." Alvarenga, "Rethinking the Ethics of Power," 364. During this period, the Hernández Martínez regime introduced a series of policies intended to defend the interests of coffee producers and exporters. These included a 50 percent exchange depreciation between 1932–1934, a moratorium on the external debt, the creation of a state Mortgage Bank to assist coffee growers, and the establishment of the Comisión de Defensa del Café Salvadoreño in 1934. For a more detailed discussion, see Victor Bulmer-Thomas, *The Political Economy of Central America Since 1920* (Cambridge: Cambridge University Press, 1987), 72–75.

27. Alvarenga, "Rethinking the Ethics of Power," 337. The *cédula patriótica* guaranteed that the bearer "no sustenta ideas subversivas ni anárquicas, y que merece confianza por parte de las autoridades en virtud de tener arraigo y ser ventajosamente conocida." But since not everyone could fork out one hundred *colones,* such papers could be purchased only by a few, by those, in Castaneda's words, who belong to the class that deserves special treatment ("un elemento para impartir las seguridades y garantías que esa clase de ciudadanos merecen").

28. Minister of Government Castaneda insisted that the state of siege in effect since the peasant uprising did not place any limits on freedom of the press as long as it did not publish subversive (communist) ideas that threatened internal order or the country's "democratic institutions." Ibid., 338.

29. "Memoria de Gobernación . . . para 1932," 333.

30. See, for example, "Memorias del Ministerio de Gobernación . . ." for the years 1933, 1934, 1936, and 1939, *Diario Oficial* 116/55 (7 March 1934), 118/43 (21 February 1935), 122/61 (18 March 1937), and 128/61 (13 March 1940). See also, "Manifiesto de Maximiliano Hernández Martínez al asumir la presidencia el 1.03.35," *Diario Oficial*

118/50 (2 March 1935) and "Mensaje del presidente Maximiliano Hernández Martínez a la Asamblea Nacional," *Diario Oficial* 122/35 (15 February 1937).

31. El Salvador, "Mensaje de Maximiliano Hernández Martínez ante la Asamblea Nacional durante la apertura de sesiones," *Diario Oficial* 114/34 (10 February 1933).

32. El Salvador, Ministerio de Defensa, *Memoria para 1946* (San Salvador: Imprenta Nacional, 1947), 64.

33. According to the minister of defense, the *patrullas* assisted in the maintenance of public order, they looked after telephone and telegraph lines, railroads, and country roads, and they cooperated with the authorities in the persecution of criminals. El Salvador, "Memoria del Ministerio de Guerra, Marina y Aviación de 1935," *Diario Oficial* 120/52 (3 March 1936). The minister of defense in 1946 underlined that the *patrullas* operated "without affecting public funds at all." El Salvador, Ministerio de Defensa, *Memoria para 1946* (San Salvador: Imprenta Nacional, 1947), 64.

34. Most every yearly report of the minister of war/defense from 1930 until the 1970s underlines the important role of schooling of recruits in the formation of the country's citizens. The teaching was undertaken by military officers who were supervised by the Ministry of Education.

35. A minister of war was very clear on this point: "our soldiers come mostly from the rural population and enter the barracks, therefore, without most of the knowledge they need for the better performance of their duties." El Salvador, Ministerio de Guerra, Marina y Aviación, *Memoria de 1940* (San Salvador: Imprenta Nacional, 1941). A few years later, the minister of defense stated that "military service is the foundation of the preparation that citizens require so that they can execute the most sacred of their civic duties, which is the defense of the fatherland." El Salvador, Ministerio de Defensa, *Memoria de 1946* (San Salvador: Imprenta Nacional, 1947).

36. For example, one prerequisite to enlist in the Guardia Nacional was prior military service and reading, writing, and mathematics skills. "Reglamento de la ley orgánica de la Guardia Nacional." *Diario Oficial* 120/31 (7 February 1936).

37. Alvarenga, "Reshaping the Ethics of Power," 366–72.

38. El Salvador, "Decreto ejecutivo de estatuto orgánico de la Asociación Cívica Salvadoreña," *Diario Oficial* 119/186 (26 August 1935).

39. See El Salvador, Ministerio de Guerra, Marina y Aviación, *Memoria para 1932* (San Salvador: Imprenta Nacional, 1933); and "Decreto ejecutivo de estatuto orgánico de la Asociación Cívica Salvadoreña."

40. Alvarenga, "Reshaping the Ethics of Power," 375–76.

41. El Salvador, Ministerio de Guerra, Marina y Aviación, *Memoria para 1932* (San Salvador: Imprenta Nacional, 1933).

42. Legislative decrees in *Diario Oficial* 120/1 (2 January 1936) and 128/4 (5 January 1940). The size of the military in 1930 also stood at three thousand. *Diario Oficial* 109/223 (6 October 1930).

43. El Salvador, Ministerio de Defensa Nacional, *Anuario Militar de 1942* (San Salvador: Imprenta Nacional, 1943).

44. See, for example, the courses offered at the Escuela Militar. The proportion of strictly military to general courses offered is as follows: in 1933, 8:25; in 1936, 5:33; and 1939, 8:41. *Diario Oficial* 114/28 (31 January 1933), 120/12 (15 January 1936), and 126/33 (11 February 1939).

45. Astilla, "The Martínez Era," 167–80.

46. Robert Varney Elam, "Appeal to Arms: The Army and Politics in El Salvador, 1931–1964," Ph.D. diss., University of New Mexico, 1968, 46–47.

47. "Constitución política de la República," *Diario Oficial* 126/39 (20 January 1939), Article 135. Previous to this, mayors were elected. Hernández Martínez said that the direct appointment of mayors would promote harmony and rid the municipalities of so much bickering. "Mensaje de Maximiliano Hernández Martínez a la Honorable Representación Nacional," *Diario Oficial* 126/40 (20 February 1939).

48. The only official statement referred to the "nearly unanimous" vote by the people for Hernández Martínez. "Mensaje del presidente Andrés I. Menéndez a la Asamblea Nacional el 12.02.35," *Diario Oficial* 118/35 (12 February 1935). General Menéndez occupied the presidency in late August 1934 so that Hernández Martínez could seek election without violating the constitutional provision against reelection.

49. "Memoria del Ministerio de Gobernación . . . de 1939," *Diario Oficial* 128/61 (13 March 1940).

50. "Decreto de la Asamblea Nacional Constituyente que elige presidente de la república a Maximiliano Hernández Martínez," *Diario Oficial* 126/17 (23 January 1939).

51. Asamblea Nacional Constituyente, "Decreto mediante el cual se elige a Maximiliano Hernández Martínez presidente de la república," *Diario Oficial* 136/50 (29 February 1944). See also "Reformas a la Constitución Política," *Diario Oficial* 136/47 (25 February 1944).

52. During 1934, for example, the government reported only one case of "subversion," when a few men were arrested with explosive materials that they planned to use "to create terror in the country." "Memoria del Ministerio de Gobernación, Trabajo, Fomento, Agricultura, Beneficiencia y Sanidad de 1934," *Diario Oficial* 118/43 (21 February 1935). As the legislative assembly stated in March 1935 when it lifted the state of siege in effect since January 1932, "[reina] en el país la más completa paz y tranquilidad, como resultado de una actuación política y administrativa conciliadora y ajustada a las leyes, norma implantada por el Jefe Supremo del Estado, que cuenta con la simpatía y apoyo firme de la opinión pública." *Diario Oficial* 118/58 (12 March 1935). However, there was no conciliation in the case of a lieutenant and his civilian accomplices accused of a "communist" plot to overthrow the government: the lieutenant was executed by firing squad and the civilians sent to jail for long prison terms. "Memoria del Ministerio de Guerra, Marina y Aviación de 1936," *Diario Oficial* 122/70 (6 April 1937).

53. "Decreto legislativo que levanta el estado de sitio vigente desde el 20 de enero de 1932," *Diario Oficial* 118/58 (12 March 1935); "Memoria del Ministerio de Gobernación . . . de 1936" *Diario Oficial* 122/61 (18 March 1937); "Prórroga del estado de sitio decretado el 8.12.41," *Diario Oficial* 136/56 (7 March 1944). The minister of government stated in his year-end report for 1933 that the state of siege remained in effect because the government "considered it more humane and patriotic to prevent than to repress." El Salvador, "Memoria del Ministerio de Gobernación . . . de 1933," *Diario Oficial* 116/55 (7 March 1934).

54. "Decreto ejecutivo prohibiendo actividad comunista," *Diario Oficial* 109/178 (12 August 1930); "Reformas al código penal que especifican la naturaleza de reuniones ilícitas," *Diario Oficial* 109/194 (1 September 1930); and "Reglamento para efectuar reuniones y manifestaciones de tipo político," *Diario Oficial* 109/244 (30 October 1930).

55. "Constitución Política de la República," *Diario Oficial* 126/15 (20 January 1939), articles 47 and 48; "Reformas a la Constitución Política de la República," *Diario Oficial* 136/47 (25 February 1944).

56. "Memoria del Ministerio de Gobernación . . . de 1939," *Diario Oficial* 128/61 (13 March 1940). To supervise these agreements, a press office was set up, which the minister

said would ensure freedom of the press but would not allow it to degenerate into disorder ("libertinaje").

57. See, for example, S. Ciudad Real, gobernador político de Sonsonate, to José Eufracio Guzmán, secretario general del Comité Pro-Patria, 14 August 1934, Archivo Nacional, sección Gobernación, unclassified.

58. See Fernanda Arévalo, presidente del comité local del Pro-Patria, to presidente del comité departamental del Partido Nacional Pro-Patria, San Antonio del Monte, 26 August 1934, Archivo Nacional, sección Gobernación, unclassified; in this letter, Arévalo informs the departmental chief of the party that he has registered eighty voters who will back Maximiliano Hernández Martínez. See also letter from Lisandro Larín Zepeda, presidente del comité departamental del Pro-Patria, to presidente del Comité Central del Partido Nacional Pro-Patria, Sonsonate, 6 October 1934, Archivo Nacional, sección Gobernación, unclassified; Larín provides a breakdown of the ten thousand individuals registered in the party in all of Sonsonate and claims that another five thousand are expected to join shortly. At year's end, the secretary of the departmental committee informed the national party authorities that 20,864 individuals had signed up with Pro-Patria in the department of Sonsonate. Joaquín E. Guzmán to Presidente de Directiva Suprema del Partido Nacional Pro-Patria, Sonsonate, 31 December 1934, Archivo Nacional, sección Gobernación, unclassified.

59. Lizandro Larín Zepeda, Presidente del Comité Departamental Pro-Patria, to Presidente Directiva Suprema del Partido Nacional Pro-Patria, Sonsonate, 30 December 1934, Archivo Nacional, sección Gobernación, unclassified.

60. "Ley reglamentaria de elecciones," *Diario Oficial* 126/44 (24 February 1939).

61. Castro Morán, *Función política del ejército salvadoreño,* 167.

62. "Un voto de confianza," carbon copy of flier issued by the Juventud Militar, February 1944, Biblioteca Manuel Gallardo, colección recortes de 1944. For a detailed account of the events leading to Hernández Martínez's overthrow, see Patricia Parkman, *Nonviolent Insurrection in El Salvador: The Fall of Maximiliano Hernández Martínez* (Tucson: University of Arizona Press, 1988).

63. "Declaraciones del señor Presidente antenoche," *El Gran Diario* 5, 1575 (7 June 1944).

64. Castro Morán, *Función política del ejército salvadoreño,* 170–73. According to Castro Morán, the most active officers in opposition to the regime were those who had graduated from the military school after 1930, while the older ones generally were supportive of Hernández Martínez.

65. "Declaraciones del señor Presidente antenoche," *El Gran Diario,* 7 May 1944. Hernández Martínez was convinced that the problems he faced were exclusively of an urban nature, since the peasants were a happy lot. As he said, "Continue to work, my friends, for the welfare of all. Be happy and content, just like the peasants as they work in their fields, happy and dedicated to their labors and tasks; in this manner, the war of nerves will be over quickly."

66. "Manifiesto de la Fuerza Armada al pueblo salvadoreño," 7 May 1944, Biblioteca Manuel Gallardo, colección recortes de 1944.

67. See, for example, a flier addressed to soldiers, *guardias,* and policemen by "el pueblo salvadoreño" that asked them not to fire upon civilians because soldiers and policemen were part of the people, too. It stated that the people have placed their trust in the men in uniform. "Que no disparen contra la población civil, porque es un crimen," 2 June 1944, Biblioteca Manuel Gallardo, colección recortes de 1944. See also a flier that lists the achievements of the movement headed by Romero: the right to a free vote, an

impartial military establishment, and the "friendship" between rich and poor (so that "unfortunate events like that of 1932" would not happen again). "Salvadoreño: al fin volviste a ser un Hombre libre," June or July 1944, Biblioteca Manuel Gallardo, colección recortes de 1944.

68. Partido Unión Demócrata (PUD), "Manifiesto al pueblo salvadoreño," flier with no date but probably July or August 1944. Biblioteca Manuel Gallardo, colección recortes de 1944.

69. "¡Pueblo católico!" September 1944, Biblioteca Manuel Gallardo, colección recortes de 1944. This anti-Romerista flier warns all good Catholics to vote for any party but not for the Romeristas, because under their outwardly innocent appearance lurks "the communist serpent." Another flier underlines the Russian and Mexican influence behind the local communist movement. "Muera el comunismo!," 24 September 1944, Biblioteca Manuel Gallardo, colección recortes de 1944.

70. "Manifiesto del Coronel Osmín Aguirre y Salinas a la Nación Salvadoreña," 21 October 1944, Biblioteca Manuel Gallardo, colección recortes de 1944. It is not clear whether Hernández Martínez was directly involved in the coup; however, Aguirre and the other senior officers involved were allies of Martínez and shared his commitment to continued military rule. See Elam, "Appeal to Arms," 107–15.

71. See flier dated 30 October 1944 that calls for a general strike, claiming that Aguirre's government was on the verge of collapse because of international censure and lack of support among the officer corps. "Al pueblo salvadoreño. El gobierno usurpador del chacal Osmín Aguirre y Salinas está tambaleando," Biblioteca Manuel Gallardo, colección recortes de 1944.

72. Castaneda Castro's retirement from the military by President Hernández Martínez allowed his supporters to insist that Castaneda Castro did not qualify as a bona fide "martinista." *Al Día—Semanario de Información,* 1/3 (27 February 1945).

73. See "Manifiesto al Pueblo Salvadoreño proclamando la candidatura del señor general don Salvador Castaneda Castro por el partido 'Unión Social Democrática,'" 1944 (no date but probably November or December), Biblioteca Manuel Gallardo, colección recortes de 1944. In some instances, the general's program appears identical to that of the Romeristas, including promises of social security legislation, respect for basic political freedoms, and improvement of conditions in military barracks and officers' messes.

74. See "Manifiesto del Coronel Osmín Aguirre y Salinas," which states in part that his government is made up of individuals who "bring together the greatest amounts of popular opinion . . . [in representation of] a legitimate majority in accordance with the purest democratic principles." See also a flier entitled "Boletín Oficial del Ministerio de Defensa Nacional" denouncing an invasion of "three thousand . . . enemies of the people" from Guatemala that sought to overthrow the government, which has "the support of the immense majority of honest Salvadorans." 15 December 1944, Biblioteca Manuel Gallardo, colección recortes de 1944.

3. THE NEW ARMED FORCES OF THE REVOLUTIONARY GOVERNMENT

1. In early 1948 negotiations were underway with the International Bank for Reconstruction and Development (IBRD) to borrow $75 million for the construction of the first hydroelectric dam on the Lempa River, even though the Salvadoran government, aware of the sensitivities of public opinion against foreign loans, issued a statement to the contrary. *La Prensa Gráfica* (9 April 1948).

2. Mariano Castro Morán, *Función política del ejército salvadoreño en el presente siglo* (San Salvador: UCA Editores, 1987), 203. Castro Morán states that the 1948 coup completely

sidelined the "traditional" military faction and enthroned the younger officers who had graduated from the military school in the early 1930s.

3. By 1948 the reformist Guatemalan regime of president Juan José Arévalo was consolidated firmly and the Costa Rican rebels under José Figueres had just overthrown the conservative government of Teodoro Picado.

4. Castro Morán, *Función política del ejército salvadoreño*, 201. In Castro Morán's own words, "From this event onwards, the military conspirator has been aware that his life will be respected."

5. Speech by Castaneda Castro on the "Día del soldado" (Soldier's Day), *La Prensa Gráfica* (8 May 1948). See also his speech on Panamerican Day, *La Prensa Gráfica* (15 April 1948).

6. See *La Prensa Gráfica* of 14.12.48 for a complete transcript of the decree. According to the American chargé in El Salvador, Murat Williams, Castaneda "had chosen this week because the strongest opponent to his continuing, [Defense Minister] General Mauro Espinola Castro, was in the hospital recovering from an appendectomy." U.S. Department of State, *Foreign Relations of the United States* (1948) vol. 9, 116–17. The papal nuncio, dean of the diplomatic corps, along with U.S. embassy officials and the Costa Rican and Honduran ambassadors, participated in the negotiations. U.S. Department of State, *Foreign Relations of the United States* (1948) 118.

7. *La Prensa Gráfica* (15 December 1948).

8. *La Prensa Gráfica* (16 December 1948). Another speaker was major Oscar Bolaños, perhaps the key player in Castaneda's overthrow, who denied that the insurgent movement was a coup d'etat; instead, he referred to it as a "movement of renovation" that sought a new organization of the state, which "is today so backward."

9. *La Prensa Gráfica* (16 December 1948) and (22 December 1948).

10. *La Prensa Gráfica* (28 December 1948).

11. *La Prensa Gráfica* (14 March 1949).

12. "Proclama del Consejo de Gobierno Revolucionario," Castro Morán, *Función política del ejército salvadoreño*, 382–83.

13. *La Prensa Gráfica* (23 May 1948).

14. *La Prensa Gráfica* (13 March 1949).

15. *Boletín del Ejército* 2/17 (19 May 1950).

16. "Ley de sindicatos," reprinted in *Boletín del Ejército* 2/28 (18 August 1950).

17. Two Guatemalans were expelled from El Salvador for espousing "marxist thinking" at a labor union meeting. *Boletín del Ejército* 2/44 (20 October 1950).

18. In fact, the regime considered social security and public housing one of its crowning achievements. *Boletín del Ejército* 5/46 (14 December 1956). The number of people benefitted was not significant in comparison to those who had no home or regular employment. In two years (1956–1958), for example, the government's agencies provided permanent housing for 7,110 people. President José María Lemus, "Mensaje en el X aniversario de la revolución salvadoreña," *Mensajes y discursos—1957* (San Salvador: Ministerio de Cultura, 1958), 464.

19. See, for example, an editorial in *Boletín del Ejército* 2/2 (27 January 1950). It states that teachers and soldiers are "the two strongest forces capable of advancing, in great measure, the progress of the nation."

20. El Salvador, *Ley transitoria electoral* (San Salvador: Imprenta Nacional, 1950).

21. *Hispanic American Report* 2 (September 1949): 11.

22. "Decreto de convocatoria a elecciones de constituyente y presidente de la república," *Boletín del Ejército* 2/4 (10 February 1950).

23. *La Prensa Gráfica*, 12 April 1950.

24. *Hispanic American Report* 3, no. 5 (May 1950).

25. El Salvador, *Constitution of 1950* (Washington, D.C.: Pan American Union, 1961), 24–25, 27.

26. *Boletín del Ejército* 3/7 (13 March 1951). Although the Communist Party was proscribed after the 1932 uprising, it continued to exist underground, maintaining safe houses in San Salvador.

27. "Los enemigos de la revolución deben tener mucho cuidado," *Diario Latino* (15 December 1951).

28. "Mensaje del señor Presidente de la República al pueblo salvadoreño," *Diario Latino* (27 September 1952). See also a communiqué of the Ministry of Defense, which claims that various rich individuals had raised about US$800,000 to finance a coup d'etat. Although they had been freed due to lack of evidence, the communiqué reiterates the regime's conviction "that there had been a conspiracy." *Boletín del Ejército* 4/34 (26 September 1952).

29. See *Hispanic American Report* 5, no. 10 (November 1952) and 6, no. 2 (March 1953). The last individuals arrested in September and October 1952 were released in May 1953 without having been charged.

30. "Ley de defensa del orden democrático y constitucional," *La Prensa Gráfica* (28 November 1952)

31. *Hispanic American Report* 5, no. 5 (June 1952).

32. *Hispanic American Report* 8, no. 12 (January 1956).

33. One candidate was disqualified when legal charges were leveled against him; as it happens, electoral law did not permit anyone involved in a lawsuit to be a candidate for office. Two other candidates were disqualified for supposedly not presenting all of the proper documentation. See *Hispanic American Report* 9, no. 2 (March 1956).

34. The opposition presidential candidates called a press conference to present evidence of fraudulent electoral registries. They also claimed that their sympathizers were being hounded and even jailed by the authorities. However, they refrained from demanding an investigation because, as they claimed, the entire government and electoral apparatus was in the hands of the PRUD. *La Prensa Gráfica* (2 March 1956).

35. Statement by the secretary general of the PRUD, José María Peralta Salazar, *La Prensa Gráfica* (1 March 1956)

36. *La Prensa Gráfica* (14 May 1956).

37. *La Prensa Gráfica* (18 May 1956).

38. "Memoria presentada por el presidente José María Lemus ante la Asamblea Legislativa," *Boletín del Ejército* 9/35 (27 September 1957).

39. "Discurso del presidente José María Lemus ante la Asamblea Legislativa en su sesión inaugural," *Boletín del Ejército* 10/18 (20 June 1958). In an interview given around this time to the magazine *Visión* and transcribed in *Boletín del Ejército* 11/23 (3 July 1959), Lemus insisted that the opposition's problem was that it just had not organized, even though it had all the conditions and facilities for doing so.

40. One of Lemus's yearly speeches before the legislative assembly is very eloquent in this regard. He said that "an enormous sector of the population that lives in the rural areas has not achieved the benefits of a program of social improvement that has raised the well-being of the cities. . . . This peasant population . . . in its current state can turn into the most fertile and appropriate ground for the activities of agitators and perturbers of social peace." "Memoria presentada por el presidente José María Lemus ante la Asamblea Legislativa," *Boletín del Ejército* 9/35 (27 September 1957).

41. See, for example, the strongly anticommunist and anti-Soviet editorials under the title "El comunismo: la religión del mal" ("Communism: the religion of evil") that appeared in the *Boletín del Ejército* 3/20 (29 June 1951) and three following issues.

42. *Boletín del Ejército* 4/39 (5 November 1952).

43. *La Prensa Gráfica* (7 October 1960). In his statements to the press, Lemus insisted that the struggle against communism would be fought principally on the economic field in order to raise the living standards of "the less favored classes."

44. See, for example, an editorial in the *Boletín del Ejército* 7/7 (4 March 1955), which states that "subversive ideas [ideas disolventes]" found "good soil to grow on due to the illiterate masses' inability to think [analizar]."

45. See, for example, a communiqué issued by AGEUS (Asociación General de Estudiantes Universitarios Salvadoreños) in March 1956, which states that opposition candidates for office are the same as the government's candidates, because all the opposition leaders were at one time part of the regime. Furthermore, they argued, those who bankroll the government party also contribute to the opposition. Thus, the people must organize around truly democratic organizations if they want things to change. *La Prensa Gráfica* (2 March 1956).

46. Reference to the military as the "mailed fist of the people" (brazo armado del pueblo) was used first in Decree 1 of the CGR on 16 December 1948. In translating the term we have used some license because a literal translation (the "armed arm of the people") not only sounds strange but makes little sense in English.

47. Ricardo Gallardo suggests that giving the military the responsibility to impede presidential reelection was tantamount to creating a fourth branch of government since the military could decide when and how the constitution was being violated. Ricardo Gallardo, *Las constituciones de El Salvador,* tomo 2 (Madrid: Instituto de Cultura Hispánica, 1961), 211.

48. In addition to the regular instruction in literacy and mathematics that recruits received in the barracks, after 1950 the ministry of defense also distributed material to combat alcoholism and even had the recruits read Alberto Masferrer's "El dinero maldito," a tract published in the 1920s that is highly critical of materialist values and unbridled capitalism. Recruits also received training in improved agricultural methods since most were individuals "whose life is given over entirely to agriculture that they practice with primitive methods." *Boletín del Ejército* 2/6 (24 February 1950). A more political motivation for education in the military was expressed in 1952: "[the recruits] are taught their civic duties in such a manner that when they leave the barracks they cannot be fooled easily by political operators and individuals with extremist ideas." *Boletín del Ejército* 4/21 (20 June 1952).

49. See, for example, the issue of the *Boletín del Ejército* 4/21 (20 June 1952) that has an editorial that speaks of the unity between soldiers and teachers.

50. President Osorio said as much during his speech on Soldier's Day (Día del soldado): "[Among the accomplishments of the revolution] that which refers to the inalterable public order is perhaps the most important." *La Prensa Gráfica* (8 May 1956).

51. *Boletín del Ejército* 9/30 (23 August 1957). An editorial in this same issue states that the objective of the agreement with the United States is to create a "technical police force."

52. *La Prensa Gráfica* (3 March 1949).

53. *Boletín del Ejército* 2/9 (17 March 1950). See also a speech by Colonel Lemus, then minister of the interior, in *Boletín del Ejército* 2/13 (21 April 1950). The military cooperative still functions today as one of the most important retail outlets in the country.

54. El Salvador, Ministerio de Defensa Nacional, *Memoria de 1951* (San Salvador: Imprenta Nacional, 1951); and *Boletín del Ejército* 10/1 (24 January 1958).

55. *Boletín del Ejército* 5/19 (29 May 1953). The agreement to send a military mission to El Salvador was signed in September 1954, after the Guatemalan crisis had been resolved. Don Etchison, *The United States and Militarism in Central America* (New York: Praeger Publishers, 1975), 129.

56. See "Memorandum by Gordon S. Reid of the Office of Middle American Affairs to the Deputy Assistant Secretary of State for Inter-American Affairs (Woodward), 18 June 1953," in U.S. Department of State, *Foreign Relations of the United States, 1952–1954*, vol. 4, 1000–05. Reid states that "the primary job [of the United States] in El Salvador will be to encourage the Salvadorans to defend themselves against the Guatemalan onslaught. To accomplish this will mean that we must give every consideration to the Salvadoran request for arms and other security and intelligence measures."

57. For the Salvadoran position in regard to the Guatemala military, see *Boletín del Ejército* 4/13 (18 April 1952), which also reports on the visit of a Guatemalan military delegation to San Salvador in April 1952 to decorate some Salvadoran officers; the Guatemalan officer that headed the mission referred to the events of 1944 (in Guatemala) and 1948 (in El Salvador) as "crusades" led by their "military youths" *[juventudes militares]*. For the Salvadoran government's role in the negotiations following the overthrow of the Arbenz government, see *Boletín del Ejército* 5/25 (9 July 1954).

58. *Boletín del Ejército* 9/17 (17 May 1957).

59. El Salvador, Ministerio de Defensa, *Memoria de 1954* (San Salvador: Imprenta Nacional, 1954), 152–53; *Memoria de 1956* (San Salvador: Imprenta Nacional, 1956), 88–90; *Memoria de 1958* (San Salvador: Imprenta Nacional, 1958), 37.

60. Etchison, *The United States and Militarism in Central America,* table 4, 95. The amount in question was under $50,000.

61. In 1952, the minister of defense, Colonel Oscar A. Bolaños, stated that most recruits came from rural areas because the military wished to cooperate with the national literacy campaign. El Salvador, Ministerio del Defensa, *Memoria para 1952* (San Salvador: Imprenta Nacional, 1952), 75.

62. El Salvador, Ministerio del Defensa, *Memoria de 1955* (San Salvador: Imprenta Nacional 1955), 273; and *Memoria de 1956* (San Salvador: Imprenta Nacional, 1956), 228.

63. *Memoria de 1955,* 273.

64. According to data in Etchison's study, the military reserves of El Salvador stood at around thirty thousand at the beginning of the 1970s, but it is not clear if this figure also includes the *patrullas cantonales*. Etchison, *The United States and Militarism in Central America,* 121.

65. *Hispanic American Report* 9, no. 10 (November 1956); Victor Bulmer-Thomas, *The Political Economy of Central America Since 1920* (Cambridge: Cambridge University Press, 1987), 155–70.

66. See, for example, Colonel Lemus's speech before the legislative assembly in August 1958. *Boletín del Ejército* 10/27 (29 August 1958).

67. Lemus was quite direct about the problem of rural workers: "[Their] current salaries are low to begin with and I ask you not to lower it because it is at the limit. A reduction of one cent can mean social ferment and the government would face many problems that it wishes to avoid at all cost." *Boletín del Ejército* 10/42 (12 December 1958). In August 1959, Lemus introduced legislation to establish a minimum wage for rural workers; however, the proposed measure created tensions with a group of large coffee

producers from Ahuachapán. Roberto Turcios, *Autoritarismo y modernización 1950–1960* (San Salvador: Ediciones Tendencias, 1993), 170–72.

68. *Hispanic American Report* 12, no. 7 (September 1959) and 12, no. 8 (October 1959).

69. *Boletín del Ejército* 11/19 (5 June 1959).

70. *Hispanic American Report* 12, no. 11 (January 1960) and 12, no. 12 (February 1960). On 14 December 1959 a military parade in San Salvador celebrating the anniversary of the 1948 coup was disrupted by rock-throwing demonstrators. See Turcios, *Autoritarismo y modernización*, 160–61.

71. *Hispanic American Report* 13, no. 4 (June 1960).

72. In fact, in July the Central Electoral Council (CCE) had rejected an application by PRAM to become a legally recognized party. The CCE reasoned that PRAM was committed to destroying democracy and installing a revolutionary regime and thus could not participate in the country's electoral contests. *Hispanic American Report* 13, no. 7 (September 1960).

73. *Hispanic American Report* 13, no. 8 (October 1960). For a detailed discussion of the disturbances leading up to the October 1960 coup, see also Turcios, *Autoritarismo y modernización*, 161–78.

74. The three officers were Colonel César Yánes Urías, Lieutenant Colonel Miguel Angel Castillo, and Major Manuel Antonio Rosales. The civilians were Fabio Castillo, René Fortín Magaña, and Ricardo Cáceres; Castillo had been dean of the medical school of the national university and the other two had taught law there. According to Turcios, another group of officers led by Major Roberto López Trejos had also been plotting together with a group of civilians to overthrow Lemus; however, Osorio, who was aware of their plans, struck first. Ironically, most of the civilians aligned with López Trejos ended up as members of the new junta. Turcios, *Autoritarismo y modernización*, 173–78.

75. Interview with Ivo Priamo Alvarenga (San Salvador, 23 May 1995). Alvarenga was a student leader who participated actively in the demonstrations prior to the overthrow of Colonel Lemus. In his opinion, electoral fraud and imposition were the predominant issues underlying the political ferment before the coup.

76. *La Prensa Gráfica* (27 October 1960). In strictly legal terms, the junta explained that it had acted under Article 112 of the Constitution of 1950, which called for citizen rebellion when the sitting government violated the constitution's provisions. See also a communiqué by the junta that states that Lemus's regime "had disregarded . . . the fundamental rights of the citizen." *La Prensa Gráfica* (17 November 1960).

77. *La Prensa Gráfica* (29 October 1960).

78. *La Prensa Gráfica* (1 November 1960).

79. Statement by the minister of the interior underlining "the absolute impartiality and neutrality" of the government. *La Prensa Gráfica* (5 November 1960). Colonel César Yanez Urías, a member of the junta, made a similar pledge a few weeks later. *La Prensa Gráfica* (21 December 1960).

80. The university student association (Asociación General de Estudiantes Universitarios Salvadoreños, AGEUS) and the labor confederation (Confederación General de Trabajadores Salvadoreños, CGTS) gave their open support to the junta and demanded the removal of municipal and other authorities who were supposedly blocking the junta's efforts. *La Prensa Gráfica* (18 November 1960).

81. The three members of the electoral commission had no obvious party affiliation but were well known for their democratic positions; one of the members was Guillermo Manuel Ungo, who later would become leader of the Salvadoran social democrats and a

prominent figure within the coalition of political parties and guerrilla organizations that confronted successive Salvadoran governments during the 1980s. *La Prensa Gráfica* (9 December 1960). The congress charged with producing a draft of a new electoral law would have representation of the principal lawyers' association, university law faculty, law students' association, and political parties in existence over the last ten years, as well as those parties in the process of organizing. *La Prensa Gráfica* (13 December 1960).

82. A few days after the coup, exiles began to return from neighboring countries, including members of the Communist Party. *La Prensa Gráfica* (28 October 1960).

83. *La Prensa Gráfica* (8 December 1960) and 3 January 1961).

84. *La Prensa Gráfica* (23 and 28 November 1960). In general, the Christian Democrats defined themselves as a third force, between liberalism and communism, and appealed for support from all sectors of society, according to a communiqué they published in *La Prensa Gráfica* (5 December 1960).

85. *La Prensa Gráfica* (2 November 1960).

86. Ibid. (20 January 1961).

87. Ibid. (5 January 1961).

88. Ibid. (14 December 1960; 16 December 1960; and 27 December 1960).

89. Ibid. (17 December 1960).

90. Ibid. (20 December 1960).

91. Ibid. (22 December 1960).

92. Ibid. (16 December 1960).

93. Ibid. (19 November 1960; 25 December 1960; and 28 December 1960). The *partidas secretas* have been a constant of the Salvadoran state and are still part of the annual budget. Under current law, the president of the republic can make use of them for whatever is deemed necessary and need provide no accounting of such expenditures.

94. *La Prensa Gráfica* (20 December 1960).

95. See statement by the junta's minister of defense, Colonel Alonso Castillo Navarrete, who insisted that the junta represented a solid bloc between the military and the people. *La Prensa Gráfica* (13 November 1960). See also a statement by the junta's minister of foreign affairs, Rolando Déneke, underlining the junta's "truly national and authentically democratic" credentials. *La Prensa Gráfica* (17 November 1960).

96. The minister of economics had to disclaim that there were plans to nationalize the central bank or any private bank, the junta reiterated its respect for private property and western, representative democracy, and the minister of defense declared that the military would remain vigilant to prevent the introduction of communist literature and propaganda. See *La Prensa Gráfica* (18 November 1960; 22 November 1960; 23 November 1960; 10 January 1961; and 17 January 1961).

97. *La Prensa Gráfica* (22 January 1961).

98. *La Prensa Gráfica* (18 November 1960; 19 November 1960; and 20 November 1960). According to Tommie Sue Montgomery, U.S. officials had a direct hand in the coup. She cites as evidence testimony given by Fabio Castillo (civilian junta member) before the U.S. Congress in 1976. Castillo claimed that members of the U.S. military mission openly encouraged officers to carry out a countercoup and were present at the San Carlos barracks on the day of the coup. Tommie Sue Montgomery, *Revolution in El Salvador: From Civil Strife to Civil Peace* (Boulder: Westview Press, 1995), 52–53.

99. *La Prensa Gráfica* (21 November 1960).

100. *La Prensa Gráfica* (23 November 1960 and 17 January 1961).

101. *La Prensa Gráfica* (24 January 1961).

102. Colonel Lemus's response to a series of questions posed by *Life en español*

(reproduced by *Boletín del Ejército* 11/47 [15 January 1960]) is interesting in this regard. He openly admitted the military's preponderant presence and underlined the role of the new military officer, trained formally and extensively to enable him to undertake responsibilities outside of the strictly military field. For Lemus, little difference existed between civilians and military officers.

103. See, for example, Oscar Osorio, *Mensaje dirigido al pueblo salvadoreño el 14 de septiembre de 1953* (San Salvador: Imprenta Nacional, 1953), 8–9.

4. THE ERA OF NATIONAL CONCILIATION

1. The civilian members of the deposed junta were sent abroad, as was ex-President Oscar Osorio. The two military members of the junta also were exiled as military attaches in the Salvadoran embassies in Mexico and Italy. *La Prensa Gráfica* (27 January 1961 and 12 February 1961).

2. The plotters seem to have come primarily from the general staff school. *La Prensa Gráfica* (27 January 1961). Ivo Priamo Alvarenga considers that the rebel officers were far better prepared academically than those who supported the October coup; they were called the "coroneles doctores" in reference to their advanced schooling. Interview with Alvarenga (San Salvador, 9 June 1995).

3. *La Prensa Gráfica* (26 January 1961). A more subtle argument was made by Colonel Mariano Castro Morán, who joined the *directorio* when Colonel Rivera stepped down to run for president; Castro Morán claimed that the military was the only institution that had survived "the legal catastrophe" caused by the October junta and thus was obliged to set things right. El Salvador, *Mensaje de los señores miembros del Directorio Cívico Militar de El Salvador el 2 de enero de 1962* (San Salvador: Imprenta Nacional, 1962), 6.

4. "Proclama de la Fuerza Armada," *La Prensa Gráfica* (5 February 1961).

5. Statement by the minister of the interior, Colonel Francisco José Sol, when he announced that state-owned lands would be divided up among campesinos. *La Prensa Gráfica* (13 February 1961). Colonel Rivera also announced that communism would be countered with "measures of social justice." *La Prensa Gráfica* (14 February 1961).

6. *Hispanic American Report* 14, no. 2 (April 1961).

7. Ibid., no. 3 (May 1961).

8. Ibid., no. 4 (June 1961).

9. Ibid., no. 9 (November 1961).

10. Ibid., no. 10 (December 1961).

11. The political parties met with the directorio the very next day after the coup but made it clear that they were not expressing support for the directorio nor approving its choice of cabinet ministers. The Christian Democrats put out a statement of their own denying they had anything to do with the coup itself. *La Prensa Gráfica* (27 January 1961).

12. *La Prensa Gráfica* (29 January 1961). The Christian Democrats demanded proportional representation, clean voter rolls, and state financing for parties, among others. *La Prensa Gráfica* (28 February 1961).

13. El Salvador, Directorio Cívico Militar, "Ley electoral," *Diario Oficial* 192 (12 September 1961), articles 3, 20, 119, and 121.

14. Ibid., article 71.

15. *La Prensa Gráfica* (28 January 1961).

16. *La Prensa Gráfica* (14 February 1961).

17. *La Prensa Gráfica* (26 February 1961) and *Hispanic American Report* 14, no. 3 (May 1961).

18. *Hispanic American Report* 14, no. 7 (September 1961).

19. *La Prensa Gráfica* (3 February 1961) and *Hispanic American Report* 14, no. 6 (August 1961).

20. Statements by the minister of defense, Colonel Armando Molina Mena, *La Prensa Gráfica* (19 February 1961). Colonel Molina said that the military was committed "to putting an end, once and for all, to that absurd gap between the army and the people that bad regimes created and maintained" in the past.

21. *Hispanic American Report* 14, no. 9 (November 1961).

22. For a detailed description of the organization and functioning of the PCN, see Alastair White, *El Salvador* (London: Ernest Benn Limited, 1973), especially chapter 7.

23. See White, *El Salvador*, 199–200, for a summary of the PDC's stance.

24. Interview with Héctor Dada (San Salvador, 10 August 1995). As one of the historic leaders of the PDC up until the 1980s, Mr. Dada recounts meetings with military officers who expressed their concern toward the Christian Democrats because no constitutional or political provisions existed to allow the government to declare the party illegal.

25. For a good summary of political parties in the 1960s, see White, *El Salvador*, 200–05.

26. *Hispanic American Report* 14, nos. 10–11 (December 1961 and January 1962).

27. *Hispanic American Report* 14, no. 12 (February 1962).

28. It should be noted that Mr. Cordón was the only civilian to occupy the executive office of El Salvador between the overthrow of Arturo Araujo in 1931 and the appointment by the legislature of Alvaro Magaña in 1982.

29. See the Social Democrats' communiqué in *La Prensa Gráfica* (4 March 1962). Their indictment of the armed forces' role reflected the predicament of all civilian political groups: "While officers in active service campaign on behalf of one of their own; while the security forces in their entirety, such as the *Guardia Nacional*, encouraged by their director, provide activists for a given party; while an 'official party' exists and receives funds from the public treasury; while the armed forces as an institution do not abandon the field of politics, retire to their barracks, and limit their activities to their prescribed technical functions, political liberty and electoral purity are impossible."

30. *La Prensa Gráfica* (20 and 22 March 1962).

31. Ibid. (5 and 9 March 1962).

32. Ibid. (15 and 28 March 1962).

33. Ibid. (8 March 1962).

34. "Mensaje del teniente coronel Julio A. Rivera al pueblo salvadoreño," paid communiqué in *La Prensa Gráfica* (30 March 1962). See also a communiqué of the PCN in *La Prensa Gráfica* (13 March 1962), which makes similar points and discounts all of the opposition parties as "mere oligarchies or small opportunistic groups."

35. *La Prensa Gráfica* (30 April and 1 May 1962).

36. *Hispanic American Report* 15, no. 9 (November 1962).

37. El Salvador, Teniente Colonel Julio A. Rivera, *Informe Presidencial—Primer año de gobierno (1 de julio de 1963)* (San Salvador: Imprenta Nacional, 1963), 67.

38. *Hispanic American Report* 15, no. 10 (December 1962).

39. Ibid., 16, no. 6 (August 1963).

40. Ibid., 16, no. 11 (January 1964).

41. Ibid., 17, no. 3 (May 1964).

42. *New York Times*, 15 March 1964.

43. El Salvador, Teniente Colonel Julio A. Rivera, *Informe Presidencial—Tercer año de gobierno (1 de julio de 1965)* (San Salvador: Imprenta Nacional, 1965).

44. *New York Times,* 21 January and 15 March 1966.

45. See James Dunkerley, *Power in the Isthmus* (London: Verso Press, 1988), 356–57, for an analysis of the ideological stance of the PDC and the PAR.

46. See David Browning, *El Salvador: Landscape and Society* (Oxford: Oxford University Press, 1971), chapter 6, for a discussion of land use in mid-twentieth century El Salvador.

47. See Robert G. Williams, *Export Agriculture and the Crisis in Central America* (Chapel Hill: University of North Carolina Press, 1986), especially 55–65.

48. *New York Times,* 5 and 7 March 1967.

49. *New York Times,* 12 March and 21 June 1968.

50. *New York Times,* 21 June 1968; White, *El Salvador,* 205. After the 1968 elections, two-thirds of the country's population lived in municipalities that had come under the control of the PDC. Interview with Héctor Dada, San Salvador, January 8, 1996.

51. Data on troop size is from Don Etchison, *The United States and Militarism in Central America* (New York: Praeger Publishers, 1975), 120–21; figure on annual recruitment is from Willard Barber and C. Neale Ronning, *Internal Security and Military Power: Counterinsurgency and Civic Action in Latin America* (Columbus: Ohio State University Press, 1966), 186.

52. Data on military spending can be found in El Salvador, Dirección General de Estadística y Censos, *Anuario Estadístico,* for years in question. Data on troop size and U.S. military assistance is from Etchison, *The United States and Militarism in Central America,* 95–98 and 120–21.

53. El Salvador, Ministerio de Defensa y Seguridad Pública, *Memoria de labores de 1963* (San Salvador: Imprenta Nacional, 1963), 79; and Barber and Ronning, *Internal Security and Military Power,* 120.

54. El Salvador, Ministerio de Defensa, *Memoria de labores de 1966* (San Salvador: Imprenta Nacional, 1966), 27–30; and *Memoria de labores de 1971* (San Salvador: Imprenta Nacional, 1971), 33–39.

55. Most of the planning and execution of civic action projects involved the military's engineering battalion and gave priority to building repairs and the construction of rural roads, sports fields, and bridges. Barber and Ronning, *Internal Security and Military Power,* 121.

56. El Salvador, Ministerio de Defensa, *Memoria de labores de 1966,* 33–35.

57. Barber and Ronning, *Internal Security and Military Power,* 181–82.

58. White, *El Salvador,* 207.

59. Ibid. Not until 1975 did the government specifically mention ORDEN as a "state institution." El Salvador, Ministerio de Defensa, *Memoria de labores de 1975* (San Salvador: Imprenta Nacional, 1975), 15–19.

60. See White, *El Salvador,* 207–09, for a detailed analysis of how the official party and the paramilitary organization worked to keep the rural areas under control and to ensure that rural voters toed the official party line. For a more recent account of ORDEN's origins, including the U.S. role in its creation, see Allan Nairn, "Behind the Death Squads," *The Progressive* (May 1984): 20–29. The heart of Nairn's article is based on an interview with "Chele" Medrano, ORDEN's founder.

61. A compelling analysis of population growth and land concentration in both El Salvador and Honduras is found in William H. Durham, *Scarcity and Survival in Central America* (Stanford: Stanford University Press, 1979).

62. Williams, *Export Agriculture and the Crisis in Central America,* 65.

63. See, for example, Marco Virgilio Carías and Daniel Slutsky, eds., *La guerra inútil: Análisis socioeconómico del conflicto entre Honduras y El Salvador* (San José, Costa Rica: EDUCA, 1971); and Thomas Anderson, *The War of the Dispossessed: Honduras and El Salvador, 1969* (Lincoln: University of Nebraska Press, 1981).

64. President Sánchez Hernández recognized one year after the war that the Salvadoran soldier had gone into battle with only the limited gear of an army in peacetime. Fidel Sánchez Hernández, *Informe rendido por el señor Presidente de la República ante la Asamblea Legislativa el 1 de julio de 1970 al cumplirse el tercer año de su gobierno* (San Salvador: Imprenta Nacional, 1970), 10.

65. Fidel Sánchez Hernández, "Discurso improvisado pronunciado el día 6 de agosto de 1969 en homenaje a la Fuerza Armada Salvadoreña," in *Discursos del señor Presidente de la República*, tomo 3 (San Salvador: Publicaciones del Departamento de Relaciones Públicas de Casa Presidencial, 1970), 25.

66. *La Prensa Gráfica* (24 June 1969).

67. Fidel Sánchez Hernández, "Mensaje dirigido al pueblo salvadoreño en relación con los actos de agresión de Honduras a El Salvador, 14 de julio de 1969," in *Discursos del Señor Presidente de la República*, 9.

68. Fidel Sánchez Hernández, "Mensaje dirigido al pueblo salvadoreño, 18 de julio de 1969," in *Discursos del Señor Presidente de la República*, 12. In his words, "our struggle is not a war of conquest but a crusade for human dignity. The humble Salvadoran persecuted in Honduras is the symbol of all men and all minorities who are harassed and oppressed in the four corners of the world."

69. Fidel Sánchez Hernández, "Mensaje al ejército salvadoreño con motivo de la victoria, 26 de julio de 1969," in *Discursos del Señor Presidente de la República*, 16–17.

70. Fidel Sánchez Hernández, "Mensaje al pueblo salvadoreño en el día del triunfo, 30 de julio de 1969," in *Discursos del Señor Presidente de la República*, 20. President Sánchez Hernández made the case for the military's special concern for the rural population in the following terms: "We, the members of the armed forces, proudly recognize our popular origins and we are conscious of the needs and wishes of the people. We know that those peasants who defended with gun in hand the homes of the Salvadorans, and those who remained here working, but willing nonetheless to march to the front lines, deserve a better fate, a more dignified life." Fidel Sánchez Hernández, "Mensaje con motivo de celebrarse el Día del Soldado Salvadoreño," in *Discursos del Señor Presidente de la República*, 63.

71. Fidel Sánchez Hernández, "Discurso pronunciado el 15 de septiembre de 1969 con ocasión de celebrarse la independencia política de Centroamérica," in *Discursos del Señor Presidente de la República*, 35.

72. Fidel Sánchez Hernández, "Discurso pronunciado al inaugurar el congreso de reforma agraria el 5 de enero de 1970," in *Discursos del Señor Presidente de la República*, 49–50.

73. Of particular significance is the statement made by President Sánchez Hernández in a speech commemorating independence from Spain: "What our founding fathers did for us is of less interest than what we are willing to do for our descendants. More than the well-justified emotions that we feel for the glory of dead Salvadorans, we should be shaken by the pain of so many compatriots who live in misery." Fidel Sánchez Hernández, "Discurso pronunciado el 15 de septiembre de 1969 con ocasión de celebrarse la independencia política de Centroamérica," in *Discursos del Señor Presidente de la República*, 33–36.

74. Fidel Sánchez Hernández, "Discurso pronunciado al inaugurar el congreso de reforma agraria el 5 de enero de 1970," in *Discursos del Señor Presidente de la República,* 50.

75. White, *El Salvador,* 205.

76. For a more detailed discussion of the educational reforms under Sánchez Hernández, see Stephen Webre, *José Napoleón Duarte and the Christian Democratic Party in Salvadoran Politics: 1960–1972* (Baton Rouge: Louisiana State University Press, 1979), 151–52. On the issue of land reform, President Sánchez Hérnandez had announced early on in his government that any land reform measure would affect only the property rights of owners of uncultivated and underutilized lands. Fidel Sánchez Hernández, *Informe rendido por el señor Presidente de la Repúblic,* 7–8.

77. The UDN was founded by individuals who had splintered off the PAR and other noncommunist groupings but also included members of the Communist Party of El Salvador. In this manner, the Communists were able to participate in the political process without violating the constitutional provisions that expressly prohibited communist political activities. See James Dunkerley, *Power in the Isthmus: A Political History of Modern Central America* (London: Verso, 1988), 360; and White, *El Salvador,* 205.

78. The constitution stipulated that in the event that no candidate received an absolute majority of votes the legislative assembly would elect the president. *Latin America* 6, no. 9 (3 March 1972): 69.

79. Juan Hernández Pico et al., *El Salvador: Año político 1971–1972* (San Salvador: Publicaciones de la Universidad Centroamericana José Simeón Cañas, 1973), 14–15.

80. Ibid., 48–51.

81. A detailed and fascinating analysis of the 1972 election results can be found in Hernández Pico et al., *Año político,* 52–79.

82. See, for example, Ronald H. McDonald, "Electoral Behavior and Political Development in El Salvador," *Journal of Politics* 31, no. 2 (May 1969): 397–419.

83. Interview with Héctor Dada, 4 January 1996. Actually, the Christian Democrats were not formally a member of the international Christian Democratic movement but maintained frequent contacts with the latter.

84. El Salvador, Ministerio de Defensa y Seguridad Pública, *Memoria de labores de 1961* (San Salvador: Imprenta Nacional, 1961), 3.

85. El Salvador, Ministerio de Defensa y Seguridad Pública, *Memoria de labores de 1964* (San Salvador: Imprenta Nacional, 1964), 6–9. The minister of defense spoke of the support the military gave to "una verdadera conciliación nacional," clearly meaning the policies espoused by the PCN. See also *Memoria de labores de 1969* (San Salvador: Imprenta Nacional, 1969), 10, which underscores the role of the military in maintaining "the organization of the republic."

86. El Salvador, Ministerio de Defensa y Seguridad Pública, *Memoria de labores de 1963* (San Salvador: Imprenta Nacional, 1963), 6.

87. El Salvador, Ministerio de Defensa y Seguridad Pública, *Memoria de labores de 1967* (San Salvador: Imprenta Nacional, 1967), 8. In his words, the common belief that the military was the great elector "has been erased, perhaps forever, from public opinion."

88. Fidel Sánchez Hernández, *Discurso pronunciado por el señor Presidente de la República y Comandante General de la Fuerza Armada con motivo del "Día del Soldado Salvadoreño" el 7 de mayo de 1969* (San Salvador: Imprenta Nacional, 1969), 4–9.

89. In 1966, the minister of defense flatly stated that the security forces guaranteed "the inviolability of the private property of Salvadoran citizens." El Salvador, Ministerio de Defensa y Seguridad Pública, *Memoria de labores de 1966* (San Salvador: Imprenta Nacional, 1966), 69. See also White, *El Salvador,* especially 193–97, for an analysis of the relations between civilians and military officers.

90. For a detailed analysis of U.S. participation in security concerns in El Salvador in the 1960s, see Michael McClintock, *The American Connection: State Terror and Popular Resistance in El Salvador* (London: Zed Books, 1985), especially 196–214.

5. THE POLITICAL CRISIS OF THE 1970S

1. Out of approximately 144,000 votes cast, some seventy-five thousand were null, as compared to less than seventy thousand valid votes divided between the PCN and PPS. For a detailed discussion of the elections, see Stephen Webre, *José Napoleón Duarte and the Christian Democratic Party in Salvadoran Politics: 1960–1972* (Baton Rouge: Louisiana State University Press, 1979), 158–76.

2. Juan Hernández Pico et al., *El Salvador: Año político 1971–72* (San Salvador: Universidad Centroamericana, 1973), 24–25. See also Cap. Francisco Emilio Mena Sandoval, *Del ejército nacional al ejército guerrillero* (San Salvador: Arcoiris Editores, 1992), 79–82.

3. The best treatments of the 1972 coup can be found in Hernández Pico et al., *Año político,* and Webre, *José Napoleón Duarte.*

4. Quoted in Hernández Pico et al., *Año político,* 128.

5. In their proclamation, rebel officers pointed to the absence of constitutional order and government corruption as well as electoral fraud as justifications for the coup. Ibid., 131–32.

6. Enrique Baloyra, *El Salvador en transición* (San Salvador: UCA Editores, 1982). For a good summary of the different interpretations of the coup, see Edgar Jiménez, "El golpe del 15 de octubre de 1979 y la crisis política nacional," in Edgar Jiménez et al., eds., *El Salvador: Guerra, política y paz (1979–1988)* (San Salvador: CINAS, 1988), 63–82.

7. Enrique Baloyra, "Reactionary Despotism in Central America," *Journal of Latin American Studies* 15, no. 2 (1983): 315.

8. For example, see Fernando Flores Pinel, "El golpe de estado en El Salvador: Un camino hacia la democratización?," *Estudios Centroamericanos* nos. 372–73 (1979): 885–904; and Italo López Vallecillos, "Rasgos sociales y tendencias políticas en El Salvador: 1969–1979," *Estudios Centroamericanos* nos. 372–73 (1979): 863–84.

9. Victor Bulmer-Thomas, *The Political Economy of Central America Since 1920* (Cambridge: Cambridge University Press, 1987), 188.

10. For a good discussion of the impact of the cotton boom on the peasantry in El Salvador, see Robert Williams, *Export Agriculture and the Crisis in Central America* (Chapel Hill: University of North Carolina Press, 1986), 52–73.

11. James Dunkerley, *Power in the Isthmus: A Political History of Modern Central America* (London: Verso, 1988), 192.

12. For an excellent discussion of Salvadoran migration to Honduras and the origins of the Soccer War, see William Durham, *Scarcity and Survival in Central America* (Stanford: Stanford University Press, 1979).

13. Charles Brockett, *Land, Power and Poverty* (Boulder: Westview Press, 1990), 75.

14. Bulmer-Thomas, *The Political Economy of Central America,* 185.

15. Ibid., 192–99.

16. For a more detailed discussion of the popular mobilization that occurred during the late 1960s and early 1970s, see Brockett, *Land, Power and Poverty,* 148–53; Dunkerley, *Power in the Isthmus,* 364–68; Phillip Berryman, *The Religious Roots of Rebellion* (London: SCM Press Ltd., 1984), chapter 5; and Tommie Sue Montgomery, *Revolution in El Salvador: From Civil Strife to Civil Peace* (Boulder: Westview Press, 1995), chapter 4.

17. According to the minister of defense, the army received "recruits completely ignorant of military service" and four months later produced model soldiers. Ministerio

de Defensa y Seguridad Pública, *Memoria 1974* (El Salvador: Imprenta Nacional, 1974), 43.

18. For a discussion of U.S. security assistance programs and their impact, see Michael McClintock, *The American Connection: State Terror and Popular Resistance in El Salvador* (London: Zed Books, 1985), 196–222.

19. El Salvador, Ministerio de Defensa y Seguridad Pública, *Memoria—1975* (San Salvador: Imprenta Nacional, 1975), 19–20, 37–43.

20. El Salvador, Ministerio de Defensa y Seguridad Pública, *Memoria—1977* (San Salvador: Imprenta Nacional, 1977), 3–5.

21. El Salvador, Ministerio de Defensa y Seguridad Pública, *Memoria—1979* (San Salvador: Imprenta Nacional, 1979), 23.

22. Dunkerley, *Power in the Isthmus,* 363–64.

23. See Montgomery, *Revolution in El Salvador,* chaps. 3–4.

24. According to both Montgomery and Stanley, citing confidential informants, Romero threatened to stage a coup if Molina went ahead with the reform plan. Montgomery, *Revolution in El Salvador,* 68, and William Stanley, "The Elite Politics of State Terrorism in El Salvador," Ph.D. diss., Massachusetts Institute of Technology, September 1991, 240–45.

25. Stephen Webre, *José Napoleón Duarte and the Christian Democratic Party in Salvadoran Politics: 1960–1972* (Baton Rouge: Louisiana State University Press, 1979), 193–95.

26. In August 1969, Sánchez Hernández established an agrarian commission to study the issue and make recommendations. A few months later, the national assembly convoked the National Agrarian Congress with representatives from the government, private sector, labor, and political opposition parties. Although the private sector withdrew from the Congress, it continued its work, approving a list of recommendations on various issues related to a projected reform plan. In his opening address at the Congress, Sánchez Hernández underlined the "unavoidable necessity" of agrarian reform. Webre, *José Napoleón Duarte,* 122–30.

27. Ibid., 189–90.

28. *Latin America Political Report,* 4 March 1977.

29. López Vallecillos, "Rasgos sociales," 871.

30. Stanley, "Elite Politics," 269.

31. Ibid., 296–97.

32. Ministerio de Defensa y Seguridad Pública, *Memoria de 1977* (San Salvador: Imprenta Nacional, 1977), 89.

33. Rivera, who graduated in the ninth promotion (1939), was succeeded by Sánchez Hernández of the eighth promotion (1938). Similarly, Molina, of the nineteenth promotion (1949), tapped Romero of the eighteenth promotion (1948).

34. Sara Gordon, *Crisis política y guerra en El Salvador* (Mexico, D.F.: Siglo 21, 1989), 159.

35. Lt. Col. José Guillermo García was appointed president of ANTEL in 1974; Lt. Col. Carlos Eugenio Vides Casanova was appointed president of INSAFI (Instituto Salvadoreño de Fomento Industrial) in 1975; Lt. Col. Nicolás Carranza was appointed a technical manager of ANTEL in 1974; and Lt. Col. Jaime Abdul Gutiérrez also served as a manager of ANTEL during the Molina government. These officers came to be known as the Equipo Molina. For a list of officers appointed to positions within public institutions during the Molina and Romero governments, see Carlos Andino Martínez,

"El estamento militar in El Salvador," *Estudios Centroamericanos* nos. 369–70 (July-August 1979): 625–27.

36. Interview with Maj. (ret.) Alvaro Salazar Brenes, San Salvador, 9 July 1993.

37. Mena Sandoval, *Del ejército nacional al ejército guerrillero,* 85–99.

38. Castro Morán, *Función política del ejército,* 269.

39. Nicolás Mariscal, "Militares y reformismo en El Salvador," *Estudios Centroamericanos* nos. 351–52 (January-February 1978): 18–19.

40. Stanley, "Elite Politics," 242–43.

41. Interview with Col. Benjamín Ramos, Intelligence Chief of the First Brigade during the 1979 coup, San Salvador, 22 March 1994; interview with Gen. Jaime Abdul Gutiérrez, member of the first junta, San Salvador, 6 July 1993.

42. See also Adolfo Arnoldo Majano, "El Golpe de Estado de 1979: Una Oportunidad Perdida," unpublished ms., 18 May 1989.

43. James Dunkerley, *The Long War* (London: Verso, 1982), 127; and Dermot Keogh, "The United States and the Coup d'Etat in El Salvador, 15 October 1979: A Case Study in American Foreign Policy Perceptions and Decision-making," in Keogh, ed., *Central America: Human Rights and U.S. Foreign Policy* (Cork: Cork University Press, 1985), 34.

44. Castro Morán, *Función política del ejército,* 266.

45. For example, during the Romero government, Col. García was relegated to command the relatively unimportant Fifth Brigade in San Vicente.

46. Stanley, "Elite Politics," 294–95. Stanley writes that this second group of officers "were reportedly seriously considering the prospect of naming a civilian banker and confidant of the military, Alvaro Magaña, as president or as a junta member." (294). This, however, seems highly unlikely, given the presidential ambitions of García and officers' general distrust of civilians.

47. Stanley, "Elite Politics," 321.

48. Guerra y Guerra was serving as an aide to President Romero. He had spent 1970–76 abroad, studying for a master's degree in electrical engineering at Ohio State University. Because of his lengthy absence, many officers viewed him as something of an "outsider."

49. For example, see Keogh, "The United States and the Coup," and Montgomery, *Revolution in El Salvador.*

50. For example, see Stanley, "Elite Politics," Castro Morán, *Función política del ejército,* Mena Sandoval, *Del ejército nacional,* Majano, "El Golpe de Estado," and Keogh, "The United States and the Coup." Gutiérrez, on the other hand, argues that García and Vides enjoyed a degree of leadership within the armed forces that could not be ignored. According to him, "we couldn't leave them out in the cold." Interview with Gutiérrez.

51. For a detailed account of the vote, see Keogh, "The United States and the Coup," 40–45.

52. Ibid., 31–33.

53. Interview with Col. Ramos.

54. See Montgomery, *Revolution in El Salvador,* and Keogh, "The United States and the Coup."

55. Dunkerley, *The Long War,* 128–29, and Baloyra, *El Salvador en Transición,* 121–22.

56. Guerra y Guerra denies that any such support was sought. See Raymond Bonner, *Weakness and Deceit* (New York: Times Books, 1984), 155.

57. According to Tommie Sue Montgomery, the plotters were in direct contact with the U.S. embassy on the day of the coup. Guerra y Guerra sought the help of the military

attaché, Col. Jerry Walker, in trying to get Gen. Romero out of the country. This information is based on interviews Montgomery conducted with Col. Walker in late 1979–early 1980. Personal communication with the authors.

58. Stanley, "Elite Politics," 342–43.

59. "Proclama de la Fuerza Armada de El Salvador—15 de Octubre de 1979," in Tomás Guerra, *El Salvador: Octubre Sangriento* (San Jose: Centro Victor Sanabria, 1979), 16.

60. "Proclama de la Fuerza Armada de la República de El Salvador—15 de Octubre de 1979," in Castro Morán, *Función política del ejército*, 412–15.

61. Interviews with Ramos and Gutiérrez.

62. In exchange for a number of economic concessions on the part of the junta and its announcement of the dissolution of ORDEN, the Bloque Popular Revolucionario ended its occupation of government ministries. Dunkerley, *The Long War*, 142.

63. Baloyra, *El Salvador en transición*, 131–32.

64. Castro Morán, *Función política del ejército*, 416–19.

65. For a more detailed discussion of the crisis, see Montgomery, *Revolution in El Salvador*, 128–29; William Stanley, *The Protection Racket State: Elite Politics, Military Extortion, and Civil War in El Salvador* (Philadelphia: Temple University Press, 1996), 184–85; and Mena Sandoval, *Del Ejército Nacional*, 191.

66. Quoted in Laurie Becklund, "Salvadoran Death Squads: Deadly Other War," *Los Angeles Times*, 18 December 1983.

67. David Browning, "Agrarian Reform in El Salvador," *Journal of Latin American Studies* 15, no. 2 (1983): 399–405.

68. Interview with Ramos. Ramos participated in the capture of D'Aubuisson. See also, McClintock, *The American Connection*, 372–73; and Castro Morán, *Función política del ejército*, 319–20.

69. Stanley, "Elite Politics," 441–42.

70. The Christian Democrats threatened—to no avail—to resign from the junta if D'Aubuisson was set free.

71. FBIS, "Defense Minister's Confirmation," Diario de Hoy, San Salvador, 14 May 1980, FBIS-Central America, 15 May 1980: 2–3.

72. Castro Morán claims the vote was 310 to 210 for Gutiérrez. Our vote totals come from a document presented to us by an officer who was present during the assembly.

73. Dunkerley, *The Long War*, 159.

74. See Laurence Simon and James Stephens, *El Salvador Land Reform, 1980–1981: Impact Audit* (Boston: Oxfam America, 1982).

75. Brockett, *Land, Power and Poverty*, 155–56.

76. Interview with Salazar Brenes.

77. "Crónica del mes," *Estudios Centroamericanos* no. 374 (December 1979): 1089. See also McClintock, *The American Connection*, 257–58.

78. Stanley, "Elite Politics," chap. 6.

79. Mena Sandoval, *Del ejército nacional*, 188. After refusing to obey Gutiérrez, Mena Sandoval was sent to the Second Brigade in Santa Ana. During the FMLN's "final" offensive in January 1981, Mena Sandoval led an abortive revolt in the Second Brigade.

80. Interview with Salazar Brenes.

81. Dunkerley, *The Long War*, 169.

82. FBIS, "Majano Explains Position," Radio Cadena JSU, San Salvador, 4 September 1980, FBIS-Central America, 5 September 1980: 3–4; FBIS, "Radio Station Seized," ACAN-EFE, Panama City, 5 September 1980, FBIS-Central America, 5 September 1980: 5–6.

83. "Civiles de la Junta Revolucionaria de Gobierno se dirigen a los oficiales de la Fuerza Armada de la República," *Estudios Centroamericanos* no. 383 (September 1980): 909–10.

84. Baloyra, *El Salvador en Transición,* 159–60.

85. Stepan, in his study of the Peruvian military's reformist experiment in 1968, uses the concept of "programmatic consensus" to refer to the extent of "prior doctrinal consensus about the general need for, and the specific content of" reformist policies. Stepan, *The State and Society: Peru in Comparative Perspective* (Princeton: Princeton University Press, 1978), chap. 4.

86. Interview with Salazar Brenes.

87. For example, Mena Sandoval led an aborted uprising at the Second Brigade in Santa Ana during the FMLN's "final" offensive in January 1981. Mena Sandoval, however, had a history of insubordination throughout his military career. See Mena Sandoval, *Del ejército nacional.*

88. Majano points out that a new conception of the armed forces was never thoroughly discussed prior to the coup and was not laid out in the Proclama. Majano, "El Golpe de Estado," 72.

89. Baloyra, "Reactionary Despotism," 316.

90. SS 7097, 11 December 1979, National Security Archive, *El Salvador 1977–1984: The Making of U.S. Policy* (Alexandria, Va.: Chadwyck-Healey, 1989).

91. Baloyra, "Reactionary Despotism," 313.

92. Ibid., 315.

93. Rouquié, *The Military and the State,* 38.

6. THE MILITARY AND DEMOCRATIZATION DURING THE 1980S

1. Adam Przeworski, "Democracy as a Contingent Outcome of Conflicts," in Jon Elster and Rune Slagstad, eds., *Constitutionalism and Democracy* (Cambridge: Cambridge University Press, 1988), 61.

2. Ibid.

3. Ibid., 62.

4. Ibid., 63.

5. Terry Karl, "Exporting Democracy: The Unanticipated Effects of US Electoral Policy in El Salvador," in Nora Hamilton et al., eds., *Crisis in Central America* (Boulder: Westview Press, 1988), 187. Przeworski argues, on the contrary, that democracy "cannot be a result of a substantive compromise, but it can be a result of an institutional compromise" (64). While I would agree that an institutional compromise was fundamental in the Salvadoran case, it was not a sufficient basis for a democratic transition. Because of the deep societal divisions resulting from the war, a substantive compromise was also essential.

6. See the article by Joel Millman, "El Salvador's Army: A Force Unto Itself," *New York Times Magazine,* 10 December 1989. ANTEL was an especially prized commodity, given its role in wiretapping telephone conversations of political opposition figures.

7. *Diario Oficial,* "Acuerdo 2," 1 June 1984.

8. Interview with Ramos.

9. For a useful discussion of military prerogatives, see Stepan, *Rethinking Military Politics,* 93–127.

10. Interview with Col. Mauricio Vargas, deputy chief of staff, San Salvador, 14 June 1992.

11. Interview with Col. John Waghelstein, commander, U.S. MILGROUP in El Salvador (1982–83), in Max Manwaring and Court Prisk, eds., *El Salvador at War: An Oral*

History of Conflict from the 1979 Insurrection to the Present (Washington, D.C.: National Defense University Press, 1988), 224.

12. Beatrice Edwards and Gretta Tovar Siebentritt, *Places of Origin: The Repopulation of Rural El Salvador* (Boulder: Lynne Rienner Publishers, 1991), 63–64.

13. Interview with Col. Joseph Stringham, commander, U.S. MILGROUP in El Salvador (1983–84), in Manwaring and Prisk, *El Salvador at War,* 227.

14. Benjamin Schwarz, *American Counterinsurgency Doctrine and El Salvador* (Washington, D.C.: RAND, 1991), 52.

15. Edwards and Siebentritt, *Places of Origin,* 64.

16. Ibid., 65.

17. Sen. Mark Hatfield, Rep. Jim Leach, and Rep. George Miller, "Bankrolling Failure: United States Policy in El Salvador and the Urgent Need for Reform," Report to the Arms Control and Foreign Policy Caucus (Washington, D.C.: November 1987), 9.

18. Schwarz, *American Counterinsurgency Doctrine,* 52.

19. A. J. Bacevich et al., *American Military Policy in Small Wars: The Case of El Salvador* (Washington, D.C.: Pergamon-Brassey's International Defense Publications, 1988), 45.

20. Ibid., 41.

21. Interview with Col. John Ellerson, commander, U.S. MILGROUP in El Salvador (1986–87), in Manwaring and Prisk, *El Salvador at War,* 336–39.

22. Bacevich et al., *American Military Policy,* 41.

23. Schwarz, *American Counterinsurgency Doctrine,* 55.

24. Bacevich et al., *American Military Policy,* 40.

25. For a discussion of the evolution of popular movements during the 1980s, see Montgomery, *Revolution in El Salvador,* 191–95.

26. See James Scott, *Weapons of the Weak: Everyday Forms of Resistance* (New Haven: Yale University Press, 1985).

27. Karl, "Exporting Democracy," 174–78.

28. José Z. García, "El Salvador: Recent Elections in Historical Perspective," in John Booth and Mitchell Seligson, eds., *Elections and Democracy in Central America* (Chapel Hill: University of North Carolina Press, 1989), 73.

29. Interview with Gutiérrez. According to Gen. Gutiérrez, the Reagan administration, which viewed the elections as an opportunity to remove the military from power, opposed the PDC proposal.

30. Ibid. Also see Duarte's discussion of the political stalemate in José Napoleón Duarte, *Duarte: My Story* (New York: G. P. Putnam's Sons, 1986), 183–85.

31. Interview with Gutiérrez. According to Gutiérrez, he chose Magaña from a list of three names presented to him by U.S. Ambassador Deane Hinton. In Honduras, the military succeeded in imposing one of its own, Gen. Paz García, as provisional president following the April 1980 Constituent Assembly elections.

32. Interview with Alejandro Duarte, President Duarte's son and member of the negotiating commission, San Salvador, 22 July 1992.

33. Tim Golden, "Duarte Kidnapping is 'test of fire,'" *Miami Herald,* 10 October 1985.

34. Jeffrey Paige, "Coffee and Power in El Salvador," *Latin American Research Review* 28, no. 3 (1993): 18.

35. Ibid., 19.

36. Joel Millman, "El Salvador's Army: A Force Unto Itself," *New York Times Magazine,* 10 December 1989, 97.

37. Ibid.

38. Schwarz, *American Counterinsurgency Doctrine,* 19–20.

39. Millman, "A Force Unto Itself," 97.

40. Confidential interview with high-ranking officer who participated in the investigation. See Schwarz, *American Counterinsurgency Doctrine,* 28–29.

41. Christopher Dickey, "Behind the Death Squads," *New Republic,* 26 December 1983, 19–20.

42. "Documento de relación entre el gobierno demócrata cristiano y las fuerzas armadas—concepto y políticas," 24 May 1984, San Salvador. The agreement was never made public nor circulated among the officer corps. One of the authors had the opportunity to read over a copy of the document in possession of one of the persons responsible for drafting portions of the agreement. He also confirmed its content with Duarte's son, Alejandro, who participated in drafting the agreement.

43. For a discussion of the positive contribution of pacts in furthering democratic consolidation, see Guillermo O'Donnell and Philippe Schmitter, *Transitions from Authoritarian Rule: Tentative Conclusions About Uncertain Democracies* (Baltimore: John Hopkins University Press, 1986), 3–71. For a contending view, see Frances Hagopian, "'Democracy by Undemocratic Means?' Elites, Political Pacts, and Regime Transition in Brazil." *Comparative Political Studies* 23, no. 2 (July 1990): 147–70.

44. O'Donnell and Schmitter, *Transitions from Authoritarian Rule,* 69.

45. Rouquié, *The Military and the State,* 374–75.

46. Hagopian arrives at the same conclusion regarding the impact of pacts in Brazil's transition. Hagopian, "Democracy by Undemocratic Means?"

47. Deborah Barry et al., "Low Intensity Warfare': The Counterinsurgency Strategy for Central America," in Nora Hamilton et al., eds., *Crisis in Central America* (Boulder: Westview Press, 1988), 80–88.

48. Michael McClintock, *The American Connection,* 315.

49. FBIS, "Ochoa 7 Jan. Interview," Radio Cadena YSKL, San Salvador, 7 January 1983, FBIS-Central America, 10 January 1983: 2–3.

50. Interview with Ret. Gen. Adolfo Blandón, San Salvador, 17 June 1992.

51. United Nations, *De la locura a la esperanza: Informe de la Comisión de la Verdad* (New York, 1993), 151–55.

52. Christopher Dickey, "Behind the Death Squads," *The New Republic,* December 26, 1983, 20.

53. Cynthia Arson, *Crossroads: Congress, the Reagan Administration, and Central America* (New York: Pantheon Books, 1989), 135.

54. FBIS, "Military Reshuffle Officially Announced," FBIS-Central America, 28 November 1983.

55. Five officers from the 1963 *tanda* received key commands as a result of the November 1983 shake-up. See FBIS, "COPEFA Announces Changes in Army Command," FBIS-Central America, 29 November 1983.

56. Ibid., 133.

57. "Trouble on Two Fronts," *Time Magazine,* 12 December 1983.

58. Lydia Chavez, "US Presses Salvador to Act on Men Tied to Death Squads," *New York Times,* 5 November 1983.

59. FBIS, "Military Leaders Support Vides on Death Squads," FBIS-Central America, 20 December 1983.

60. Ibid., 130–42. See also, Laurie Becklund, "Salvadoran Death Squads: Deadly

Other War," *Los Angeles Times,* December 18, 1983; and Bernard Gwertzman, "Salvador Curbs Death Squads, US Aides Say," *New York Times,* 1 January 1984.

61. Stanley, "Elite Politics," 493–98.

62. Confidential interview with high-ranking officer who served in the Duarte government.

63. Members of the *tandona* commanded the elite counterinsurgency battalions, several detachments, and a few brigades. Col. René Emilio Ponce occupied the key position of chief of operations of the Estado Mayor.

64. FBIS, "Duarte Announces Col. Staben's Reinstatement," FBIS-Central America, 8 May 1986.

65. FBIS, "Blandón Announces Changes in High Command," FBIS-Central America, 5 July 1988; FBIS, "Vargas, Others Reassigned in Military Reshuffle," FBIS-Central America, 1 November 1988.

66. Interview with Ret. Gen. Adolfo Blandón.

67. "Estudio de Estado Mayor sobre la Fuerza Armada como Institución Fundamental de la Seguridad Nacional," San Salvador, 15 September 1988. The authors acquired a copy of the memorandum from one of its authors.

68. Millman, "A Force Unto Itself," 97.

69. Karl, "Exporting Democracy," 185.

70. Montgomery, *Revolution in El Salvador,* 215.

71. For more on the divisions within the coffee elite and their political implications, see Paige, "Coffee and Power," and Daniel Wolf, "ARENA in the Arena: Factors in the Accommodation of the Salvadoran Right to Pluralism and the Broadening of the Political System," unpublished manuscript, 20 January 1992, San Salvador.

72. Tom Gibb and Frank Smyth, *El Salvador: Is Peace Possible? A Report on the Prospects for Negotiations and United States Policy* (Washington, D.C.: Washington Office on Latin America, April 1990).

73. For example, whereas in 1983 there were 920 officers, by 1987 there were 1,652.

74. Stanley, *The Protection Racket State,* 246.

75. Montgomery, *Revolution in El Salvador,* 217–20.

76. According to the Truth Commission Report, those present included: Col. René Emilio Ponce, chief of staff; Col. Juan Orlando Zepeda, vice minister of defense; Col. Inocente Montano, vice minister of public security; Col. Francisco Elena Fuentes, commander of the First Brigade; and Gen. Rafael Bustillo, commander of the air force. United Nations, *De la locura a la esperanza: Informe de la Comisión de la Verdad para El Salvador* (New York, March 1993), 44–50.

77. Confidential interview with senior officer.

78. George Vickers, "The Political Reality After Eleven Years of War," in Joseph Tulchin and Gary Bland, eds., *Is There a Transition to Democracy in El Salvador?* (Boulder: Lynne Rienner Publishers, 1992), 40.

79. The Kissinger Commission recommended a major increase in military aid to El Salvador.

80. Fitch, "Military Professionalism," 24.

81. A good overview of human rights abuses in El Salvador during the 1980s can be found in Americas Watch, *El Salvador's Decade of Terror* (New Haven: Yale University Press, 1991). See also, United Nations Truth Commission report, *De la locura a la esperanza.*

82. Americas Watch, *El Salvador's Decade of Terror,* 17–18.

83. Schwarz, *American Counterinsurgency Doctrine,* 35.

84. Ibid., 35–36.

85. The entire battalion had just completed two days of a ten-day Special Forces training course, which was interrupted by the FMLN's November offensive.

86. Arson, *Crossroads*, 71.

87. Ibid.

88. For a more detailed discussion of the massacre, see the UN Truth Commission report, *De la locura a la esperanza*, 76–81.

89. An officer who headed up a commission in February 1989 charged with investigating some of the worst incidents of human rights abuses during the war provided one of the authors with a copy of Cap. Figueroa Morales's sworn affidavit.

90. The Truth Commission report claims that León Linares knew of the assassination of the Jesuits in November 1989 and participated actively in the subsequent cover-up. United Nations, *De la locura a la esperanza*, 44–50.

91. See ibid., 82–88.

92. Kenneth Freed, "Qualye Gives Salvador Ultimatum on Rights," *Los Angeles Times*, 4 February 1989, and "US Plea Fails to Stem Salvador Killings," *Los Angeles Times*, 9 March 1989.

93. Interview with Col. Benjamín Ramos, 22 March 1994, San Salvador.

94. According to Ramos, the commission's findings were almost identical to those of the United Nations Truth Commission, which was established under the provisions of the January 1992 peace accords. Ibid.

95. Confidential interview.

96. U.S. General Accounting Office, *El Salvador: Transfers of Military Assistance Fuels* (Washington, D.C.: USGAO, August 1989).

97. U.S. General Accounting Office, *El Salvador: Accountability for U.S. Military and Economic Aid* (Washington, D.C.: USGAO, September 1990), 14.

98. See especially Howard Kurtz and Edward Cody, "US Probes Sale of Faulty Bullets to Salvador Army," *Washington Post*, 28 September 1984; and Edward Cody, "US Case Involving Sale of Faulty Ammunition is Test for Salvadoran Army," *Washington Post*, 23 August 1986.

99. Cody, "US Case," A14.

100. Vides Casanova and Rivera were both members of the 1957 *tanda*.

101. Cody, "US Case," A19.

102. Schwarz, *American Counterinsurgency Doctrine*, 18–19.

103. Interview with Col. Mark Hamilton, U.S. Military Group commander, San Salvador, 10 July 1992.

104. Millman, "A Force Unto Itself."

105. Bacevich et al., *American Military Policy*, 26.

7. THE ARMED FORCES AFTER THE PEACE ACCORDS

1. George Vickers, "The Political Reality After Eleven Years of War," in Joseph Tulchin and Gary Bland, eds., *Is There a Transition to Democracy in El Salvador?* (Boulder: Lynne Rienner Publishers, 1992), 39. On the negotiations leading to the peace accords, also see Terry Karl, "El Salvador's Negotiated Revolution," *Foreign Affairs* 71, no. 2 (1992): 147–64.

2. Karl, "El Salvador's Negotiated Revolution," 156–57.

3. United Nations, *Acuerdos de paz* (New York: UN Department of Public Information, 1992).

4. United Nations, "Mexico Agreements" (New York: UN Department of Public Information, 1991).

5. Ibid.

6. George Vickers and Jack Spence et al., *Endgame* (Cambridge, Mass.: Hemisphere Initiatives, 1992), 12.

7. Interview with Gen. Mauricio Vargas, deputy chief of staff, San Salvador, 14 June 1992.

8. United Nations, "Report of the Secretary-General on the United Nations Observer Mission in El Salvador," UN Document S/25812, 26 May 1993, New York, 10. Also see William Stanley, *Risking Failure: The Problems and Promise of the New Civilian Police in El Salvador* (Boston: HI/WOLA, 1993), 17.

9. The brigade has approximately two thousand troops. About two hundred are former Treasury Police and most of the remainder are former guardsmen. During the summer of 1993, the brigade accepted its first contingent of regular conscripts. Interview with Col. Angel Eliseo Ramos Escalante, commander of the Special Brigade for Military Security, San Salvador, July 15, 1993.

10. Vickers and Spence, *Endgame*, 16.

11. Stanley, *Risking Failure*, 12.

12. Ibid., 12, 20.

13. Ibid., n. 28. Not until August 1993 did the Ministry of Defense agreed to hand over the remainder of the pistols still in its possession.

14. Vickers and Spence, *Endgame*, 10.

15. The civilian members of the commission were Abraham Rodríguez, a prominent businessman and former personal advisor to President Duarte; Eduardo Molina, one of the founding members of the Christian Democratic Party; and Reynaldo Galindo Pohl, an elder statesman who had served in several governmental and international posts over the years. The two military members of the commission, former Defense Ministers Gen. Eugenio Vides Casanova and Gen. Rafael Humberto Larios, only had access to the commission's deliberations and recommendations but not to the investigative phase of its work. They also had no vote.

16. Seventy-six were to be removed from active duty and twenty-six were to be transferred to other posts.

17. The FMLN had until 31 October to demobilize its forces fully. However, in October the FMLN announced that it was postponing the demobilization of the final 40 percent of its forces until the government complied with the commission's recommendations and with provisions of the accords related to the land issue.

18. Vickers and Spence, *Endgame*, 12.

19. United Nations, "Letter of 7 January 1993 to the President of the Security Council from the Secretary General," UN Document S/25078, New York, 13 January 1993.

20. "El Salvador: todavía no se completa depuración," *Inforpress Centroamericana*, 4 February 1993, 4–5.

21. The Truth Commission was established under the accords to investigate and to recommend prosecution of the most egregious human rights violations that occurred during the civil war. Its members included Belisario Betancur, former president of Colombia; Reinaldo Figueredo, former foreign minister of Venezuela; and Thomas Buergenthal, professor of law and honorary president of the Inter-American Institute for Human Rights.

22. Initially, President Cristiani did not accept Ponce's offer to resign.

23. United Nations, *De la locura a la esperanza: Informe de la Comisión de la Verdad para*

El Salvador (New York, March 1993). The Truth Commission report also detailed the FMLN's involvement in human rights violations and recommended that some of its leaders be barred from public office.

24. Members of the *tandona* completed their thirty years of service during 1993, making them eligible for retirement at that time. Thus, by delaying their removal until June 1993, these officers were able to retire with honors and with pensions intact. On the contrary, if they had been removed from active duty at the end of 1992 as agreed upon, they would have been denied some of these privileges.

25. Confidential interview with senior officer, San Salvador, 29 July 1992.

26. Paul Zagorski, *Democracy vs. National Security: Civil-Military Relations in Latin America* (Boulder: Lynne Reinner Publishers, 1992), 64.

27. David Pion-Berlin, "Military Autonomy and Emerging Democracies in South America," *Comparative Politics* 25, no. 1 (October 1992): 83–102.

28. Interview with Col. José Humberto Corado Figueroa, then chief of operations of the Estado Mayor, San Salvador, 28 July 1992.

29. President Cristiani was to appoint the members of the Academic Council by May 11, 1993; however, the appointments were not made until July 31, 1993.

30. Interviews with Lic. Joaquín Samayoa, vice rector of the UCA, San Salvador, 19 July 1993; and with Col. Jaime Gúzman Morales, chief of staff, Estado Mayor, San Salvador, 30 July 1993.

31. Interview with Samayoa.

32. Several officers interviewed pointed out that the Universidad Militar, for example, has an academic council with civilian members. However, these are handpicked by the military and consist of professors who teach at the military academy or university. Traditionally, this has meant professors who hold politically conservative viewpoints and are viewed as "friends" of the military establishment.

33. Zagorski, *Democracy vs. National Security*, 65.

34. United Nations, *De la locura a la esperanza*, 144.

35. Gobierno de El Salvador, "Ley de Servicio Militar y Reserva de la Fuerza Armada," San Salvador, 31 July 1992.

36. Interview with Col. Luis Alejandre Sintes, chief of the Military Division of ONUSAL, San Salvador, 6 July 1993.

37. Vickers and Spence, *Endgame*, 13.

38. The Atlacatl Battalion was responsible for the Mozote massacre in December 1981, and several of its members were directly implicated in the Jesuit murders in November 1989.

39. Interview with Col. Luis Alejandre Sintes.

40. Interview with Col. Juan Ernesto Méndez Rodríguez, chief of civil affairs, Estado Mayor, San Salvador, 23 July 1993.

41. See the article by Joel Millman, "El Salvador's Army: A Force Unto Itself," *New York Times Magazine*, 10 December 1989.

42. Confidential interview with former senior government official.

43. El Salvador, Ministerio de Defensa Nacional, *Memoria de 1992* (San Salvador: Imprenta Nacional, 1992) and *Memoria de 1993* (San Salvador: Imprenta Nacional, 1993). This increase is also reflected in monthly summaries of ACM activities obtained for February 1992, March 1993, and May 1993.

44. Interview with Col. Roberto Tejada Murcia, vice minister of defense, San Salvador, 13 July 1993.

45. The government created the SRN in January 1992 to administer the implementation of the PRN.

46. United Nations, *Acuerdos de paz,* 3 (author's translation).

47. Peter Sollis, *Reluctant Reforms: The Cristiani Government and the International Community in the Process of Salvadoran Post-war Reconstruction* (Washington, D.C.: WOLA, June 1993), 38.

48. Interview with Col. Rudy Jones, commander of U.S. MILGROUP, San Salvador, 26 July 1993.

49. "Statement of General George A. Joulwan, Commander in Chief, United States Southern Command, Before the Senate Armed Services Committee," 21 April 1993.

50. Public Law 102–391, Sec. 530, "Assistance for El Salvador," 102d Congress, 6 October 1992.

51. See Sollis, *Reluctant Reforms,* 37.

52. Interview with Col. Corado, San Salvador, 4 August 1993.

53. Quoted in ONUSAL, *IX Informe del Director de la División de Derechos Humanos al Secretario General: Agosto 1993-Octubre 1993* (San Salvador: ONUSAL, 1993), 25.

54. Confidential interview.

55. Confidential interview.

56. Rouquié, *The Military and the State,* 346.

57. Sollis, *Reluctant Reforms,* 38.

58. These observations are based on a confidential interview with a senior officer from the outgoing High Command.

59. Interview with Gen. Vargas.

60. Interview with Col. Corado.

61. Interview with Col. Gúzman.

62. The 1993 defense budget represented a 6.4 percent drop from 1992. For 1994, the Cristiani government requested the same amount as for 1993.

63. The Clinton administration only requested $3.8 million for 1994.

64. An example of the strain on resources was the High Command's decision to open only three of thirty scheduled recruiting offices around the country during 1993. Interview with Col. Alejandre Sintes.

65. "Discurso de entrega de mando del Ministro de la Defensa Nacional, General de Division René Emilio Ponce," *La Prensa Gráfica,* 1 July 1993; and *La Prensa Gráfica,* 2 July 1993.

66. Col. José Humberto Corado Figueroa, "Perspectivas de las relaciones civiles-militares en El Salvador" (San Salvador: CENITEC, 7 October 1993). In a second interview with one of the authors, Corado reaffirmed his views regarding civilian oversight of the armed forces. He was adamantly opposed to a civilian defense minister, did not support giving legislators more access to the details of the defense budget, and opposed civilian oversight of military education. Interview with Col. Corado, minister of defense, San Salvador, 4 August 1993.

67. "Ausencia de la Fuerza Armada y Auge de la Criminalidad," *Revista Militar,* July 1993, San Salvador.

68. Bustillo's candidacy was short-lived. He resigned as the PCN's candidate on 1 September 1993 after party leaders refused to hand over control of the party to him. The PCN's eventual candidate was Roberto Escobar García, a retired general and lawyer.

69. IUDOP, "La Comisión de la verdad y el proceso electoral en la opinión pública salvadoreña," *Estudios Centroamericanos,* 537–38 (Julio-Agosto 1993): 714–15; and *La Prensa Gráfica,* 1 October 1993.

70. For an excellent analysis of the process of developing the PNC, see Stanley, *Risking Failure.*

71. ONUSAL, *IX Informe del Director de la Division de Derechos Humanos al Secretario General: Agosto-Octubre 1993* (San Salvador: ONUSAL, 1993).

72. Interviews, Nueva Granada, Usulután, 18 March 1994.

73. Interviews, Christian base community, Mejicanos, 17 March 1994.

74. This section borrows heavily from Jack Spence and George Vickers, *A Negotiated Revolution? A Two Year Progress Report on the Salvadoran Peace Accords* (Cambridge, Mass.: Hemisphere Initiatives, March 1994), 18–22.

75. The Land Bank was responsible for purchasing and transferring the lands.

76. Jack Spence et al., *El Salvador: Elections of the Century* (Cambridge, Mass.: Hemisphere Initiatives, July 1994), 5.

77. *La Prensa Gráfica,* 18 March 1994.

78. Spence et al., *El Salvador,* 7.

79. Because of the TSE's questionable total registration figures, there are no definitive figures for overall turnout.

80. Personal observation in Chalatenango and conversations with electoral observers on election day.

81. Richard Stahler-Sholk, "El Salvador's Negotiated Transition: From Low Intensity Conflict to Low Intensity Democracy," *Journal of Interamerican Studies and World Affairs* 36, no. 4 (winter 1994): 1–59.

82. Spence et al., *El Salvador,* 37–38.

83. *Inforpress Centroamericana,* 17 February 1994.

84. *Inforpress Centroamericana,* 2 June 1994.

85. Margaret Popkin, *Justice Delayed: The Slow Pace of Judicial Reform in El Salvador* (Cambridge, Mass.: Hemisphere Initiatives, December 1994), 10.

86. Spence and Vickers, *A Negotiated Revolution?,* 11.

87. Popkin, *Justice Delayed,* 10.

88. *Inforpress Centroamericana,* 13 October 1994.

89. Ibid.

90. "Informe del Grupo Conjunto para la Investigación de Grupos Armados Ilegales con Motivación Política," *Inforpress Centroamericana,* 11 and 18 August 1994.

91. *Inforpress Centroamericana,* 25 August 1994.

92. "Informe del Grupo Conjunto," *Inforpress Centroamericana,* 18 August 1994.

93. This section is based on the report by Jack Spence et al. *The Salvadoran Peace Accords and Democratization: A Three Year Progress Report and Recommendations* (Cambridge, Mass.: Hemisphere Initiatives, March 1995), 17–19.

94. Interview with Col. Juan Ernesto Méndez Rodríguez, chief of civil affairs (C–5), San Salvador, 23 July 1993.

95. David Dye et al., *Contesting Everything, Winning Nothing: The Search for Consensus in Nicaragua, 1990–1995* (Cambridge, Mass.: Hemisphere Initiatives, November 1995).

96. Unemployment and underemployment rates were estimated at over 50 percent in 1993. Ibid.

97. On the gangs, see the report by Mike O'Connor, "A New US Import in El Salvador: Street Gangs," *New York Times,* 3 July 1994.

98. *Inforpress Centroamericana,* 21 March 1996, 11 April 1996, and 2 May 1996.

99. *La Prensa Gráfica,* 21 September 1996. The program to expand the *juntas de vecinos* was so controversial that Alvaro de Soto, undersecretary general of the United Nations, made them an issue during his visit to El Salvador in September 1996. Under

pressure from de Soto, the Calderón Sol government agreed to dismantle the 114 existing juntas and to desist from organizing any new ones.

8. CONCLUSIONS: THE ROAD AHEAD

1. *Inforpress Centroamericana,* 21 March 1996, 8.

2. While the military *fuero* was in force, military officers accused of common crimes were tried in military courts.

3. *Latin American Weekly Report,* 3 October 1996; *New York Times,* 20 September 1996.

4. Daniel Premo, "The Nicaraguan Armed Forces in Transition, 1990–1995," Latin American Studies Association Congress, unpublished paper, September 1995; and David Dye et al., *Contesting Everything, Winning Nothing: The Search for Consensus in Nicaragua, 1990–1995* (Cambridge, Mass.: Hemisphere Initiatives, November 1995).

5. Dye, *Contesting Everything.*

6. Premo, "The Nicaraguan Armed Forces in Transition."

7. J. Mark Ruhl, "Redefining Civil-Military Relations in Honduras," *Journal of Interamerican Studies and World Affairs* 38, no. 1 (spring 1996): 33–66.

8. Ibid.

9. Richard Millet, "An End to Militarism? Democracy and the Armed Forces in Central America," *Current History* 94, no. 589 (February 1995): 74.

10. Adam Przeworski, *Democracy and the Market: Political and Economic Reforms in Eastern Europe and Latin America* (Cambridge: Cambridge University Press, 1991).

11. David Pion-Berlin, "Military Autonomy and Emerging Democracies in South America," *Comparative Politics* 25, no. 1 (October 1992): 83–102.

12. Jorge Zaverucha, "The Degree of Military Political Autonomy During the Spanish, Argentine and Brazilian Transitions," *Journal of Latin American Studies* 25, no. 2 (May 1993): 283–99.

13. Alfred Stepan, *Rethinking Military Politics,* 128–45.

14. Agriculture's share of total GDP declined from 30.3 percent in 1984 to 8.9 percent in 1993. Victor Bulmer-Thomas, *The Political Economy of Central America Since 1920* (Cambridge: Cambridge University Press, 1987), 271; and Economist Intelligence Unit, *Country Profile: Guatemala, El Salvador, 1994–95* (London: Economist Intelligence Unit Ltd., 1995), 1–59.

15. Interview with Benjamín Ramos, Centro DEMOS, 22 March 1994, San Salvador.

16. The authors are grateful to Tommie Sue Montgomery for this observation.

17. For example, the PCN representative on the subcommission of COPAZ (the commission set up to verify implementation of the peace accords) that worked on the new civilian police was (retired) General Adolfo Blandón, former chief of staff. The PDC relied heavily on the expertise of (retired) Colonel López Nuila, the former vice minister of public security, to develop its position regarding the new police.

18. Przeworski, *Democracy and the Market,* 29.

19. Wendy Hunter, "Politicians Against Soldiers: Contesting the Military in Postauthoritarian Brazil," *Comparative Politics* 27, no. 4 (July 1995): 439.

20. Ibid., 440.

21. Ibid.

BIBLIOGRAPHY

OFFICIAL PUBLICATIONS
El Salvador

Dirección General de Estadísticas y Censos, *Anuario Estadístico.* (Issued yearly.)

El Salvador. *Ley Transitoria Electoral.* San Salvador: Imprenta Nacional, 1950.

El Salvador. *Constitution of 1950.* Washington, D.C.: Pan American Union, 1961.

El Salvador. *Mensaje de los señores miembros del Directorio Cívico Militar de El Salvador el 2 de enero de 1962.* San Salvador: Imprenta Nacional, 1962.

El Salvador. *Informe Presidencial—Primer año de gobierno (1 de julio de 1963).* San Salvador: Imprenta Nacional, 1963.

El Salvador. *Informe Presidencial—Tercer año de gobierno (1 de julio de 1965).* San Salvador: Imprenta Nacional, 1965.

Gobierno de El Salvador. "Ley de Servicio Militar y Reserva de la Fuerza Armada." San Salvador, 31 July 1992.

Ministerio de Defensa. *Memoria.* San Salvador: Imprenta Nacional (Issued yearly. This ministry's name varied over time: Ministerio de Guerra, Marina y Aviación, Ministerio de Defensa, Ministerio de Defensa y Seguridad Pública, and, finally, Ministerio de Defensa Nacional.)

Ministerio de Gobernación. *Memoria.* San Salvador: Imprenta Nacional (Issued yearly).

Ministerio de Planificación y Coordinación del Desarrollo Económico y Social. *Indicadores Económicas y Sociales.* San Salvador: Imprenta Nacional (Issued yearly.)

Other Sources

Agency for International Development. *U.S. Overseas Loans, Grants and Assistance from International Organizations.* Published yearly.

United Nations. *Acuerdos de paz.* New York: UN Department of Public Information, 1992.

————. *De la locura a la esperanza: Informe de la Comisión de la Verdad para El Salvador.* New York, March 1993.

————. "Letter of 7 January 1993 to the President of the Security Council from the Secretary General." UN Document S/25078. New York, 13 January 1993.

————. "Mexico Agreements." New York: UN Department of Public Information, 1991.

————. "Report of the Secretary-General on the United Nations Observer Mission in El Salvador." UN Document S/25812. New York, 26 May 1993.

U.S. Arms Control and Disarmament Agency. *World Military Expenditures and Arms Transfers, 1995.* Washington, D.C.: Government Printing Office, April 1996.

U.S. Department of State. *Foreign Relations of the United States.* Washington, D.C.: Government Printing Office. Published yearly.

U.S. Foreign Affairs and National Defense Division. *El Salvador, 1979–1989: A Briefing Book on U.S. Aid and the Situation in El Salvador.* Washington, D.C.: 28 April 1989.

U.S. General Accounting Office. *El Salvador: Accountability for U.S. Military and Economic Aid.* Washington, D.C.: USGAO, September 1990.

———. *El Salvador: Transfers of Military Assistance Fuels.* Washington, D.C.: USGAO, August 1989.

U.S. Library of Congress, Congressional Research Service. *El Salvador Under Cristiani: U.S. Foreign Assistance Decisions.* Washington: 20 July 1993.

NEWSPAPERS AND JOURNALS

Al Día—Semanario de Información
Boletín del Ejército
Diario Latino
Diario Oficial
El Gran Diario
Estudios Centroamericanos
Hispanic American Report
Inforpress Centroamericana

La Prensa Gráfica
Latin American Political Report
Latin American Weekly Report
Los Angeles Times
Revista Militar
New York Times
Washington Post

BOOKS, ARTICLES, AND UNPUBLISHED MANUSCRIPTS

Abrahamsson, Bengt. *Military Professionalism and Political Power.* Beverley Hills: Sage Publications, 1972.

Aguero, Felipe. "The Military and Limits to Democratization," in Mainwaring et al., eds., *Issues in Democratic Consolidation: The New South American Democracies in Comparative Perspective.* Notre Dame: University of Notre Dame Press, 1992.

Aguilera, Gabriel. *El fusil y el olivo: La cuestión militar en Centroamérica.* San José: DEI, 1989.

Alvarenga, Ana Patricia. "Reshaping the Ethics of Power: A History of Violence in Western Rural El Salvador, 1880–1932." Ph.D. diss., University of Wisconsin-Madison, 1994.

Americas Watch. *El Salvador's Decade of Terror.* New Haven: Yale University Press, 1991.

Anderson, Thomas P. *Matanza: El Salvador's Communist Revolt of 1932.* Lincoln: University of Nebraska Press, 1971.

———. *The War of the Dispossessed: Honduras and El Salvador, 1969.* Lincoln: University of Nebraska Press, 1981.

Andino Martínez, Carlos. "El estamento militar en El Salvador." *Estudios Centroamericanos* nos. 369–70 (July-August 1979): 625–27.

Arson, Cynthia. *Crossroads: Congress, the Reagan Administration, and Central America.* New York: Pantheon Books, 1989.

Astilla, Carmelo F. E. "The Martínez Era: Salvadoran-American Relations, 1931–1944." Ph.D. diss., Louisiana State University, 1976.

Bacevich, A. J., et al. *American Military Policy in Small Wars: The Case of El Salvador.* Washington, D.C.: Pergamon-Bassey's International Defense Publications, 1988.

Baloyra, Enrique. *El Salvador en transición.* San Salvador: UCA Editores, 1982.

———. "Reactionary Despotism in Central America." *Journal of Latin American Studies* 15, no. 2 (1983): 315.

Barber, Willard, and C. Neale Ronning. *Internal Security and Military Power: Counterinsurgency and Civic Action in Latin America.* Columbus: Ohio State University Press, 1966.

Barry, Deborah, et al. "'Low Intensity Warfare': The Counterinsurgency Strategy for Central America," in Nora Hamilton et al., eds., *Crisis in Central America.* Boulder: Westview Press, 1988.

Becklund, Laurie. "Salvadoran Death Squads: Deadly Other War." *Los Angeles Times*, 18 December 1983.

Benítez, Raul. *La teoría militar y la guerra civil en El Salvador.* San Salvador: UCA Editores, 1989.

Berryman, Phillip. *The Religious Roots of Rebellion.* London: SCM Press Ltd., 1984.

Bonner, Raymond. *Weakness and Deceit.* New York: Times Books, 1984.

Brockett, Charles. *Land, Power and Poverty.* Boulder: Westview Press, 1990.

Browning, David. *El Salvador: Landscape and Society.* Oxford: Oxford University Press, 1971.

———. "Agrarian Reform in El Salvador." *Journal of Latin American Studies* 15, no. 2 (1983): 399–405.

Bulmer-Thomas, Victor. *The Political Economy of Central America Since 1920.* Cambridge: Cambridge University Press, 1987.

Carías, Marco Virgilio, and Daniel Slutsky, eds. *La guerra inútil: Análisis socioeconómico del conflicto entre Honduras y El Salvador.* San José, Costa Rica: EDUCA, 1971.

Castro Morán, Mariano. *Función política del ejército salvadoreño en el presente siglo.* San Salvador: UCA Editores, 1987.

Chalmers, Douglas. "The Politicized State in Latin America," in James Malloy, ed., *Authoritarianism and Corporatism in Latin America.* Pittsburgh: University of Pittsburgh Press, 1977.

Chavez, Lydia. "US Presses Salvador to Act on Men Tied to Death Squads." *New York Times*, 5 November 1983.

Ching, Erik. "Una apreciación de la insurrección del 32." *Tendencias* 44 (Septiembre 1995): 28–31.

Cody, Edward. "US Case Involving Sale of Faulty Ammunition is Test for Salvadoran Army." *Washington Post*, 23 August 1986.

Corado Figueroa, Col. José Humberto. "Perspectivas de las relaciones civiles-militares en El Salvador." San Salvador: CENITEC, 7 October 1993.

Danopoulus, Constantine. "Military Dictatorships in Retreat: Problems and Perspectives," in Danopoulos, ed., *The Decline of Military Regimes.* Boulder: Westview Press, 1988.

Dickey, Christopher. "Behind the Death Squads." *New Republic*, 26 December 1983.

Duarte, Jose Napoleon. *Duarte: My Story.* New York: G. P. Putnam's Sons, 1986.

Dunkerley, James. *The Long War.* London: Verso, 1982.

———. *Power in the Isthmus.* London: Verso, 1988.

Durham, William H. *Scarcity and Survival in Central America.* Stanford: Stanford University Press, 1979.

Dye, David, et al. *Contesting Everything, Winning Nothing: The Search for Consensus in Nicaragua, 1990–1995.* Cambridge, Mass.: Hemisphere Initiatives, November 1995.

Economist Intelligence Unit, *Country Profile: Guatemala, El Salvador, 1994–95* (London: Economist Intelligence Unit Ltd., 1995).

Edwards, Beatrice, and Gretta Tovar Siebentritt. *Places of Origin: The Repopulation of Rural El Salvador.* Boulder: Lynne Rienner Publishers, 1991.

Elam, Robert Varney. "Appeal to Arms: The Army and Politics in El Salvador, 1931–1964." Ph.D. diss., University of New Mexico, 1968.

Etchison, Don. *The United States and Militarism in Central America.* New York: Praeger Publishers, 1975.

Foreign Broadcast Information Service (FBIS). "Blandon Announces Changes in High Command." FBIS-Central America. 5 July 1988.

————. "COPEFA Announces Changes in Army Command." FBIS-Central America. 29 November 1983.

————. "Defense Minister's Confirmation." Diario de Hoy, San Salvador. 14 May 1980. FBIS-Central America. 15 May 1980: 2–3.

————. "Duarte Announces Col. Staben's Reinstatement." FBIS-Central America. 8 May 1986.

————. "Majano Explains Position." Radio Cadena JSU, San Salvador. 4 September 1980. FBIS-Central America. 5 September 1980: 3–4.

————. "Military Leaders Support Vides on Death Squads." FBIS-Central America. 20 December 1983.

————. "Military Reshuffle Officially Announced." FBIS-Central America. 28 November 1983.

————. "Ochoa 7 Jan. Interview." Radio Cadena YSKL, San Salvador. 7 January 1983. FBIS-Central America. 10 January 1983: 2–3.

————. "Radio Station Seized." ACAN-EFE, Panama City. 5 September 1980. FBIS-Central America. 5 September 1980: 5–6.

————. "Vargas, Others Reassigned in Military Reshuffle." FBIS-Central America. 1 November 1988.

Fidel, Kenneth, ed. *Militarism in Developing Countries*. New Brunswick, N.J.: Transaction Books, 1975.

Finer, S. E. *The Man on Horseback: The Role of the Military in Politics,* 2d ed. Boulder: Westview Press, 1988.

Fitch, J. Samuel. "The Political Consequences of US Military Aid to Latin America." *Armed Forces and Society* 5, no. 3 (1979): 360–86.

————. "Military Professionalism, National Security and Democracy: Lessons Learned from the Latin American Experience." *Pacific Focus* 6 (1989): 99–147.

Flores Pinel, Fernando. "El golpe de estado en El Salvador: Un camino hacia la democratización?" *Estudios Centroamericanos* nos. 372–73 (1979): 885–904.

Freed, Kenneth. "Quayle Gives Salvador Ultimatum on Rights." *Los Angeles Times,* 4 February 1989.

————. "US Plea Fails to Stem Salvador Killings." *Los Angeles Times,* 9 March 1989.

Gallardo, Ricardo. *Las constituciones de El Salvador*. Madrid: Instituto de Cultura Hispánica, 1961.

García, José Z. "El Salvador: Recent Elections in Historical Perspective," in John Booth and Mitchell Seligson, eds., *Elections and Democracy in Central America*. Chapel Hill: University of North Carolina Press, 1989.

————. "The Tanda System and Institutional Autonomy of the Military," in J. Tulchin and G. Bland, eds., *Is There a Transition to Democracy in El Salvador?* Boulder: Lynne Reinner Publishers, 1992.

Garretón, Manuel. *The Chilean Political Process*. Boulder: Westview Press, 1989.

Gibb, Tom, and Frank Smyth. *El Salvador: Is Peace Possible? A Report on the Prospects for Negotiations and United States Policy*. Washington, D.C.: Washington Office on Latin America, April 1990.

Golden, Tim. "Duarte Kidnapping is 'Test of Fire.'" *Miami Herald,* 10 October 1985.

Goodman, Louis, et al. *The Military and Democracy: The Future of Civil-Military Relations in Latin America*. Lexington, Mass.: Lexington Books, 1990.

Gordon, Sara. *Crisis política y guerra en El Salvador*. México, D. F.: Siglo 21 1989.

Grieb, Kenneth J. "The United States and the Rise of General Maximiliano Hernández Martínez." *Journal of Latin American Studies* 3, no. 2 (1970): 151–72.

Guerra, Tomás. *El Salvador: Octubre Sangriento.* San José: Centro Victor Sanabria, 1979.

Guidos Vejar, Rafel. *El ascenso del militarismo en El Salvador.* San Salvador: UCA Editores, 1980.

Gwertzman, Bernard. "Salvador Curbs Death Squads, US Aides Say." *New York Times,* 1 January 1984.

Habermas, Jurgen. *The Theory of Communicative Action.* Vols. 1 and 2. Boston: Beacon Press, 1984, 1985.

Hagopian, Frances. "'Democracy by Undemocratic Means?' Elites, Political Pacts, and Regime Transition in Brazil." *Comparative Political Studies* 23, no. 2 (July 1990): 147–70.

Hamilton, Nora, et al., eds. *Crisis in Central America.* Boulder: Westview Press, 1988.

Hatfield, Sen. Mark, Rep. Jim Leach, and Rep. George Miller. "Bankrolling Failure: United States Policy in El Salvador and the Urgent Need for Reform." Report to the Arms Control and Foreign Policy Caucus. Washington, D.C.: November 1987.

Hernández Pico, Juan, et al. *El Salvador: Año político 1971–72.* San Salvador: Publicaciones de la Universidad Centroamericana José Simeón Cañas, 1973.

Hunter, Wendy. "Politicians Against Soldiers: Contesting the Military in Postauthoritarian Brazil." *Comparative Politics* 27, no. 4 (July 1995): 425–43.

Huntington, Samuel. *The Soldier and the State: The Theory and Politics of Civil-Military Relations.* Cambridge: Harvard University Press, 1957.

———. *Political Order in Changing Societies.* New Haven: Yale University Press, 1968.

International Institute for Strategic Studies. *The Military Balance 1978–1994.* London: IISS, 1994.

IUDOP. "La Comisión de la verdad y el proceso electoral in la opinión pública salvadoreña." *Estudios Centroamericanos* 537–38 (Julio-Agosto 1993): 711–34.

Jimenez, Edgar. "El golpe del 15 de octubre de 1979 y la crisis política nacional," in Edgar Jimenez et al., eds., *El Salvador: Guerra, política y paz (1979–1988).* San Salvador: CINAS, 1988.

Jimenez, Edgar, et al., eds. *El Salvador: Guerra, política y paz (1979–1988).* San Salvador: CINAS, 1988.

Karl, Terry. "Exporting Democracy: The Unanticipated Effects of US Electoral Policy in El Salvador," in Nora Hamilton et al., eds., *Crisis in Central America.* Boulder: Westview Press, 1988.

———."El Salvador's Negotiated Revolution." *Foreign Affairs* 71, no. 2 (1992): 147–64.

Keogh, Dermot. "The United States and the Coup d'Etat in El Salvador, 15 October 1979: A Case Study in American Foreign Policy Perceptions and Decision-Making," in Keogh, ed., *Central America: Human Rights and U.S. Foreign Policy.* Cork: Cork University Press, 1985: 21–69.

Kruijt, Dirk, and Edelberto Torres-Rivas, eds. *América Latina: militares y sociedad.* San José: FLACSO, 1991.

Kurtz, Howard, and Edward Cody. "US Probes Sale of Faulty Bullets to Salvador Army." *Washington Post,* 28 September 1984.

Lemus, José María. *Mensajes y discursos — 1957.* San Salvador: Ministerio de Cultura, 1958.

Linz, Juan, and Alfred Stepan. *The Breakdown of Democratic Regimes.* Baltimore: Johns Hopkins University Press, 1978.

López Vallecillos, Italo. "Rasgos sociales y tendencias políticas en El Salvador: 1969–1979." *Estudios Centroamericanos* nos. 372–73 (1979): 863–84.

Lowy, Michael, and Eder Sader. "The Militarization of the State in Latin America." *Latin American Perspectives* 12, no. 4 (fall 1985).

Majano, Adolfo Arnoldo. "El Golpe de Estado de 1979: Una Oportunidad Perdida." Unpublished manuscript. 18 May 1989.

Manwaring, Max, and Court Prisk, eds. *El Salvador at War: An Oral History of Conflict from the 1979 Insurrection to the Present.* Washington, D.C.: National Defense University Press, 1988.

Mariscal, Nicolás. "Militares y reformismo en El Salvador." *Estudios Centroamericanos* nos. 351–52 (January-February 1978): 18–19.

McClintock, Michael. *The American Connection: State Terror and Popular Resistance in El Salvador.* London: Zed Books, 1985.

McDonald, Ronald H. "Electoral Behavior and Political Development in El Salvador." *Journal of Politics* 31, no. 2 (May 1969): 397–419.

Mena Sandoval, Cap. Francisco Emilio. *Del ejército nacional al ejército guerrillero.* San Salvador: Arcoiris Editores, 1992.

Millet, Richard. *Guardians of the Dynasty.* Maryknoll, N.Y.: Orbis Books, 1977.

———. "An End to Militarism? Democracy and the Armed Forces in Central America." *Current History* 94, no. 589 (February 1995): 71–75.

Millman, Joel. "El Salvador's Army: A Force Unto Itself." *New York Times Magazine,* 10 December 1989.

Montgomery, Tommie Sue. *Revolution in El Salvador: From Civil Strife to Civil Peace.* Boulder: Westview Press, 1995.

Nairn, Allan. "Behind the Death Squads." *The Progressive* (May 1984): 20–29.

National Security Archive. *El Salvador 1977–1984: The Making of U.S. Policy.* Alexandria, Va.: Chadwyck-Healey, 1989.

Needler, Martin. "El Salvador: The Military and Politics." *Armed Forces and Society* 17, no. 4 (summer 1991): 568–88.

Nun, José. "The Middle-Class Military Coup," in Claudio Veliz, ed., *The Politics of Conformity in Latin America.* London: Oxford University Press, 1967.

O'Connor, Mike. "A New US Import in El Salvador: Street Gangs." *New York Times,* 3 July 1994.

O'Donnell, Guillermo. *Modernization and Bureaucratic Authoritarianism.* Berkeley: Institute for International Studies, 1973.

O'Donnell, Guillermo, and Philippe Schmitter. *Transitions from Authoritarian Rule: Tentative Conclusions.* Baltimore: Johns Hopkins University Press, 1986.

ONUSAL. *IX Informe del Director de la División de Derechos Humanos al Secretario General: Agosto-Octubre 1993.* San Salvador: ONUSAL, 1993.

Osorio, Oscar. *Mensaje dirigido al pueblo salvadoreño el 14 de septiembre de 1953.* San Salvador: Imprenta Nacional, 1953.

Paige, Jeffrey. "Coffee and Power in El Salvador." *Latin American Research Review* 28, no. 3 (1993): 18.

Parkman, Patricia. *Nonviolent Insurrection in El Salvador: The Fall of Maximiliano Hernández Martínez.* Tucson: University of Arizona Press, 1988.

Peña Trejo, Salvador, with Joaquín Castro Canizales (Quino Caso). "Narración histórica de la insurreción militar del 2 de diciembre de 1931." *Diario Latino,* 2 June 1964.

Pérez Brignoli, Héctor. "Indios, comunistas y campesinos: La rebelión de 1932 de El Salvador." *Cuadernos Anuarios* 5. San José: Escuela de Historia, Universidad de Costa Rica, 1991.

Pion-Berlin, David. "Military Autonomy and Emerging Democracies in South America." *Comparative Politics* 25, no. 1 (October 1992): 83–102.

Popkin, Margaret. *Justice Delayed: The Slow Pace of Judicial Reform in El Salvador.* Cambridge, Mass.: Hemisphere Initiatives, December 1994.

Poulantzas, Nicos. *State, Power, Socialism.* London: New Left Books, 1978.

Premo, Daniel. "The Nicaraguan Armed Forces in Transition, 1990–1995." Unpublished paper delivered at the Latin American Studies Association Congress, September 1995.

Przeworski, Adam. "Democracy as a Contingent Outcome of Conflicts," in Jon Elster and Rune Slagstad, eds., *Constitutionalism and Democracy.* Cambridge: Cambridge University Press, 1988.

———. *Democracy and the Market: Political and Economic Reforms in Eastern Europe and Latin America.* Cambridge: Cambridge University Press, 1991.

Putnum, Robert. "Toward Explaining Military Intervention in Latin American Politics." *World Politics* 20 (October 1967): 83–110.

Rouquié, Alain. *The Military and the State in Latin America.* Berkeley: University of California Press, 1987.

Ruhl, J. Mark. "Redefining Civil-Military Relations in Honduras." *Journal of Interamerican Studies and World Affairs* 38, no. 1 (spring 1996): 33–66.

Saloman, Leticia. *Militarismo y reformismo en Honduras.* Tegucigalpa: Editorial Guaymuras, 1982.

Sánchez Hernández, Fidel. *Discurso pronunciado por el señor Presidente de la República y Comandante General de la Fuerza Armada con motivo del "Día del Soldado Salvadoreño" el 7 de mayo de 1969.* San Salvador: Imprenta Nacional, 1969.

———. *Discursos del Señor Presidente de la Republica.* San Salvador: Publicaciones del Departamento de Relaciones Públicas de Casa Presidencial, 1970.

———. *Informe rendido por el señor Presidente de la República ante la Asamblea Legislativa el 1 de julio de 1970 al cumplirse el tercer año de su gobierno.* San Salvador: Imprenta Nacional, 1970.

Schwarz, Benjamin. *American Counterinsurgency Doctrine and El Salvador.* Washington, D.C.: Rand Corporation, 1991.

Scott, James. *Weapons of the Weak: Everyday Forms of Resistance.* New Haven: Yale University Press, 1985.

Simon, Laurence, and James Stephens. *El Salvador Land Reform, 1980–1981: Impact Audit.* Boston: Oxfam America, 1982.

Sollis, Peter. *Reluctant Reforms: The Cristiani Government and the International Community in the Process of Salvadoran Post-war Reconstruction.* Washington, D.C.: WOLA, June 1993.

Spence, Jack, et al. *El Salvador: Elections of the Century.* Cambridge, Mass.: Hemisphere Initiatives, July 1994.

———. *The Salvadoran Peace Accords and Democratization: A Three Year Progress Report and Recommendations.* Cambridge, Mass.: Hemisphere Initiatives, March 1995.

Spence, Jack, and George Vickers. *A Negotiated Revolution? A Two Year Progess Report on the Salvadoran Peace Accords.* Cambridge, Mass.: Hemisphere Initiatives, March 1994.

Stahler-Sholk, Richard. "El Salvador's Negotiated Transition: From Low-Intensity Conflict to Low-Intensity Democracy." *Journal of Interamerican Studies and World Affairs* 36, no. 4 (winter 1994): 1–59.

Stanley, William. "The Elite Politics of State Terrorism in El Salvador." Ph.D. diss., Massachusetts Institute of Technology, 1991.

———. *Risking Failure: The Problems and Promise of the New Civilian Police in El Salvador.* Boston: HI/WOLA, 1993.

———. *The Protection Racket State: Elite Politics, Military Extortion, and Civil War in El Salvador.* Philadephia: Temple University Press, 1996.

Stepan, Alfred. *The Military in Politics: Changing Patterns in Brazil.* Princeton: Princeton University Press, 1971.

———. "The New Professionalism of Internal Warfare and Military Role Expansion," in Stepan, ed., *Authoritarian Brazil: Origins, Policies and Future.* New Haven: Yale University Press, 1973.

———. *The State and Society: Peru in Comparative Perspective.* Princeton: Princeton University Press, 1978.

———. *Rethinking Military Politics: Brazil and the Southern Cone.* Princeton: Princeton University Press, 1988.

Turcios, Roberto. *Autoritarismo y modernización: El Salvador 1950–1960.* San Salvador: Ediciones Tendencias, 1993.

Vagts, Alfred. *A History of Militarism.* Greenwich: Meridian Books, Inc., 1959.

Valenzuela, J. Samuel. "Democratic Consolidation in Post-Transitional Settings," in Mainwaring et al., eds., *Issues in Democratic Consolidation: The New South American Democracies in Comparative Perspective.* Notre Dame: University of Notre Dame Press, 1992.

Vickers, George. "The Political Reality After Eleven Years of War," in Joseph Tulchin and Gary Bland, eds., *Is There a Transition to Democracy in El Salvador?* Boulder: Lynne Rienner Publishers, 1992.

Vickers, George, and Jack Spence, et al. *Endgame.* Cambridge, Mass.: Hemisphere Initiatives, 1992.

Webre, Stephen. *José Napoleón Duarte and the Christian Democratic Party in Salvadoran Politics: 1960–1972.* Baton Rouge: Louisiana State University Press, 1979.

Welch, Claude. *No Farewell to Arms? Military Disengagement from Politics in Africa and Latin America.* Boulder: Westview Press, 1987.

White, Alistair. *El Salvador.* London: Ernest Benn Limited, 1973.

Williams, Robert G. *Export Agriculture and the Crisis in Central America.* Chapel Hill: University of North Carolina Press, 1986.

Wilson, Everett Alan. "The Crisis of National Integration in El Salvador, 1919–1935." Ph.D. diss., Stanford University, 1970.

Wolf, Daniel. "ARENA in the Arena: Factors in the Accommodation of the Salvadoran Right to Pluralism and the Broadening of the Political System." Unpublished manuscript, 20 January 1992, San Salvador.

Wolpin, Miles. "External Political Socialization as a Source of Conservative Military Behavior in the Third World," in Kenneth Fidel, ed., *Militarism in Developing Countries.* New Brunswick, N.J.: Transaction Books, 1975.

Zagorski, Paul. *Democracy vs. National Security: Civil-Military Relations in Latin America.* Boulder: Lynne Reinner Publishers, 1992.

Zaverucha, Jorge. "The Degree of Military Political Autonomy During the Spanish, Argentine and Brazilian Transitions." *Journal of Latin American Studies* 25, no. 2 (May 1993): 283–99.

INDEX